M000165243

BETWEEN TWO WORLDS: THE WORLD BANK'S NEXT DECADE

Richard E. Feinberg and contributors

Gerald K. Helleiner
Joan M. Nelson
Sheldon Annis
John F. H. Purcell
Michelle B. Miller
Charles R. Blitzer
Howard Pack

Series Editors:
Richard E. Feinberg
Valeriana Kallab

Transaction Books
New Brunswick (USA) and Oxford (UK)

Copyright © 1986 by Overseas Development Council, Washington, D.C.

All rights reserved under International and Pan-American Copyright Conventions. No part of this book may be reproduced or transmitted in any form or by any means, electronic or mechanical, including photocopying, recording, or any information storage and retrieval system, without prior permission in writing from the publisher. All inquiries should be addressed to Transaction Books, Rutgers—The State University, New Brunswick, New Jersey 08903.

Library of Congress Catalog Number: 86-50513
ISBN: 0-88738-123-5 (cloth)
ISBN: 0-88738-665-2 (paper)
Printed in the United States of America

Library of Congress Cataloging-in-Publication Data

Between two worlds.

(U.S.-Third World policy perspectives; no. 7)
1. World Bank.
I. Feinberg, Richard E.
II. Series.
HG3881.5.W57B48   1985   332.1'532   86-50513
ISBN 0-88738-123-5
ISBN 0-88738-665-2 (pbk.)

Between Two Worlds: The World Bank's Next Decade

Acknowledgments

Series Editors:
Richard E. Feinberg
Valeriana Kallab

Project Associate:
Mary L. Williamson

Assistant Editors:
Carol J. Cramer
Patricia A. Masters

The Overseas Development Council gratefully acknowledges the assistance of the Ford, William and Flora Hewlett, and Rockefeller Foundations, whose financial support contributes to the preparation and dissemination of the policy analysis presented in ODC's U.S.-Third World Policy Perspectives series.

On behalf of the ODC and the contributing authors, the series editors wish to express thanks to members of the ODC Program Advisory Committee who encouraged and helped to plan the swift preparation of this policy study, and to the many experts who commented on the drafts of chapters either independently or at the several working sessions held to discuss the issues addressed in this volume.

Special thanks for administrative liaison and coordination in the production of this volume are also due to Lisa M. Cannon and Ingeborg Bock.

Contents

Foreword

This year marks the beginning of a new stage in the work of the World Bank group—the International Bank for Reconstruction and Development, the International Development Association, and the International Finance Corporation. Established in the aftermath of World War II to finance the rebuilding of war-torn Europe, the Bank, over the ensuing decades, has evolved into the international system's most important development institution.

A 'new era' at the World Bank is signaled by two separate events. First, the Bank's member governments have assigned it the lead role in dealing with the debt crisis that has preoccupied policy makers in both developed and developing countries since 1982. Developing-country debt now totals nearly $1 trillion. By mid-1985, slow growth in the developing countries was damaging the economies and interests of both the Third World and the industrial nations. In response, U.S. Treasury Secretary James Baker proposed a series of initiatives (which quickly became known as the "Baker plan") to restore growth as the end goal of dealing with the debt of Third World countries; his proposal singled out the World Bank (along with the Inter-American Development Bank) for the prime role in guiding the process of adjustment with growth in the major debtor countries.

At the same time, the World Bank's president, A.W. Clausen, having guided the Bank through one of the most difficult periods in its history, announced that he would step down when his term ended in mid-1986. His successor, the distinguished former U.S. Congressman Barber Conable, will become the sixth president the World Bank has had since it was established. Thus, the Bank will be under new leadership precisely when it has been given an unprecedentedly important role in the management of a global economy caught in the throes of the challenging crisis of development and debt.

The Bank's new charge and leadership prompted the Overseas Development Council—which has long been concerned with the Bank's role in international development—to plan this special volume in its U.S.-Third World Policy Perspectives series. *Between Two Worlds: The World Bank's Next Decade* is designed to analyze the policy issues that the Bank's new president will encounter when he takes office in July 1986; hence the open-letter format of our recommendations. It is of course our intent to focus much wider attention on the challenges facing the Bank, its member states, and its new leadership as they address the difficult problems of restoring growth and assuring its more equitable distribution to the three-quarters of the world's people living in the developing world.

The Bank clearly does not take on this task alone, but its role—among the other multilateral and national agencies—is unique and critical. The issues before the Bank are of considerable direct importance to the Overseas Development Council's prime audience: decision makers in the public and private sectors in the United States. It was a U.S. initiative that led to the Bank's current leadership position, with all of the attendant expectations. It will be important, therefore, for both Congress and the executive branch to offer full political and financial support for the Bank in the period ahead.

This Policy Perspectives was written and produced in a very short period of time. In the course of its preparation, a large number of people commented on drafts of the policy papers and participated in discussions of the main conclusions. In addition, the authors conducted extensive interviews with World Bank officials, and had access to a wide range of Bank documents. As is usual, the views expressed in this volume—some of which are of course controversial—are those of the authors and do not necessarily represent the views of the ODC as an organization or of the individual officers of its Board, Council, or staff. The analyses, views, and recommendations contained herein are presented in the hope of making an important contribution to the serious consideration and debate of issues that merit policy makers' attention.

On behalf of the Council, I would like to extend special thanks to the Rockefeller Foundation, and particularly to John Stremlau and Catherine Gwin, for the grant that enabled us to take on the preparation of this volume—and for having encouraged its preparation in the first place. The continuing program support of the Ford, William and Flora Hewlett, and Rockefeller Foundations for the work of the Overseas Development Council has also contributed to this special project.

June 1986

John W. Sewell, *President*
Overseas Development Council

Between Two Worlds:
The World Bank's Next Decade

Overview

An Open Letter to the World Bank's New President

Richard E. Feinberg

You have been appointed to what one of your predecessors, Robert McNamara, calls the "best job in the world." As the premier development finance institution, the World Bank houses an extraordinary collection of first-class economists and has the clout associated with an annual loan level of over $15 billion. You inherit an agency that has earned a reputation in industrial countries for professional competency and financial soundness, and that is respected in the Third World for its fairness and good will.

You take charge when the World Bank is being thrust into an unprecedented, and potentially very powerful, global role. As a result of the twin crises of development and debt, the Bank finds new opportunities for influence in Third World countries and on international capital markets. Desperate for help, debtors and creditors alike are willing to devolve a portion of previously guarded management prerogatives to a capable international agency, and the Bank alone is fit for the task. In the midst of a development crisis of historic proportions, a crisis both material and spiritual that has devastated national economies and the development models upon which they were constructed, the Bank has been charged by industrial-country governments and creditors with helping the Third World combine wrenching reforms in basic economic structures with renewed growth. Simultaneously, the Bank has been assigned the enormous job of reinvigorating badly shaken international capital markets by working with debtor nations to repair their economies and by providing new incentives to lenders.

Up to now, the Bank's power over this agenda has been more potential than realized. The Bank needs a strong guiding hand to restructure its relations with the International Monetary Fund, private capital markets, and the Reagan administration in ways that recognize both the constraints on Bank actions and the Bank's capacity for global leadership. A redefinition of Bank-Fund relations is required to correct for the relative decline in Bank stature occasioned by the Fund's more assertive response to the debt crisis. The scope and nature of Bank relations with international lenders and investors are evolving rapidly and call for innovative and at times forceful Bank initiatives. And finally, as the Bank positions itself for new influence, the smoothing over of past tensions with the White House will be an especially delicate task.

Many Bank staff are in an anxious and defensive mood. They feel that the Reagan administration, by initially labeling the Bank anti-capitalist, impeded it from responding more effectively to Third World needs, only to criticize the Bank recently for not doing more to manage the debt crisis. The new call for Bank leadership in the international economy has raised fears that the institution's independence and integrity will be subordinated to the interests of the commercial banks and the U.S. Treasury. Many of the Bank's four thousand professionals are also frustrated by internal divisiveness over development ideology and bureaucratic turf. One of your highest priorities will no doubt be to overcome this uncertainty of purpose and restore a clear sense of direction and mission among the staff.

The Bank's Next Decade: Four Critical Roles in a Dynamic Environment

This overview and the policy papers that follow were prepared in the frank hope of providing a set of fresh ideas on where you might take the Bank during the next decade. The complexity of the issues confronting the Bank will present you with a series of tough conceptual and policy dilemmas. The issues addressed in this letter and throughout the study include:

- **Is there more that the Bank can do to tackle the chronic debt crisis?**

- **How can the Bank manage "conditionality" so as to be simultaneously an effective agent for resource transfers and a force for structural adjustment in developing nations? And can the Bank square its inherent interna-**

tionalism with the Third World's aspirations for national sovereignty?

- What relationship should the Bank have with the International Monetary Fund? What can be done to overcome the long-standing resistance to more familial ties between the two Bretton Woods sisters?

- How can the Bank maintain its historic concern for equity and poverty alleviation even as it seeks to promote efficiency and the expansion of private sectors within developing countries?

- Whose Bank is it, in the final analysis? Should the Bank primarily be the servant of its most powerful stockholders, or should it seek to mediate between North and South—to be a bridge between two worlds?

Our thinking on these questions has been guided by a vision of the Bank as performing *four critical roles* in the future global political economy:

First, the Bank can be a **coordinator** of global capital flows, pulling together a widening array of official and private lenders and investors behind projects and programs, especially in the more debt-ridden nations. As coordinator, the Bank can combine its traditional role of financial intermediary between taxpayers and bond-buyers in the North and borrowers in the South with the roles of investment banker and strategic planner—helping to design country-specific strategies by forging macro analyses and projects with attainable financial resources.

Second, the Bank can function as a **mediator** of political and economic differences between industrialized and developing countries. The Bank can strive to reduce international tensions by reinforcing a shaky international economy while providing a forum where even the weaker nations have some voice in the debate about their economic and political futures.

Third, the Bank should be a **stabilizer** in the global economy, working to reduce the sharp gyrations in global capital flows that have unhinged so many developing economies. By launching new, more flexible financial instruments, upgrading countries' management of their external accounts, and helping to shape a more open and less conflictive trading system, the Bank can contribute to steadier global growth.

Fourth, the Bank can be the leading **intellectual center** for thinking about development. Employing the single largest concentration of economists specializing in the Third World, it can gather data globally, synthesize research done outside its walls, and bring its own brainpower to bear on emerging problems. By disseminating its findings worldwide, the Bank can substantially affect the development agenda.

These roles are complementary and mutually reinforcing. While they are not entirely new to the Bank, fulfilling them in today's more complex world will require both an internal restructuring of the Bank and innovative approaches to Bank programs.

The Bank has continuously altered its programs in response to changes in the international environment. In the years following its establishment at the Bretton Woods Conference in 1944, the International Bank for Reconstruction and Development (IBRD) concentrated its energies on contributing to the reconstruction of war-torn Europe. In the 1950s, in keeping with the expressed needs of its clients in Latin America and Asia—and with the then conventional theories of development—the Bank built roads, hydroelectric power facilities, and ports. In 1961, its soft-loan window—the International Development Association (IDA)—was opened to lend on concessional terms to poorer developing countries, especially in South Asia, that could not afford the near-market interest rates charged by the IBRD. In the 1970s, the Bank found that the benefits of growth were not "trickling down" to the poor majority in many developing societies, and chose to devote a rising proportion of its resources to projects directly targeted for poverty alleviation.

In the 1980s, "policy-based lending" ascended the stage: The Bank began rapid disbursement of balance-of-payments support to countries that agreed to alter specified economic policies. This form of lending was a response to three big problems. As a result of the global recession in the early 1980s and the contraction of private capital markets, many developing countries badly needed quick injections of foreign exchange. At the same time, the Bank's traditional project approach was running into trouble: Foreign-exchange and fiscal squeezes deprived governments of the financial means to initiate new World Bank projects, many of which had to be cancelled; equally alarming, a growing number of projects, particularly in rural Africa, were failing. Voices in both the North and South rose in crescendo to argue that many countries were pursuing flawed development strategies that impeded the success of even well-designed projects.

Before commenting on the future of this significant Bank initiative, it is important to consider what is both a symptom and a cause of the slowdown in Third World growth: the debt crisis.

The World Bank and the Debt Crisis

It would be unfair to fault the Bank for failing to foresee the debt crisis. Few predicted the gravity of the global recession of the early 1980s or foresaw soaring interest rates and the sudden retreat of the commercial banks. Still, the Bank's record might have been better. Its data on cumulative debt underestimated the problem and consistently ran one to two years behind events. Bank projections of global growth rates and of the growth of Third World economies and exports were overly optimistic; in 1981, the Bank was working with growth rates of between 4.1 per cent and 5.3 per cent for the 1980–85 period—well above the actual rate of 3 per cent. With these flawed expectations and data base, the Bank repeatedly misjudged debt-servicing capacities. While individual country studies often did note a potential debt problem, they typically concluded that, with adequate external aid and good domestic policies, a happy ending was within reach. Country economists did not want to discourage their clients or their foreign lenders, and judgments of "not creditworthy" also would have raised inconvenient doubts about the Bank's own lending program.

When the debt crisis first broke and threatened the very stability of the international financial system, the Bank arguably was obliged to join opinion leaders in issuing assurances that the problem was only one of short-term liquidity. But after an intense internal debate, Bank management seemingly convinced itself that most nations could surmount their debt problems within a few years through a combination of import restraint, export-led growth, and continued if slowed commercial bank lending. The Bank took a back seat to the IMF, not sufficiently anticipating that severe austerity would de-fund the investment projects that were the Bank's stock in trade as well as play havoc with nations' development plans. In retrospect, the Bank should have issued pointed warnings regarding the long-term problems posed by the crisis instead of painting a reassuring face over it. Now that the mural has been chipped away, many in the Bank argue that the institution should have foreseen that prolonged austerity would cut down on investment and therefore eventually on exports, miring many countries in a no-growth trap. Furthermore, rather than relying on the wishful thinking that private banks would resume lending, the Bank might have warned that the commercial banks had experienced a severe jolt, and that the resulting financing gap might have to be filled largely by official sources.

Instead, for over two years the Bank stood on the sidelines while many countries in Latin America and Africa lost the gains won by a decade or more of development efforts. The Bank's gross disbursements to fourteen highly indebted countries rose from \$2.7 billion in 1982 to \$3.9 billion in 1985, a significant jump in percentage terms, but still a tiny increment compared to these nations' financial requirements. Even today, while the Bank's regional divisions are seized with the debt problem, management has not yet spoken out with a clear voice on the major North-South issue of the 1980s. Instead, drawing attention to the damage that the debt burden is wreaking on development has been left to U.N. agencies, the regional development banks, and private voluntary organizations. The Inter-American Development Bank in particular has focused on the problem of reverse resource transfer: From 1982 through 1985, Latin America transferred some \$106 billion in net resources (defined as the difference between new capital inflows and amortization, interest payments, and profit remittances) to foreign creditors and investors. The World Bank's own most recent debt tables, which exclude interest payments on short-term debt, disclosed that for all developing countries the resource drain has been growing steadily worse, from negative \$8 billion in 1983 to an estimated negative \$22 billion in 1985; prior to 1983, net flows were solidly positive—standing at a positive \$19 billion as recently as 1981.

Even if thoroughly restructured, the debt overhang will cast a looming shadow on the growth prospects of many developing nations. But it is imperative that the debt crisis be permanently deflated—for the sake of the debtors as well as the commercial banks and the World Bank. Without such a shift, investment rates will remain low in many debt-ridden nations and economic actors will continue to be preoccupied by short-term financial turmoil. The Bank will be unable either to catalyze adequate financial resources to pursue investment projects or to persuade clients to attempt necessary but costly long-term reforms. Furthermore, prolongation of the debt crisis endangers the prospects for new World Bank funding in the U.S. Congress, where populist lawmakers will argue that the Bank's monies will merely go to servicing the debts owed to large Wall Street banks.

Need for a World Bank Initiative

The industrial countries' current economic well-being creates a propitious climate for new initiatives to alleviate the debt problem. It is too late to talk of a preemptive strike on debt, but the oil-price crash provides an opportunity for all parties to abandon defensive postures. As World Bank President, you may want to place priority on seeking the intensified personal involvement of Secretaries James Baker and George Shultz, and of Chairman Paul Volcker, as the first step in a multinational effort to attack the debt problem and extend help both to newly afflicted oil-exporting nations and to countries that have endured multiple years of austerity policies and economic recession.

A World Bank Initiative might encompass the following actions:

1. Amend the welcome "Program for Sustained Growth" announced by Secretary Baker last fall in Seoul to include equity. IMF and World Bank conditionality should explicitly address the distribution of the domestic benefits and costs of adjustment programs and should provide interested governments with ideas on how to protect the more vulnerable groups.

2. Establish target figures for reducing the resource drain that is afflicting many developing nations. The country targets should be consistent with reasonable rates of economic expansion. Increased official flows are part of the answer, but there should also be a renewed effort to narrow the gap between the interest bill being paid to commercial banks and the amount of new money they are willing to extend. The Baker plan stopped short of establishing the necessary mechanisms and procedures for inducing sufficient private bank cooperation. Concerted action now is required on the part of official lenders, central banks, and bank regulatory authorities to alter the banks' current preference to delay until reforms are well under way. When heavily indebted nations agree to World Bank structural adjustment programs, commercial banks generally should promptly respond by extending parallel loans or foregoing some interest payments, since up-front financing greatly increases the likelihood of successful economic reform.

3. Adopt a genuinely case-by-case approach to debt which concentrates on speeding up the renewal of creditworthiness for some countries but which admits that others simply *cannot* carry their existing burdens and resume economic growth. For this latter category, a portion of a country's debt may have to be written off to restore order to its financial transactions. Country financial agreements should include contingency clauses to allow for changing levels of debt relief or new loans to reflect, for example, shifting interest rates and commodity prices. Financial packages tailored to each country could build on methods that the private capital markets have been developing for chipping away at accumulated debt, including debt-for-equity swaps, the conversion of debt into local currency, and the sale of discounted loans on secondary markets.

4. Tap Japan's $50-billion trade surplus to provide growth capital to the Third World. Beyond bond flotations on Japanese capital markets and Japan's periodic contributions to IBRD and IDA programs, the World Bank could focus on Japanese banks and investors in promoting its guarantee and insurance programs. In addition, the Bank might consider establishing a special facility for recycling Japanese surpluses, as the IMF did for Saudi Arabia in the 1970s.

5. Propose specific steps to provide developing countries with increased access to industrial nations' markets. Partly in response to World Bank persuasion, the United States recently agreed to consider making reciprocal concessions in the forthcoming trade negotiations under the General Agreement on Tariffs and Trade (GATT) to countries that have unilaterally liberalized their trade regimes as part of World Bank-supported reforms, provided that the trade reforms are permanent and concern products of interest to the United States. The Bank should seek a similar willingness from other industrial nations. Furthermore, the World Bank should cooperate with the GATT and the IMF in monitoring the macro-economic and trade policies of the industrial states to judge whether they are consistent with the export-oriented growth policies that the Bank is advocating for developing nations.

A World Bank Initiative could be a follow-on to the Baker plan, with added advantages. An emphasis on equity would introduce a traditional and critical Bank theme that would add distributive objectives to those of efficiency and growth. The goal of reducing net outflows to a level consistent with growth would come closer to meeting many countries' real capital needs. Such an emphasis on the now chronic reverse transfers of resources from poor countries to rich ones would rectify a perception sometimes held in industrialized nations that the Third World is again asking for handouts—and who but the World Bank is better suited to point out the economic illogic and moral injustice of this perverse trend in capital flows? The proposed initiative would also provide mechanisms for assuring adequate participation by the commercial banks, more flexibility in response to changing world economic conditions, and greater differentiation of financial packages to fit individual country circumstances. It would be a multilateral initiative originating with the World Bank, and could make use of Japan's economic strengths in tackling a problem every Bank member wants to overcome.

An equitable solution to the debt problem, one in which all parties are seen to be paying a cost for past mistakes, could correct a growing and disconcerting view that the Bank is following the

Fund in identifying more with the creditors than with the debtor nations. An equitable outcome could also enhance the image and reality of the Bank as a just and effective mediator between North and South.

Structural Adjustment and National Sovereignty

Policy-based lending will be a formidable test of the Bank's skills at reconciling the concerns of lenders and borrowers. The new focus on structural adjustments will be indispensable; but the results so far have been uneven, and the strategy is subject to numerous interpretations and vociferous debate.

As some of the old-timers at the Bank can testify, the phrase "structural adjustment" has had multiple incarnations in development theory. The term was originally used in the 1950s and 1960s by Latin American "structuralists" who labeled land tenure, dependence on imported technology, and the concentration of exports in one or two unstable commodities important "structural" obstacles to development. During the 1970s, in response to the drastic shifts in oil and food prices, "structural adjustment" was often used to mean raising the domestic prices of these commodities to international levels. In the 1980s, the meaning has switched once again; this time, "structuralists" seek to reorient producers toward export markets. Most recently, "structural change" is often equated with the opening up of economies to international trade and private capital flows; some take another step, arguing that external liberalization should be matched with a freeing of domestic prices, while others take yet another, pressing for privatization of the ownership of the means of production as well as the provision of social services.

The 1980s recasting of "structural adjustment" represents a remodeling of ideas that are not particularly new. They do, however, amount to a fundamental critique of the development strategies that have been followed in most Latin American and African nations. The most recent propositions are an assault on the citadel of import-substituting industrialization that has been at the heart of Latin American policies, and on the statist bias, sometimes grounded in socialist ideology, that has guided some African and Asian patterns of development.

In many developing countries, the rising generations of technocrats share elements of these critiques. Many Third World policy makers have uprooted ideologies of statism and anti-imperialism in favor of more pragmatic and discriminating approaches, preparing a potentially fertile terrain for policy-based lending. Nevertheless, these same leaders are wary of the Bank's new enthusiasm for structural adjustment programs.

You will hear these complaints from many Third World clients:

—The Bank is in danger of becoming like the IMF—pushing simplistic, standardized formulas that slight the particular history, culture, and politics of individual nations, and that are based more on preconceived ideology than on objective analysis. For instance, yes, they will say, trade liberalization may be appropriate at times, but let's remember that the relatively closed economies of Brazil, India, and China have been doing very well of late, that the debt crisis shackles many economies to trade-surplus-maximizing strategies, and that successful export promotion policies may involve significant state intervention, as the Asian successes demonstrate. And even if the global trade outlook improves, how can dozens of developing countries expand exports all at once?

—Some Bank staff are just too junior, too arrogant, or too ignorant to negotiate with senior government officials who generally know more about their own countries' economic and political realities.

—Structural adjustment programs are overly ambitious, encompass too many objectives and details, and require closely spaced assessments that come up before substantial progress can reasonably be expected.

—The size of the Bank's loans is often not commensurate with the costs and risks of the adjustments that it proposes.

If the Bank is unable to respond to these complaints, it could quickly expend its accumulated good will and find itself in conflict with many of its member governments. If the Bank declares poorly performing nations ineligible, the result could be to drive them further into financial distress and political isolation. Worse, if programs fail, the Bank's analytical credibility and its own creditworthiness could be jeopardized. In sum, the Bank's central purposes—coordinator, mediator, stabilizer, and intellectual guide— could all be compromised.

A great deal more analysis and reflection is needed on how best to avoid these pitfalls. In two subtly argued essays in this volume, Gerald Helleiner and Joan Nelson suggest some avenues of escape from the dilemmas of structural adjustment lending:

—*Let us recognize what is known and what is not.* Economists are in widespread agreement on the need for responsible fiscal and monetary policies, expanded savings and investment, and supply-side restructuring toward tradable goods through the realignment of prices and other incentives. Much less is known, however, about the dynamics of economic adjustment, about the timing and phasing of reforms—about how to get from here to there. Economists are even less prepared to advise individual nations as to what political roads to follow and what institutional mechanisms to build. Key development choices, such as income distribution, the role of government, and the selection of 'engines of growth' (for example, foreign direct investment, trade, telecommunications, or education), are heavily political and must be country-specific.

—*Dialogue is more likely than* diktat *to produce lasting reforms.* Actions taken primarily because of externally imposed conditions rather than domestic convictions are unlikely to be sustained. Policy dialogues should be more akin to participatory teamwork than to adversarial negotiation. A Bank mission's authority might sometimes be enhanced by placing at its head a distinguished international figure drawn from outside the Bank. Since policy-based lending involves the Bank in sensitive, political issues, Bank economists themselves would benefit from training courses in the art of diplomacy. Bank missions must be especially circumspect with larger, more self-confident clients, but they can sometimes be more assertive when a government lacks its own plans or analytical capabilities, or is internally divided, or heavily dependent on external donors for cash or for a high percentage of its public investment (as is often true in Africa).

—*Loan conditionality should focus on a few, select issues that must be resolved if progress is to be made toward the broad goals of the entire program.* A long list of requirements either holds an entire program hostage to a secondary issue, or is open to highly subjective assessments. Particularly when a government is already on a harmonious wave length, staff should avoid quibbling over details. The Bank has quietly but correctly moved away from ambitious structural adjustment loans (SALs) that encompass an entire national economy and is now concentrating on narrower sector loans, which are closer on a lending continuum to projects—the Bank's traditional area of expertise. The Bank also needs to review its tranching policy, to match the frequency of its assessments to the nature of the reforms under scrutiny.

—*Determination of the size of policy-based loans should be more rational and transparent.* Are loan amounts a function of the probable economic or political costs of reform, of the client's balance-of-payments needs, or of some largely predetermined country lending limit? Applying either of the first two criteria might often require much larger loans, but would make adjustment programs more viable. Bank management might also want to clarify the substantive criteria and bureaucratic mechanisms for determining country lending levels while demonstrating that the Bank can respond flexibly to changing policies and needs in individual countries.

Some Bank missions already adhere to many of these guidelines. Even if fully adopted, however, these proposals can help the Bank to steer clear of obvious obstacles; they cannot negate the basic reality that for a developing nation, structural adjustment is a very tough, prolonged task that involves a fundamental realignment of power and privilege. Given the complexity of the process, the Bank should avoid overselling its capabilities. It will have to learn from its inevitable mistakes, and be braced for the reversals of governments that leave programs in shambles and money wasted. Structural adjustment lending is a high-risk venture, but, given the evident need for quick-disbursing monies and far-reaching policy change, the Bank has no choice but to try. Fully acknowledging the dangers ahead, Gerald Helleiner suggests that the Bank devote roughly 40–45 per cent of its lending during the next several years to this challenge.

A large share of Bank resources will continue to be devoted to project loans and direct poverty alleviation. By stressing in public addresses and in-house meetings the Bank's vast experience and ongoing successes in its traditional fields, you could forge a shield against bad publicity and shorten swings in staff morale that may occur when the Bank stumbles in its new course. The spotlight has swung to follow policy-based lending, the newest addition to the Bank's repertoire, but the storehouse of other Bank achievements merits polishing up and prominent display.

The Bank and the Fund

The World Bank's partner institution, the International Monetary Fund, faces a turning point in its global role as well. In recent years, the Fund has been stripped of influence over some issues and arguably miscast on others. The collapse of the fixed-exchange-rate system in the 1970s deprived the Fund of its key function. The institution has also been stymied in its drive to create its own international currency, the SDR. At the recent Tokyo Summit, industrial-country leaders again revealed their preference for coordinating monetary and other economic policies among themselves, relegating the Fund to a "review" status. While the IMF remains the world's lender of last resort, it has not made a loan to an *industrial* country since 1977. When the debt crisis exploded in the early 1980s, the Fund successfully stabilized financial markets, but was not given the resources to carry the Third World to a new, dynamic equilibrium. Moreover, in keeping with its self-defined role as a short-term, revolving fund, the IMF now wants to retrench in the Third World: The Fund's net lending to developing countries fell from $11.4 billion in 1983 to only $0.2 billion in 1985.

Uncertainty regarding the Fund's future role is clearly a matter of concern for the World Bank. As many in the Fund now realize, it is no longer possible to maintain the old, sharp distinctions between short-term financial distress and long-term development disequilibria that served as the basis for the division of labor between the Fund and the Bank in the Third World. Countries must now cope with both finance and development problems *simultaneously, and over an extended period.* Logic might dictate that a single institution take charge of the inseparable processes of stabilization and adjustment, but institutional inertia, among other reasons, will most likely prevent a merger of the Bank and Fund. More feasible will be a new leading role for the Bank in the longstanding but uneasy cooperation between the two institutions.

From the World Bank's perspective, the ongoing IMF withdrawal from the Third World has both dark and bright sides. The Bank can more easily emerge from its senior partner's shadow, but at the cost of the Fund draining Bank clients of badly needed liquid capital. So the objective is to persuade the Fund—and its key shareholders—to accept a lead role for the Bank while at the same time the Fund prolongs its own stay in the Third World.

If recent Fund programs have not brought stability to many Latin American and African economies, the Fund administers or has potential use of a pool of about $100 billion in hard currencies, significant portions of which should remain available to support Third World economic adjustment. On financial and moral grounds, Fund abandonment of its unfinished business is not justifiable. Nor is it politically defensible for the World Bank to appear to be replenishing Fund coffers via its loans to Third World treasuries.

The IMF's recent decision to recycle its Trust Fund monies to Africa through a Structural Adjustment Facility is a step in the right direction. The Fund can also initiate a positive role for itself in some countries by accepting temporarily reduced repayments when countries experience unanticipated external shocks. The Fund's mandate to make financial resources available on a temporary basis is consistent with variations in repayment terms that make allowances for members' circumstances and swings in the global economy. The Fund should also set aside its qualms over members' "prolonged use" of its resources and be willing to negotiate a series of stand-by agreements in countries engaged in Bank-assisted policy reforms. In addition, the United States and West Germany should drop their opposition to the issuance of more SDRs: Many developing countries clearly need reserves; the United States and other nations could benefit from the stimulus to their exports; and the often-cited fear of fueling global inflation is now less relevant.

Finally, one of the most obvious yet difficult tasks awaiting you is to work with the Fund's Managing Director to forge more cooperative relationships between Bank and Fund country economists. While some Bank and Fund counterparts work well together, other associations are blocked by ideological, procedural, and bureaucratic obstacles. Fund staff need to be reminded that freeing markets and closing budget deficits, however important, do not by themselves constitute a development strategy, and that they do not have exclusive domain over such key issues as exchange rates and export taxes; that joint Bank/Fund missions and policy papers can often help to ensure consistency in analysis and prescriptions; and that information must flow two ways on a routine and timely basis. Bank staff need a greater say in designing stabilization policies to ensure that they serve the goals of long-term adjustment, growth, and poverty alleviation. The Fund's experienced macro economists should interact more with Bank experts in molding fiscal, monetary, and exchange-rate policies that reinforce the sectoral investment strategies being pursued under Bank programs. Bank-Fund relations might be further strengthened by asking some member countries to appoint a single, qualified Executive Director to both Boards; there are successful precedents.

Policing the Bretton Woods System

As the Bank flexes new muscles with its policy-based lending, it will need to reconsider its policies toward bankrupt or rebellious nations that are not meeting their financial obligations. The Bank will need to declare a feasible and constructive sanctions policy and must decide to what degree it will coordinate its enforcement mechanisms with the Fund.

Since January 1985, the IMF has declared four countries ineligible for participation in its major programs, and one of them is now ineligible for Bank lending as well. These four nations have stumbled into uncharted territory by remaining in arrears to a Bretton Woods creditor beyond the established amnesty period. A number of other countries are likely soon to join the list of outcasts as they, too, reach the bottom of their liquid reserves. The arrears problem undermines the international economic system by excluding countries instead of integrating them into global markets. Helping to reverse this trend will be a considerable challenge for the Bank.

As the rules now stand, countries that are current in their accounts with the World Bank remain eligible for new loans and disbursements on old loans regardless of their standing in the IMF. Vietnam, Guyana, and Sudan have thus received disbursements from existing project loan agreements with the Bank in FY1986, despite their *non grata* status with the Fund. The Sudan has also signed three new project loan agreements with the Bank in FY 1986. The Bank has cancelled disbursements to Liberia, but this is only because the country is also in arrears to the Bank itself. Bank policy, however, has recently been revised to institute an automatic review of the economic circumstances of any borrower declared ineligible by the Fund, with a possible presumption that such a country should no longer receive new loans.

This policy needs to be sensitive to extenuating circumstances that may become apparent during individual country reviews. The Bank need not help to create pariah states by conforming automatically with Fund policies toward troubled debtors; instead, it would do well to maintain a flexible approach to IMF-ineligible countries. When such countries have remained current in their Bank payments, a credit review is justified if it does not presume countries to be unreliable Bank clients: political factors (reflecting the Fund's unpopularity in much of the Third World) or economic considerations may well explain a country's decision to honor the preferred creditor status of the Bank but not the Fund. For example, a debtor country may have a relatively manageable World Bank debt compared to the sum it owes the Fund, as is the case with Guyana. A related problem is the reduction in IMF lending to the Third World, which has made the IMF a net resource drain for many indebted nations, adding to the pressure for debtors to delay repayments to the Fund. Under these conditions, the Bank must be careful to distinguish itself from the IMF and should seek to identify viable project and sector loans that enable it to maintain positive net capital flows to troubled debtors.

The Bank's challenge, under your leadership, will be to administer fair judgments that separate the willful offenders from countries trapped by circumstance. For example, governments that blatantly abuse Bank funding or repeatedly negotiate agreements in bad faith may be candidates for sanctions. Just as structural adjustment strategies must be tailored to individual country cases, so should punishments. These judgments are likely to arise in the cases of numerous small indebted countries that are reaching the end of their ability to repay even with structural adjustments and severely curtailed internal spending, and promise to test the mediating abilities of the Bank.

An important task will be to persuade the Fund's shareholders and administrators of the need for separate Bank and Fund policies on arrears. Your argument might emphasize that ongoing cooperation with the World Bank is a step in itself toward a country's reconciliation with and repayment of the IMF. Third World countries would also have reduced incentives to initiate innovative and risky Bank structural adjustment programs if repayment troubles on any loan from a Bretton Woods institution triggered a halt in subsequent loans. And finally, the Bank's effectiveness as an intermediary among debtor countries, commercial banks, and the IMF would be seriously compromised by any perception in the Third World that it was rubber-stamping instead of formulating impartial and reliable policy.

Readdressing Poverty

The Bank's new thrust to assist developing countries in restructuring their economies and attracting private investment should not overshadow the important contributions it can make to poverty alleviation. Growth with equitable distribution can be an achievable goal for both policy-based lending and Bank projects. But, as Sheldon Annis argues in this volume with cogent evidence, the Bank, while hardly abandoning its concern for the poor, is paying them less heed in the 1980s. While the debt crisis understandably forced governments to concentrate on immediate financial matters, the downgrading of poverty issues also reveals the force of political winds in key Northern nations and in the economics profession in the United States. One telling symbol: The Bank's research department altered the label of its office of "Employment and Income Distribution" to "Labor Markets."

In recent months, some Bank staff have sought to reassert the importance of poverty issues and have marshalled an impressive case. The Bank has learned a great deal about how to address poverty, and it makes sense to benefit from and build on that acquired knowledge. Politically, the Bank risks losing the support of some funders if it seems to be abandoning the poor. Economically, high unemployment and related social violence are drags on future societal prosperity. And if a country's economic policies are widely perceived by its own people to be unjust, the measures may not be politically sustainable, regardless of their technical merits or aggregate growth achievements: witness the experiences under the Shah of Iran, Somoza in Nicaragua, and Marcos in the Philippines.

The Bank today possesses many new resources and policy levers to add to its accumulated project expertise, and actually finds itself in a much stronger position to tackle poverty. Policy-based lending places it near the strategic center of resource allocation decisions. By affecting the investment plans of governments, the links between public and private sectors, and the workings of markets, the Bank can direct a much larger pool of resources toward poverty alleviation. Its new potential to influence macro-economic policies may prove especially valuable for stimulating new economic opportunities for the very poor, thus improving efficiency and equity simultaneously.

Often the Bank can fulfill both of these goals—for example, by arguing against state subsidies to the rich and helping governments to prevent capital flight. Unfortunately, there is at times a short-term tradeoff between growth and equitable distribution; in such cases, the Bank's role can be to help nations develop the analytical ability to understand these tradeoffs, to identify the size and characteristics of the beneficiary and losing groups, and to devise strategies to assist the most vulnerable. Gerald Helleiner recommends that the Bank's research department concentrate on crafting adjustment strategies that minimize social costs, and that provide carefully targeted compensation to those poor whose interests may be unavoidably harmed. For example, as a recent Bank policy document noted, advice to clients to increase food prices and to boost incentives to farmers might be accompanied by the suggestion that some food subsidies remain for the unemployed and for infants and mothers, within budget constraints.

Bank efforts to make public sectors more efficient can also advance equity. Through its advice on fiscal matters, the Bank can alert policy makers to inequities in existing tax systems and can suggest fairer distribution of the tax burden. Where government ownership of firms or interventions in markets have served only to suffocate initiative or to exploit the poor, privatization or decentralization of decision making may advance equity. Moreover, governments that carefully define their areas of obligation and expertise are more likely to succeed in those anti-poverty programs that they do pursue.

The choice of technology is another tool available to the Bank for improving both equity and efficiency in Third World economies. The Bank has supplied valuable research to take "appropriate technology" from a catch phrase to operational strategies. But there are always new frontiers in this field, and the debt crisis and population boom have intensified the need for innovative industrial and agricultural technologies. Howard Pack argues in this volume that the Bank should devote significant resources to providing capital to generate employment in *small- and medium-scale* enterprises. The Bank's experience in researching and disseminating technological innovations can make it the global leader in such development strategies. Pack urges the Bank to strengthen its coordinating role in industrial technology innovation by helping to fund research institutes and by forming an umbrella consultative group like the one that it administers on international agricultural research (the CGIAR). Such project work on appropriate technologies should be supplemented by sector and structural adjustment loans that reward cost-effective technology choices.

Project and program lending should also be combined to bolster the Bank's work on environmental management, an area of public policy that has direct impact on the poor. We are already witnessing the devastation of human and animal life and natural environments in Sub-Saharan Africa and elsewhere. World Bank projects and macro-economic adjustment programs can help countries manage and build resources for future development, but too often growth has come only through alarming depletion of the environment. You might consider intensifying the Bank's efforts to combine growth and environmental objectives through a threefold strategy: 1) the Bank's policy-based lending could encourage revisions in countries' pricing structures, tax codes, trade policies, and other macro-economic determinants of resource use to improve environmental conservation; 2) project loans could provide technical assistance and training for resource management; and 3) the Bank's efforts to build environmental concerns into all projects could be strengthened.

By integrating its project lending with advice on fiscal policies, public-private sector relations, technology and the environment, and other broad macro-economic and sectoral policies involved in structural adjustment, the Bank *can* help interested governments make a serious attack on poverty. Concerned governments could look to the Bank as the leading repository of knowledge on how these many policy instruments alter the distribution of income, and on how to identify and minimize tradeoffs between efficiency and equity. This potentially powerful and sophisticated approach to addressing poverty could be a key component of the proposed World Bank Initiative to combine debt relief with economic recovery and poverty alleviation.

Bureaucratic Reforms

The taking on of major new tasks naturally carries consequences for internal organization. The Bank's policy-based lending requires both a greater presence in the field and a more tightly organized review process at headquarters in Washington. To bolster its ability to work with the private sector, the Bank may also want to hire some market-tested entrepreneurs.

"Policy dialogue" between the Bank and its clients is more likely to take the form of participatory teamwork if some Bank staff build tight working relations with national policy makers by living in-country. Prolonged assignments in the field could increase the effectiveness of staff who work on such sensitive and complex political issues as public-sector decision making and other institutional reforms. A strong in-country mission is also better placed to help coordinate the many donor programs, an especially important role for the Bank in Africa, where weak bureaucracies are sometimes overwhelmed by dozens of foreign aid agencies. Bank resident missions also afford an opportunity to employ more local nationals, as a way to lower costs while training local talent. Although the Bank has recently been increasing the number of resident missions, much more could be done to buttress their capacities and power. The frequently cited danger of "clientism" (of Bank staff coming to identify more with their countries of residence than with their employer) could be reduced by routine rotation and by close integration of field missions with the regional offices in Washington.

The emergence of policy-based lending poses new issues for Bank organization in Washington for which diametrically opposed solutions are being proposed. One view is that Bank policy must be consistent across countries, and that a highly centralized and authoritative department should clear loans; the IMF's Exchange and Trade Relations (ETR) office is the model. The opposing view finds that the Fund's excessive centralization has yielded a theocracy too trapped in catechism to respond to changing circumstances or individual country realities. According to this theory, long-term development issues are particularly ill-suited to universalisms; therefore, power in the Bank should instead be located in strengthened regional divisions, whose staff is closer to circumstances on the ground.

A middle option might seek the advantages of both centralized clarity and consistency, and the creativity and specificity that can come with decentralization. While policy-based lending is still in its experimental stages, the Bank might benefit from a powerful department with highly skilled non-ideological staff that helps to develop and possibly clear new loans, draws lessons from successes and failures, and quickly feeds them back into the loan process. The Bank's Country Policy Department and the office of the Senior Vice President for Operations currently handle some of these functions, but they might better be performed in a single unit. This central brain would have considerable input in the early design of policy-based loans, and a more regular presence on loan appraisal missions. Close cooperation with the research department would be important if the latter were carrying out work on such issues as melding adjustment with equity and measuring the impact of reforms on vulnerable groups. As the Bank gains experience in policy-based lending, loan-clearance and review powers should gradually be decentralized to the offices of well-staffed regional vice presidents, which combine a broad policy perspective with detailed country knowledge and can integrate country programs with projects. Eventually the central bureau might be folded in with the research department, to study Bank-wide experience with policy-based lending and to facilitate information exchange among the regional bureaus.

The growth of policy-based lending raises important management and staffing issues. To speed loan approval, bureaucratic procedures need streamlining. Memoranda have to pass through too many approval layers: the trek from country economist to division chief to department director to chief economist to regional vice president to the operations policy staff to the senior vice president to the loan committee to the Executive Board is wasteful of time and talent. At the same time, the Bank will need more broad-gauged economists to carry out micro, sectoral, and country macroeconomic studies, and could also benefit from hiring more political scientists and anthropologists to alert the staff to institutional and cultural factors that impinge on economic change. Furthermore, the staff incentive system should be reexamined: the persistent criticism that staff are rewarded more for loan quantity than quality is especially pertinent in the case of policy-based lending. If staff are perceived to be shoveling out such loans, the Bank's credibility will be tarnished.

The Bank's venture into the private sector has further organizational and staffing implications. As John Purcell and Michelle Miller point out in this volume, responsibility for interacting with the private sector is concentrated in specific areas of the Bank, including the Energy and Industry Departments, the Treasurer's office, the co-financing program, and the International Finance Corporation (IFC). You may want to improve the coordination among these areas, and to develop mechanisms to encourage more cross-fertilization between these programs and the regional divisions. To enhance Bank relations with the private sector and fulfill the role of investment banker, the Bank would do well to hire more staff experienced in making business deals and assembling financial packages.

Two additional reforms might strengthen the Bank's ability to formulate and implement policies in the period ahead: the creation of a central policy planning staff and an upgrading of the Executive Board. Oddly enough, the Bank currently lacks a single policy planning staff that reports directly to the President. A small, carefully selected group of broad-gauged individuals who enjoy the President's confidence is crucial for issuing warning signals of impending problems, designing new policy initiatives, and ensuring consistency among policy, programs, and budgeting. Such a policy planning staff should feel secure enough to present even critical and unpopular ideas. In recent years, heterodox views have too often been close to the truth on such issues as the danger of a debt crisis, the probabilities of a commodity price slump and other instabilities in the international system, the corrupt and exploitative nature of some client regimes, especially in some African countries and in the Philippines, and the importance of the role of women in development. A good policy planning staff serves as a direct channel to the president for a wide variety of dissident views, including those being promulgated outside the Bank.

A quality Executive Board could make a major contribution to policy formulation, and could serve as your ambassadors to their nations. In your early conversations with finance ministers, you might urge them to seek the highest levels of talent in appointing their Executive Director at the Bank, as would befit the augmented importance of the institution. In return, you might steer the Board away from tedious discussions of the details of individual loans and instead seriously consult it on major policy issues.

These criticisms of current operations should not overshadow the fact that World Bank management and staff compare very favorably to those in other large bureaucracies, especially some international agencies. The political pressures you are under to make drastic staff cuts should be treated cautiously. Your first move might be to hire an outside consulting firm to review Bank organization in light of the Bank's changing programs.

The Bank's Future Lending Levels

At this point, you may be looking for an estimate of the increase in Bank capital that would be required to support the above recommendations. Such estimates of desirable future Bank lending levels sometimes begin with a calculation of the financing that developing nations will need in order to reach a certain growth rate. The World Bank is assigned the task of providing those funds that private markets and other lenders seem unlikely to cover. But today, there are too many uncertainties in the global economy—regarding commodity prices, interest rates, and OECD trade policies and growth—to assess the scale of such needs with any accuracy. Moreover, as Charles Blitzer suggests in this volume, financing needs are likely to be so great, and other sources so inadequate, that this "financing gap" methodology simply suggests that future Bank lending levels will be determined by other criteria, such as budgetary considerations in the North or the intensity of economic reform in the South.

A substantial increase in IBRD and IDA resources is clearly warranted, for three reasons in addition to that of aggregate Third World needs. First, the Bank will have to enlarge substantially the size of its policy-based loans for borrowing governments to feel that it is covering an adequate portion of the costs of painful reforms and providing enough investment resources for the reforms to work. Second, the Bank will require more resources if it is to have the leverage to catalyze private flows. Third, the IBRD's net resource transfer—disbursements minus repayments and interest—was down to $2 billion in 1985; given current trends, it may vanish by 1988. If the IBRD ceases to be a source of net resources, its very raison d'etre as a development finance agency will come into question.

Current Bank management, as you are aware, would like to have the capacity to expand the annual lending of the non-concessional IBRD to $21.5 billion (compared to $11.4 billion in FY1985)—a goal requiring that the Bank's authorized capital of $78.5 billion be increased by about $53 billion. All major donors other than the United States now favor the immediate initiation of negotiations on a new general capital increase (GCI). Concurring with this sense of urgency, Blitzer calls for a GCI of $100 billion, in order to allow the IBRD to increase net disbursements in the next five to six years by $65 billion over currently anticipated levels. While conceding that the Bank might not need this capacity, Blitzer believes the Bank should be positioned to assist nations attempting serious structural reforms. He urges retention of the 1:1 loan-to-capital "gearing" ratio; a more aggressive ratio might alarm bond buyers who are very conscious of the current poor credit ratings of many Bank clients and of the experimental nature of policy-based lending. Since capital subscriptions primarily take the form of government guarantees ("callable capital"), a GCI of course need not have a significant impact on national budgets. The Bank's proven ability to fatten its capital base through retained earnings suggests that it could do without further *paid-in* capital, although donors might want to make small, symbolic appropriations to reassure capital markets that they remain committed to the Bank's solvency.

Your predecessor was deeply disappointed at the U.S. refusal to fund the concessional IDA at levels that would allow for more than about $3 billion in annual lending. Given the fiscal crisis in the United States, you may not do much better, but it is worth a fresh try with the Administration and Congress to explain the call for a substantial IDA replenishment. The funds will be urgently needed to assist many African states that are attempting structural adjustments and striving to raise the productivity of capital. Yet there is a limit to how much of the IDA monies required for Africa can fairly and constructively be taken away from the populous, low-income Asian countries. India and China have made great strides, but they are still very poor and receive relatively little aid in per capita terms. Their capacity for market borrowing could wear thin quickly, and both are engaged in liberalizing reforms that could be helped by support from IDA.

To reawaken market interest in developing countries, the Bank under the leadership of Tom Clausen has devised creative co-financing, investment, and guarantee schemes. However, John Purcell and Michelle Miller suggest that the quantitative results have been and are likely to remain modest in the short term. Today, commercial banks are working hard to reduce their ratios of exposure to capital in many developing countries, and no amount of domestic reform is likely soon to overcome this trend and elicit large amounts of new capital. Countries with scant industry are simply not good bets for the quick creation of a vibrant stock exchange. Furthermore, there are inherent limits to the role that the World Bank can play in motivating private investment: Opportunities that offer obvious profits do not need additional stimuli; and no amount of paint can turn an obvious lemon into a gold bar. Scouting for projects that fall between these two types, and have potential but uncertain profitability, requires long and careful work.

While the Bank's efforts to promote private flows are worthwhile, it should not overestimate the probable results. The balance between private and public flows tilted too far toward the former during the 1970s, but will now have to incline sharply toward the latter, until a more stable equilibrium can be reached when developing nations regain access to private markets.

U.S. Power and Multilateral Agencies

Like your predecessors, you will have to balance two realities: you are an American citizen, in effect appointed by the White House, and subject to the close scrutiny of a U.S. government and Congress acutely aware of their 20-per cent share of the Bank's stock, but you are also the president of an international institution with 149 member countries. The Bank's president has to please its major stockholder while retaining the agency's independence and global accountability. A Bank perceived to be nothing more than an extension of the U.S. Treasury Department loses influence with its other members, but a Bank perceived to be hostile to U.S. interests will become embattled and capital-poor.

The best way to square the circle is to reaffirm that multilateralism can serve U.S. national interests. The following points might prove useful in talking to American audiences:

—Struggles earlier in the Reagan administration to unshackle U.S. power from multilateral constraints proved to have substantial costs. Unilateralist economic policies and market mechanisms failed to bring stability to exchange rates or to adequately lower interest rates, and were unable to manage Third World debt. As a result, Secretary Baker has wisely sought to rebuild cooperative decision making on such key issues as exchange rates, interest rates, and even national fiscal and monetary policies. At its root, the Baker plan is a call for prolonged and coordinated activism by industrial-country governments and the Bretton Woods agencies to stabilize the international financial system.

—The United States has close mutual interests with the other industrial countries which weigh very heavily in World Bank decision making. These interests include increasing international trade, maintaining adequate supplies of commodities, and expanding opportunities for profitable international investments. The World Bank has long sought to advance these goals, and can do so in a multilateral framework that generally is more politically acceptable than bilateral channels.

—As a result of multilateral burden-sharing, every dollar of capital paid in by the United States enables the IBRD to lend $60. (Charles Blitzer's chapter provides a detailed discussion of this multiplier effect of combining fractional paid-in capital with burden-sharing by other donors.)

American audiences will include some who may argue that multilateralism dilutes U.S. power and forces the United States to make concessions to weaker nations. The Reagan administration has in some cases enhanced U.S. influence in world affairs by adopting a forceful posture on its own, and recent U.S. policy toward the Bank is an example. Reagan's successes, however, may postpone but cannot halt the inevitable rise of other nations— Japan, West Germany, Brazil and other emerging developing countries—and the increase of their relative shares of global power. Within the Bank, as elsewhere, the United States will undergo a transition from primacy to coalition-building. The United States may retain the power to block actions, but will need the cooperation of others to forward new initiatives.

If audiences remains unsure, you might remind them that, as in the U.S. Congress, coalition-building means power-sharing and genuine consultation. For U.S. actions within the Bank, this means building regular channels of communication with groups of developing nations. It means granting some power to other industrial nations, keeping in mind our common interests in systemic growth and stability. Indeed, while the United States is correct to suggest that Japan—as a capital-rich nation living under the U.S. nuclear umbrella—ought to carry a larger burden of the foreign aid bill, Japan is justified in requesting a corresponding increase in its clout in the World Bank. (An increase in Japan's voting shares could pull the United States below the 20-per cent mark that gives it veto power on major policy matters. The logic of interdependence warrants such an adjustment, but the U.S. Congress may see it differently.)

Similarly, you might argue that, as the Bank's president, you are working to build a wide coalition that includes Washington along with other capitals in the industrial and developing countries. You are not only thinking of national governments: within countries, business and labor groups, private voluntary organizations, political parties, and state and local governments are all potential clients and supporters of a sound Bank.

An anxious U.S. audience could be assured that U.S. influence in the Bank remains substantial and is built on much more than U.S. voting power and its ability to nominate the president. Many factors guarantee that American opinions will be heard: the Bank's location in Washington, in shouting distance from the U.S. Treasury Department; the strength and attentiveness of the U.S. Executive Director's office; the use of English as the Bank's official language; and the fact that Americans account for one quarter of the higher-level professional staff, as well as of senior management.

Finally, you are bound to hear concerns in the United States that the Bank finances projects overseas that compete with domestic firms. You can, of course, point out that the Bank creates trade *opportunities*, not just trade *competition*. The Bank supports U.S. exports both directly, through credits, and indirectly, by urging governments to adopt more open trading regimes and spurring export-oriented growth to increase nations' import capacities. Strategic planning studies of individual industries, undertaken by a new research unit in the Bank, could further strengthen your case. This research would assess the global prospects of international industries and provide valuable information to developing countries while enabling the Bank to counter charges that it generates surplus production. The Bank's capacity to undertake such studies and to assimilate related work being done by others is bureaucratically fragmented and needs to be centralized, with the output publicized.

The Bank should be able to gather a loyal and diverse coalition of Americans to support its work. The Bank's promotion of international trade, of more open and efficient development strategies, and of global financial stability will appeal to U.S. firms and banks as well as to centrist politicians. The Bank's concern for resource transfers and poverty alleviation is especially important to liberals, and can be coupled with increased Bank attention to alleviating the debt burden and addressing environmental issues. Internationalists place great stock in the Bank's role as a mediator of global tensions, and as a coordinator and catalyst of financial markets. And the *real politik* school will approve of the Bank's new emphasis on conditionality and leverage.

Conclusions and Recommendations

This letter has suggested numerous ways for the Bank to fulfill its crucial functions of coordinator, mediator, stabilizer, and intellectual center. What follows is a summary of key recommendations.

Coordination

A series of failures—of private capital markets to avoid a destructive cycle of over- and under-lending, of many Third World countries to design sustainable development strategies, and of donor agencies to pool resources—has opened wide chasms that only the World Bank seems potentially capable of filling.

• By assisting nations to draw up development strategies that meet standards for international competitiveness, the Bank can help to draw in the requisite external finance.

• By continuing to invent new financial instruments that connect various sources of capital, private and public, the Bank can overcome political, informational, and other barriers to more efficient international capital flows.

• By working with other creditors in debt rescheduling and aid consortia meetings, and with other official donors within individual countries, the Bank can contribute to agreements that treat all creditors fairly and that improve the productivity of new investments.

- By undertaking strategic planning studies of individual industries, the Bank can help avoid surplus production and head off tensions among trading partners.

Mediation

The Bank is in danger of forfeiting its mediating role if it addresses itself too exclusively to its largest stockholder, or to narrow creditor interests.

- By distributing the costs of financial adjustment more equitably among the contending parties, the proposed World Bank Initiative would better situate the Bank between creditors and debtors, between North and South.

- By supporting equitable adjustment strategies, the Bank would also seek to attenuate conflict among social classes within some developing countries.

- By maintaining a certain independence from the IMF when countries fall into arrears, the Bank will be better positioned later to reconcile the Fund with recalcitrant or bankrupt member countries.

- By highlighting the virtues of multilateralism, Bank leadership can educate Americans to the value of the Bretton Woods institutions in a changing age.

Stabilization

A recurrence of the sharp gyrations in global growth and capital markets that have recently threatened the international banking system and debilitated many developing-country economies should be avoided. Working with other agencies and governments, the Bank can both help prevent further damage from past errors and strengthen the international system's capacity to avoid future shocks.

- By advocating a reduction in the net drain of resources from the Third World, and by case-by-case granting of debt relief to afflicted debtors, the Bank can lessen the weight of old debt and create conditions for renewed growth and the eventual restoration of creditworthiness.

- By substantially increasing its own net lending, and by increasing the size and number of structural adjustment loans, the Bank can make its own contribution to overcoming the severe capital shortages plaguing many Third World nations.

• By collaborating with the IMF to design stabilization-cum-adjustment programs, and by persuading key industrial nations of the wisdom of further SDR allocations, the Bank can help prevent the Fund from becoming a destabilizing influence on member nations' balances of payments.

• By working with international investors and developing-country governments, the Bank can help create the financial instruments, the development strategies, and the optimistic psychology that are the ingredients for sustainable long-term capital flows that provide a healthy balance between private and official obligations.

Intellectual Center

The twin crises of debt and development have created the opportunity to question old verities. The Bank is well placed to play a leading role in formulating new answers to changing problems.

• By continuing to improve the scope and timeliness of its debt information system, the Bank can make creditors and debtors more aware of nations' financial capacities and requirements.

• By analyzing and collating the experiences with adjustment policies, the Bank can help member nations learn from each others' successes and failures, and improve its own policy advice.

• By devoting research efforts to studying the equity implications of adjustment policies, the Bank can help countries design fairer programs, while building upon its own acquired knowledge of how to alleviate poverty.

• By designing policy-based loans through a process of dialogue rather than *diktat*, the Bank can learn from the wisdom of its members and foster the sort of genuine inquiry and open exchanges of views that are most conducive to mutual respect and the accumulation of knowledge.

If the position of World Bank president is the best job in the world, it may also be the most demanding. It requires the wisdom of the philosopher king; the finesse of the practiced diplomat; the astuteness of the coalition politician; the administrative shrewdness of the senior bureaucrat; the mastery of financial detail of the corporate treasurer—and the boldness of vision that distinguishes a true leader. We on the staff of the Overseas Development Council join the rest of the world in wishing you the best in your endeavors.

Summaries of Recommendations

Summaries of Recommendations

1. Policy-Based Program Lending: A Look at the Bank's New Role (Gerald K. Helleiner)

The World Bank's expanding program of policy-based lending is likely to be highly productive in Latin America and Sub-Saharan Africa over the next five to ten years. However, some Bank policy recommendations—ones that go beyond supply-side restructuring toward tradables, responsible fiscal and monetary policies, and efforts to raise domestic savings—are professionally and politically controversial. Neither the optimal timing nor the sequencing of adjustment policies, for example, is well understood by the economics profession. Moreover, matters on which the Bank explicitly or implicitly advises its members—including trade policies, the role of markets versus governments, the role of foreign investment and exports, and the distribution of income—are subjects of much policy debate both within the Bank and among academic economists. Optimal policies certainly vary by country, and overgeneralized prescriptions in these areas arouse concern that the Bank may be illegitimately mixing its own preferred brand of development policies with the need for medium-term balance-of-payments adjustment. Adjustment policies cannot in any case succeed unless there is understanding and commitment to them at the country level.

To facilitate the expansion of policy-based lending where it can be productive while addressing its inherent problems, the author makes the following recommendations:

1. The Bank should plan for larger increases in structural and sector adjustment lending over the next five to ten years than the 15-20 per cent of total lending now projected; it can bring the proportion back to more 'normal' levels when balance-of-payments pressures ease. It should also temporarily increase its local-cost financing and urge bilateral aid donors to alter their lending programs similarly.

2. Policy-based (or program) lending should be coordinated with debt restructuring and relief in comprehensive assessments of individual countries' financing needs, in which Paris Club creditors, aid donors, the IMF, and the Bank are all integrally involved.

3. The Bank's conditions for program lending should be confined to those relating to medium-term balance-of-payments adjustment requirements and the protection of the welfare of vulnerable groups. Even when a country's overall development strategies do not accord with staff preferences, the Bank should consistently and flexibly support step-by-step policy change in appropriate directions.

4. Bank and Fund approaches must be consistent. It would be helpful to assign one or the other a 'lead' role at the individual country level for the next three to five years—presumably the Bank for the fifteen countries identified in the Baker plan and most of Sub-Saharan Africa. An independent review of IMF-Bank interrelationships and policy-based lending could be productive.

5. 'Neutral' inputs to relationships between the international financial institutions and borrowing members, drawing on outside expertise and independent funding, should be considered to help smooth the "policy dialogue" and monitoring processes.

6. The Bank's research program on adjustment processes and policies and their effects on growth and distribution deserves strong support. In general, a more eclectic and less predictably 'pro-market' approach would improve the reputation of Bank research activity. Analysis of policies and performance of industrialized countries as they relate to adjustment in developing countries should be expanded.

2. The Diplomacy of Policy-Based Lending (Joan M. Nelson)

Since their introduction in 1980, structural adjustment loans (SALs) and sector adjustment loans have proved important additions to the World Bank's array of techniques for promoting sustainable growth. They have provided flexible and fast-disbursing credits in response to urgent needs while accelerating and improving the design of reforms. They have also strengthened governments' economic management capabilities, and facilitated the Bank's ability to encourage and coordinate aid and loans from other sources.

The Bank plans to expand its policy-based lending dramatically in the next several years. Increased aid may induce and support more vigorous reform in some countries. But the pressure to "move money" is also a threat to effective policy influence.

Medium-term structural adjustment measures of the kind that the Bank promotes entail basic realignments in relative power and privilege. They generate sustained resistance from interest groups and parts of the bureaucracy. Successful reform therefore requires equally sustained commitment from reformist elements. *The core task of the Bank's policy-based lending is to create and sustain commitment rather than to press for specific measures at a particular moment.*

Commitment is the outcome of a learning process. It takes time. The main tools for encouraging the learning process are analysis, dialogue, and persuasion. There is often a tradeoff between immediate influence on specific reforms through use of tough conditions and longer-run influence on decision processes; the latter is usually a more important goal. Reforms undertaken primarily because they are conditions for release of badly needed funds, without understanding and commitment from political leaders, are likely to wither for lack of essential complementary or follow-up measures.

Loan conditions are most effective where they focus on a few key measures that are crucial for progress toward the broad, longer-run goals of the entire program. Less detailed (not softer) conditionality at first glance appears to trade less reform for faster resource transfer. But if some of the finer points are lower priority and compliance is difficult to judge, not much reform will actually be lost.

The Bank's ability to insist on conditions varies dramatically from country to country. The larger newly industrializing countries, especially those in Latin America, have thus far resisted the macroeconomic conditionality of SALs; in these countries, the Bank's influence must rest primarily on joint analysis and its role as broker vis-à-vis other (mainly private) sources of finance. Some smaller countries have been much more compliant with Bank guidance. In some of these countries, limited local analytical capacities have led Bank staff to specify reform steps in great detail. Yet these are the very cases where developing autonomous capacity to reach and implement decisions is most crucial for sustained effective adjustment. Detailed, ongoing intervention is not likely to produce that capacity, whereas it is likely to generate growing resentment.

Increased aid may "buy" accelerated reform in some countries. And increased aid should be made available to countries that have already undertaken drastic reforms but do not have funding adequate to resume growth. In still other cases, however, the long process of building understanding and support for basic reforms is only partly accomplished and is not likely to be speeded by increased aid. But unless painful stabilization measures achieve growth, there may be a political backlash that will sabotage prospects for further reform. Conversely, after years of falling living standards, even a modest upturn can help create confidence that will facilitate continued reform. Thus, where the broad thrust of country policies is appropriate, more adequate support than has been provided in the past few years could pave the way for long-term reform even if few or no short-term changes are demanded as conditions for the aid.

3. The Shifting Grounds of Poverty-Lending at the World Bank (Sheldon Annis)

The World Bank is moving away from what it could do relatively well—investing in the poor—toward the far more problematic role of managing the global economy. It should instead use its unique combination of resources, leadership, analytical capabilities, and political clout to do something that no other institution can do as well: finance economic growth that begins with the poor.

Investing in the poor is not only right for humanitarian reasons, it is also good banking. Comparing poverty and non-poverty lending experience, the Bank has found that the poor are reliable borrowers, that poverty projects do not have higher failure rates than non-poverty projects, and that investments in human capital give rates of return at least as favorable as non-poverty investments.

This is not to imply that the Bank should return to the narrow project mode that prevailed in the 1970s. Such Bank projects tended to be excessively oriented toward "hardware" at the expense of inputs that improve quality and accessibility; they generally failed to encourage participation or to build strong linkages between grassroots organizations and the public sector level; they often benefited select groups of the poor at the expense of broader investments that could have benefited the poor majority; they often took on overly ambitious objectives that were failures in social, economic, and environmental terms; and they often diverted attention away from supposed "non-poverty" sectors that in the long run were more critical to the poor than narrowly defined "poverty projects."

The Bank of the next decade needs not only to renew the 'drumbeat' of poverty alleviation that guided its course through the 1970s, but to correct the mistakes of that period. To that end, perhaps the potentially most powerful innovation in the Bank's new tool kit is policy-based lending. Although the idea may have evolved as a means to unshackle presumed constraints on growth as part of the adjustment process, the principle can be applied far more comprehensively. The causes of low growth, debt, and poverty are not simply that poor people don't have enough incentives to produce or that they are constrained by protectionist trade policies: In too many countries, the poor don't have land, small farmers don't have access to infrastructure, workers are not protected by social security and fair labor legislation, education is scant, prices discriminate against small farmers, agricultural and settlement policies work against natural resource management, credit is often not available to the people who can best make use of it, and, in general, politics tends to stifle growth by reinforcing entrenched power and privilege. The Bank should address *these* policy challenges as it links new investments with policy reforms.

In many ways, the present era provides an excellent opportunity to initiate a truly poverty-oriented approach to development. The Bank has learned from past mistakes and now can build on its experience. It has developed powerful new tools that can strike to the roots of poverty and low growth. In addition, many Third World governments, and especially new democracies, are interested in socially equitable models of development that respond to pressures from their constituencies. And perhaps most important, the poor themselves are better educated, healthier, better organized, more experienced with institutional development—in a word, more "investable."

4. The World Bank and Private Capital (John F. H. Purcell and Michelle B. Miller)

In its programs that involve private capital, the World Bank operates on the border between the broad range of development activities that the *public sector* directly carries out with public funds from governments and official agencies (including the Bank), and those commercially attractive activities that the *private sector* undertakes in the developing world. The Bank must constantly explore the interstices between these two realms, finding "niches of opportunity" where development can be promoted through constructive interaction between government initiatives and resources, and private capital and entrepreneurship.

Beyond its reliance on borrowing from private investors to fund its lending program, the Bank interacts with private capital in three ways. First, its policy adjustment loans attempt to create a more positive environment in borrower countries for renewed commercial bank lending and foreign direct investment. Second, the Bank cofinances loans with commercial banks. Third, the International Finance Corporation (IFC), a World Bank affiliate, makes loans and equity investments in conjunction with foreign and local private sector investors in developing countries.

These programs tend to be both relatively modest in scope and fairly concentrated within the Bank's organizational structure. They share several limitations, including being difficult to replicate, relatively labor-intensive, and often only informally coordinated with major Bank programs. The authors argue that these programs must necessarily remain modest, although they could become less concentrated and their goals more coordinated with and diffused throughout the Bank.

In the case of policy-based lending, the Bank's program is constrained by the varying receptiveness of developing-country governments to enhancing the role of the private sector in their economies; it can be most effective where governments are motivated to undertake steps to strengthen private sector roles.

The Bank's co-financing program works to fill a narrow gap in existing institutions. It is neither practical nor politically acceptable for the program to compete directly for assets where private lenders are willing to go without guarantees. The Bank can offer only limited guarantees through co-financing and thus can stimulate additional loans through its program only in special cases—where the overall situation is right, where the appropriate personnel are in place to encourage the effort, or where commercial banks face persuasive external pressure to lend.

IFC is essentially a provider of venture capital; it invests in the start-up phase of a project and sells its equity once the project is creditworthy. Its scope is limited both by its mandate to fund projects that cannot get private financing but will be profitable when completed, and by its need for a highly specialized staff with qualifications different from those available elsewhere within the Bank.

A new World Bank affiliate agency, the Multilateral Investment Guarantee Agency (MIGA), awaits approval by member governments. MIGA will provide insurance against specified noncommercial investment risks, and will work to promote private investment in developing countries. The authors argue that the agency will be most effective if its activities are well coordinated with other World Bank efforts; but it, too, will face pressure not to compete with private sector agencies offering similar insurance services.

The authors do not advocate a substantial transformation of the Bank's relationship to the mix of public and private actors who participate with it in the development process. While the Bank can expand its lending in line with the Baker plan and can continue its shift toward a more policy-oriented approach aimed at a resumption of growth, it cannot be expected to leverage the amounts needed to resolve the debt crisis—let alone lend those amounts on its own. The authors also urge that the Bank avoid becoming the spearhead for an ideological emphasis on the private sector. Private capital can play a beneficial role in the development process only under certain conditions and not in all cases. While the size of capital flows is in itself an important variable, and while there is growing recognition that flows of private capital are essential to complement public sources, the more important question is where private capital goes and for what purposes it is used. The Bank's foremost role should be to provide guidelines about what policies encourage beneficial private sector participation.

Without changing its fundamental mission, the Bank can work to improve its ability to accommodate the concerns and approaches of private investors and lenders within its existing structure. The authors conclude that there is room for closer cooperation between the Bank's functional and regional units involved in policy-based lending and for more cross-fertilization between programs that have a private sector orientation. Better methods of information-sharing and coordination as well as increased inclusion in decision-making of individuals with expertise in financial markets and new instruments on the Bank's staff can increase the Bank's collective knowledge and sensitivity to the potential contribution of private capital to development.

5. Financing the World Bank (Charles R. Blitzer)

The World Bank should have the capacity to substantially expand its lending to those countries that are able to invest new resources productively. Greater World Bank financing is particularly important at the present time, when private flows to many developing countries are severely restricted because of creditworthiness problems. Restored creditworthiness will depend in large measure on demonstrated results in improving productivity and re-establishing sustainable growth. Moreover, additional World Bank lending may make it easier for countries to accelerate the often difficult process of policy reform required to restructure their economies and to use resources more productively and efficiently.

Growth in non-concessional World Bank lending will soon be effectively limited by the level of subscribed capital, and IDA lending is fully dependent on continuing appropriations from donors. The dilemma is that the need for the World Bank to increase its lending capacity coincides with a period of severe budgetary stringency in many industrialized countries, particularly in the United States, making significantly increased appropriations improbable and reduced appropriations more likely. The author suggests that this dilemma can be overcome with a two-pronged approach:

1. A large General Capital Increase (GCI), on the order of $100 billion, is recommended to increase the World Bank's capacity to make non-concessional loans. This would allow the World Bank the flexibility to increase net disbursements to $65 billion in the next five to six years—if conditions warrant and if the borrowing countries are able to use these resources productively. The budgetary costs of new capital subscriptions would be manageable if the paid-in portion were no more than 2.5 per cent, or one-third the level of the last GCI. The budgetary cost to the United States of a subscription to such a GCI would be $500 million—or $50 million annually over a ten-year period. The author concludes that increasing lending capacity through changes in the so-called 'gearing ratio' would be a mistake because the present guarantee arrangements allow the World Bank maximum flexibility in its lending program and reduce the cost of its borrowing from world capital markets. Early agreement on a GCI is also desirable due to the decline in the ratio of industrial-country subscribed capital plus the World Bank's retained earnings to its disbursed loans—a phenomenon that could have a negative impact on the cost of the Bank's borrowing.

2. In the case of concessional lending, the need for expanded lending is immediate and coincides with a period of extreme budgetary stringency; the author therefore suggests that, for the upcoming IDA replenishment, an interest-subsidy facility should be established as a substitute for the present IDA funding arrangements. The principal of loans made under this facility would be raised by the sale of bonds, with a one-to-one gearing ratio to assure investors. The interest costs on these obligations would be shared by donors and the borrowing countries. The major advantage of this system is that the use of leveraging would allow for very large reductions in initial required appropriations while permitting a significant expansion of the lending program.

For example, assuming that such a facility were organized to provide net transfers of $7 billion annually and the interest subsidy were 4.5 per cent a year, the average budgetary cost to the United States during the next five years would be $215 million. By comparison, the U.S. budgetary cost of IDA operating at $3.5 billion annually (approximately the same level as presently) would be $875 million yearly over the next five years. Although the developing countries would lose some concessionality under this proposal, they would gain through the increased investment financing that such a scheme would permit.

6. The Technological Impact of World Bank Operations (Howard Pack)

The World Bank has promoted innovative technologies in many of its activities, attaining a solid record of achievements. It has helped to finance international agricultural research centers, encouraged the provision of agricultural extension services, financed efforts to encourage low-cost housing, and funded experiments designed to determine the feasibility of labor-intensive construction methods. Its industrial lending programs have not been characterized by the same degree of innovation, although recently there has been some movement in this direction. While industrial lending is not currently a major area of funding by the World Bank, the sector is of great importance for the future of the developing countries.

The major issues facing developing-country governments with respect to industry are the improvement of productivity and the generation of new jobs. In contrast, the World Bank's efforts have been limited mainly to financing new large-scale factories, with only cursory attention given to generating employment and improving productivity in existing plants in the same sector. Greater attention to these considerations would require a larger staff and might lead to a smaller total lending program for the transitional period. Maintaining the current level of industrial-sector lending may reduce the Bank's funding of alternative, smaller projects that have higher social rates of return.

To improve World Bank achievements in industrial-sector lending, the following guidelines might be incorporated into Bank lending:

1. Increase lending to the small-scale industrial sector while reducing funding of large-scale enterprises.

2. Attempt to generate innovations useful in the small-scale sector by a mechanism to stimulate research on agriculture similar to that employed by the Consultative Group on International Agricultural Research and the set of international research institutes that it supports.

3. Encourage programs designed to improve productivity in existing enterprises. Such efforts will often preclude the need for additional investment in a sector.

4. Provide an international mechanism for stimulating trade in used equipment, including the provision of information and insurance.

5. Where the World Bank continues to finance large-scale enterprises, encourage the adoption of equipment that maximizes income and employment generated by the investment. A high priority should be given to fostering bidding competition among a variety of international purveyers of equipment and to using Third-World-based consulting engineering firms.

Between Two Worlds: The World Bank's Next Decade

Chapter 1

Policy-Based Program Lending: A Look at the Bank's New Role

Gerald K. Helleiner

Short-term demand-oriented approaches to resolving balance-of-payments difficulties, such as are typically recommended by the IMF, have been reasonably successful when applied to short-term problems originating in over-expansion of domestic demand. They have been noticeably less effective, however, in dealing with prolonged and continuing difficulties—largely external in origin—facing many developing countries in the 1980s. The Baker plan appears to signal a new perception on the part of the U.S. government that longer-run supply-side approaches are now required in the major debtor developing countries and in the low-income countries of Sub-Saharan Africa. To this end, many suggest a new leading role for the World Bank in stabilization and adjustment programs.

The International Monetary Fund (IMF) has seen its function as assisting countries to achieve "sustainable growth,"[1] leaving to the World Bank and to aid donors the pursuit of rates of growth that are "desirable" or at least "adequate." Now, however, the IMF says that, for the major debtor countries and Sub-Saharan Africa, "an appropriate adjustment strategy must pay attention to the form as well as the size of external adjustment so that growth—which is so vital to the stamina needed for adjustment—does not suffer."[2] The Fund agrees that this will require, among other things, an "enhanced role for the World Bank and other multilateral development banks reflected in increased and more effective structural adjustment lending."[3]

Those now advocating an expanded World Bank role in program lending include some who have always seen program support as particularly productive for developing-country borrowers and/or as providing useful opportunities for external policy leverage. Most of those currently favoring relative expansion of medium- and long-term program lending do not, however, see this as a permanent shift in the Bank's approach to development lending as much as a temporary response to unusually severe balance-of-payments pressures. The period during which this temporary shift is required will vary from country to country, but it is likely to range from five years in Latin America to ten years in Africa.

Sustained restoration of external balance at acceptable levels and rates of growth of domestic output requires restructuring of production—toward tradables and away from non-tradables. Such restructuring requires not only appropriate domestic incentives but also sector-specific investment. The costs of too short-term an approach and inadequate external financing have been shortfalls in the investment required for such medium-term adjustment. Demand restraint has hit investment particularly hard, both because the import content of investment spending is typically higher than that of consumption and because government recurrent expenditures and private consumption are inherently difficult to cut. Additionally, in many cases, particularly in Sub-Saharan Africa, cutbacks have meant import-strangled economies operating well below existing capacity. In Sub-Saharan African countries, where both human and physical capital stocks are depreciating under the current severe foreign-exchange constraints, high immediate returns are obtainable from the provision of foreign exchange for the rehabilitation and full utilization of efficient existing capital, prior to any prospect of fresh net investment.

Growth requires increased investment and/or increased productivity. The Baker plan provides for increased conditional program lending by the World Bank, with conditionality associated with growth objectives as well as short-term stabilization. Unfortunately, IMF and World Bank experiences with longer-term policy-based program lending—notably through the Extended Fund Facility (EFF) and the Structural Adjustment Loan (SAL) experiments—have been mixed at best. The IMF has been unable to shift significantly from its traditional demand-oriented and short-term modalities. A recent study of EFF lending found that over half these loans were cancelled for non-compliance with IMF conditions, while several more had otherwise unsatisfactory outcomes.[4] The World Bank's SAL program has had fewer cancellations, at least in part because the performance conditions are more ambivalent; but the countries covered and the record of fostering appropriate policy reform have been limited.

It is not evident that the Bank's resources, knowledge, or lending procedures are any better suited to overcoming today's deep-seated adjustment problems than those of the IMF have been in the past. It looks as if adjustment finance will continue to fall short of the required amounts. There is still only limited professional understanding of adjustment processes and of the interactions between short-term and longer-term objectives—either in terms of theory or in terms of available evidence.[5] Optimal policies for growth have long been a matter for particularly vigorous professional disagreement, whatever the apparent self-assurance of some economists within the Bank.

This chapter explores the outlook and possibilities for an expanded World Bank role in policy-based program lending. It reviews the principal instruments of such lending and their prospects. It addresses the substantive issues in medium-term adjustment policy formation and seeks to identify what is and is not agreed among professionals. Some of the institutional aspects of an expanded Bank role in policy-based program lending are considered, as are some of the implications for the Bank's research program.

Instruments of Policy-Based Program Lending

Although structural adjustment loans (SALs) have received the most attention since their inception in 1980, "sector adjustment loans" have been more important over the past two years (see Table 1). In fiscal 1985, thirteen sector adjustment loans made up 10.3 per cent of total World Bank/IDA commitments, while three structural adjustment loans accounted for less than 2 per cent of the total (down from an average of 8 per cent in the 1980–84 period). The Bank's current three-year projections suggest that, in the 1985–87 period, sector adjustment loans will account for 10–15 per cent of commitments, whereas SALs will account for only about 4 per cent.

The distinction between SALs and sector loans is not always clear. Both seek major reforms in policies and institutions,[6] with the latter typically, but not always, more narrowly focused upon specific sectors. Issue coverage in sector adjustment lending has been extremely broad in some instances, for example, in reconstruction in Ghana and Guinea-Bissau, or in trade policy in Colombia and Morocco. More usually, however, it is related to more narrowly defined areas, such as export development, agriculture, industry,

Table 1. World Bank/IDA Commitments by Major Category of Lending Instrument FY1980–85
(percentages)

	1980	1981	1984	1985
Specific Investment	60.5	49.3	41.3	49.6
Sector Operations				
Sector investment and maintenance	16.9	20.6	26.5	24.9
Financial intermediaries	15.4	18.8	13.2	11.1
Sector adjustment	0.6	1.1	8.5	10.3
Structural Adjustment and Program Loans	2.7	7.1	8.2	1.6
Technical Assistance	1.1	2.3	2.1	1.4
Emergency Reconstruction	2.3	0.6	0.3	1.0
Total	100.0	100.0	100.0	100.0

Source: World Bank and author's calculations.

energy, fertilizer, or public enterprises. Policy reforms required under the conditions of these loans typically relate to liberalization, rationalized pricing, and other efficiency-raising measures.

Sector adjustment loans are generally seen as both less complex and less intrusive than structural adjustment loans. A comprehensive SAL simply may be too complicated to negotiate in a country like Brazil, but quite feasible in Ghana or Niger. Moreover, the degree of intrusion in domestic policies that a SAL implies may be politically intolerable today for larger and more powerful countries, particularly those with major debt "leverage." It is noteworthy that, although there have been no SALs in major Latin American countries, there have been large sector adjustment loans to Brazil, Colombia, and Mexico, among others. The Bank has thus been quite pragmatic and flexible in its utilization of these alternative lending instruments in its various member countries.

Other, even larger "sector operations" include "sector investment and maintenance" loans, and loans to local financial intermediaries. Non-project loans are also available for technical assistance and for emergency reconstruction after disasters. In all, lending for specific projects now accounts for less than half of total World Bank/IDA commitments, as against 60 per cent in 1980.

The Bank has also proven adept at modifying its usual project and sector lending procedures in response to its members' changing needs. Under the fast-disbursing Special Action Program that operated from 1983 to 1985, for instance, the Bank altered the time profile of its normal lending for forty-four countries facing particularly severe balance-of-payments adjustment pressures; some of these procedures subsequently have been incorporated into regular Bank lending practices. Not all of the Bank's program finance is appropriately described as "policy-based lending"; at the same time, both program *and project* loans can be consciously directed at policy change in support of structural adjustment. Categorizations such as those of Table 1 therefore can be misleading, and the data based on them should not be taken too literally.

Since non-SAL forms of policy-based non-project finance are now of greater significance, formal, self-imposed constraints upon the proportion of Bank lending devoted to SALs (10 per cent of total lending, 30–40 per cent to any one country) no longer serve any purpose. The need for rehabilitative and adjustment-oriented program lending relative to the funding of traditional development projects varies across countries and over time. At present and for the next five to ten years, program loans are likely to be particularly productive in Latin America and Sub-Saharan Africa. Unless major modifications are made in the character of the remainder of the Bank's lending program, it is difficult to see how, in current circumstances, SAL and sector adjustment lending can sensibly be projected at only 15–20 per cent of total lending over the next few years. One could easily imagine structural adjustment and sector adjustment loans together making up 75 per cent of Bank lending in countries severely constrained by scarcity of foreign exchange. Assuming that the geographic composition of its lending remains roughly the same, this would imply that program lending of these two types alone would rise to roughly 40–45 per cent. Relaxation of limits on the extent of local-cost financing permitted in the Bank's project loans is another device that could be employed more liberally to meet the current need for more balance-of-payments finance. At the same time, the Bank should be exercising maximum influence on commercial banks, bilateral aid donors, and other sources of external finance to provide credit or assistance in *program* form. As current adjustment difficulties and debt pressures ease, the relative importance of program finance can return to more normal levels.

Overall country-level needs for external resources for medium-term adjustment programs must be assessed in a holistic fashion. Debt-servicing obligations to all creditors, including the IMF and World Bank, must be considered in their entirety and in the context of the anticipated overall balance-of-payments position. Debt restructuring and relief in which all creditors are treated equitably (though not necessarily uniformly), should continue to be elements in the external financing programs of individual countries. Indeed, debt restructuring and relief, which in effect provides immediate *program* support, should be considered as just another instrument of program lending. There is no logic in the separate convocation of Paris Club meetings and aid donor consultations. Aid agencies should meet together with Paris Club creditors, the Fund, and the Bank to consider jointly country programs and their financing requirements.

Policies for Medium-Term Adjustment and Development: How Much is Agreed?

Unlike IMF lending, the inter-country distribution of World Bank lending is not governed by rules or quotas. Whereas not all countries have a short-term balance-of-payments 'need,' presumably all could claim that they deserve and require development finance. How inter-country distribution is decided within the Bank is not obvious; and perhaps it should be made obvious.

It is possible that the Bank's shift from traditional project lending toward policy-based program lending serves to rationalize a redistribution of resources toward major debtors and/or others of whose policies the Bank approves. If such countries are to receive a 'premium,' so to speak, above the resources that they would otherwise obtain from the Bank, then such a policy should be embarked upon deliberately and openly rather than slipped in under the guise of a new approach to lending. Undoubtedly it makes sense to redirect some Bank resources to those in particular balance-of-payments difficulties. But if resources are also to be redirected toward those pursuing what the Bank considers to be appropriate adjustment policies, it will be crucial to ensure that the Bank's assessments of local policies are soundly based and do not appear to be politically or ideologically biased. Policy-based program lending will ultimately stand or fall on the credibility and effectiveness of the Bank's conditions.

What *are* the key elements of a sound macro-economic framework for structural adjustment and development? There can be general agreement on the desirability of maintaining an appropriate real exchange rate, appropriate incentive structures more generally, adequate rates of domestic savings and productive investment, and responsible fiscal and monetary policies. Typically it is not as easy, however, to achieve agreement on *how* best to move from disequilibrium situations to those of greater internal and external balance—and, therefore, on the precise meaning of "appropriate," "adequate," and "responsible" policies.

The economics profession is much more comfortable with the analysis of alternative equilibrium or steady states than it is with analysis of transitions between them. The *dynamics* of change— within which market imbalances and alterations of behavior are of the essence—are extremely difficult to model. In fact, there is no *agreed* methodological framework for analyzing the medium-term macro-economic adjustment process that is now the prime object of policy.[7] Nor is there complete understanding of the complex interactions between financial and real variables in different kinds of countries—particularly not in the current confused circumstances of rampant inflation, debt crisis, and capital flight. In short, while macro and development economists know and agree on the sorts of macro-economic conditions at which they would like to arrive—that is, sustainable external balance with reasonably stable prices and growth—they have no agreed route for getting there.

At least as important to the longer-run restoration of external (and internal) balance is the ongoing process of economic growth and development. Countries that have pursued less-than-perfect development policies (and presumably all have some room for improvement) may be able to "tighten up" under the current pressure. Improvements in allocative efficiency and x-efficiency (better management), utilization of previously underutilized resources, and encouragements to longer-run savings and productive investment may all increase medium-term and longer-term growth. Unless there are reasons for believing that previous constraints on policy have been eased, however, there may not be room for much maneuver in these respects.

Beyond these generalities concerning the requirements for structural adjustment and more rapid growth, matters become considerably more controversial. While there can still be widespread agreement on the need for greater selectivity and care in public investment and for greater efficiency and consistency in economic management in general, there are major debates about strategy and tactics in particular country cases. And both in general and in the case of particular countries, there is fundamental political as well as professional disagreement on matters such as the appropriate overall role of the state, the scope for private enterprise, the degree of "outward orientation," and the distribution of income. The heart of the problem lies in the fact that the quasi-technical (though quite difficult enough) issues relating to medium-term balance-of-payments adjustment inevitably overlap in the Bank's policy-based program lending with much more controversial and highly political issues of development strategy.

Despite these complexities, the World Bank possesses a fairly consistent approach to policy-based lending. Like the IMF, it stresses monetary and fiscal orthodoxy, appropriate real exchange rates, positive real interest rates, and avoidance of administrative controls on external transactions. As far as longer-term development strategy is concerned, the Bank urges export expansion and overall outward orientation as against import substitution; liberalization of import barriers and movement toward unified import incentives; and maximum reliance upon markets rather than government ownership or direction in the domestic economy. The Bank's primary emphasis is on price incentives and "getting the prices right," and its obvious presumption is that, even in a world of pervasive imperfections, markets can normally be trusted to achieve that objective better than governments. Even in the world of the second-best, its approach is consistently to liberalize that which can be liberalized.

Just as the IMF has been criticized for the oversimplicity and inflexibility of its short-term models and approaches, the Bank now attracts criticism for the generalized character of the development policies it recommends. Certainly its general approaches can be defended only if they are flexibly applied; as universal rules they are neither economically sound nor politically acceptable. Improved incentive systems, for instance, generate the desired responses only in an appropriate overall context. Non-price impediments may severely constrain performance *whatever* the incentive structure. In African agriculture, short-run improvements in performance are limited by inadequate marketing systems, inability to obtain key inputs or sufficient credit, absence of consumer goods on which to spend earnings, and deficient transport and storage arrangements—while inadequate land and technology frequently set bounds to longer-run prospects.[8] Where total agricultural supply response is small, as is frequently the case, the main impact of food price increases may simply be to increase poverty.[9] In any case, it is not always easy to engineer or sustain real price changes through changes in nominal variables. Price inflation can be expected to offset nominal exchange-rate devaluation substantially, and the most cost-effective route to a sustainable new real exchange rate may not be to seek to reach it in one fell swoop.

The role of interest rates also remains uncertain. Increased real rates may improve the allocative efficiency of investment, reduce capital flight, and even attract savings from abroad in economies with relatively developed financial markets. The IMF research department itself concludes, however, that: "Despite the amount of research expended on the interest responsiveness of savings in general, and in developing countries in particular, it is still uncertain whether an increase in interest rates will, on balance, raise the savings rate."[10] Nor are the advantages of full financial liberalization over "financial repression" unambiguously favorable.[11]

Few would quarrel with the aspiration to remove or reduce import controls wherever possible. They tend to introduce inefficiency and corrupt practices when they are long maintained. But the timing of their removal and/or rationalization must be determined in the overall context of the economy's circumstances. To advocate liberalization during periods of foreign-exchange crisis is to risk the imposition of even greater economic costs upon an economy already operating under stress and below capacity. Premature and ill-timed liberalization episodes will set back the prospect for greater efficiency and improved overall economic performance in the longer run.

Similarly, few would quarrel with the aim of expanding exports from foreign-exchange-constrained economies. But the prospect of all developing countries simultaneously expanding export volume in similar products, whether primary or manufactured, is one that must be analyzed in detail. Primary-product prices are likely to suffer and protectionist barriers to manufactures to increase as a result of concerted efforts at export growth. Export strategy must therefore be quite carefully constructed, and information about market prospects coordinated and made more widely available. (However difficult such contingent projections may be, the Bank has a special obligation to offer holistic assessments of market prospects under various stipulated supply-side as well as demand scenarios.) It is not good enough to argue, as some do, that only a relatively few countries will actually act on the advice to expand exports, and that the adding-up problem therefore can be ignored. Nor is it sufficient to argue, as do others, that since world prices are 'given' for small countries, they can do nothing about them and should respond to current prices as best they can. Nor does the much-cited correlation between export growth and GNP growth— never applicable to the poorest countries anyway[12]—tell very much about the direction of causation or appropriate policies for countries that seek both.[13]

The role of foreign direct investment is another source of controversy. Increased incentives and receptivity to foreign investors may simply generate quasi-rent from them if, as much of the recent evidence suggests, their investment decisions are based primarily on more fundamental locational characteristics and long-run factors.[14] In recent years, direct investment in developing countries, which has always been highly concentrated in the same countries that attracted commercial bank lending, has dropped just as far and as fast as commercial lending, and it is unlikely to resume until the overall economic outlook in these countries improves. Quite apart from the sensitivities of many countries regarding foreign ownership and control of domestic industries—and however desirable increased equity, or equity-like, finance might be—the elasticity of response by direct foreign investors to improved investment incentives in developing countries is, for the present, likely to be low.

The relative roles of prices, markets, and governments in development are particularly controversial and politically sensitive. To acknowledge the importance of prices and incentive structures is certainly not the same as to advocate the universal use of markets. In a second-best world, there can be no theoretical presumption that even "well-functioning" markets will render signals conducive to the achievement of static efficiency, let alone developmental efficiency. There can certainly be wide agreement that governments should be selective in their activities and, where possible, more efficient in managing their own enterprises. Divestment is undoubtedly appropriate in many cases; as a universal prescription, however, it is of dubious merit. Market imperfections and failures, distributional and "non-economic" objectives, and political pressures of various kinds are likely to continue to generate significant government intervention in developing-country economies; indeed, contrary to Bank orthodoxy, there is some evidence that government participation is associated with more rapid growth.[15] The political and economic efficacy of markets and governments varies across countries and in individual countries over time. Policy generalizations based on ideologically or experientially rooted perceptions can only be viewed with skepticism.

By far the most pervasive and consistent conclusion in the increasingly sophisticated economic analyses of adjustment policy alternatives is the impossibility of offering generalized prescriptions to fit all country circumstances. A recent survey of World Bank macro-economic models of developing countries sought to explore the consistency of their policy implications with the Bank's own 'conventional wisdom' regarding appropriate adjustment policies.[16] Many of the most important policies typically advocated—such as nominal devaluation and monetary and interest-rate policies—could not be analyzed at all because most of the models dealt only in real variables. That in itself reflects the relatively undeveloped state of the macro-economic modeling art in the countries in question. More striking still, however, is the inconclusiveness of many of the results.

Trade and exchange-rate policies generally "perform" as expected, although the dynamics of transitions—for example, the efficacy of nominal devaluations of various dimensions to achieve a desired real devaluation—are not addressed. "Getting prices right" (that is, in accordance with world prices) in the energy and agricultural sectors, on the other hand, may or may not be sensible structural adjustment policy. Thus in one model, of an oil-exporting country (Nigeria), Bank advice on energy prices seemed appropriate. But in another model, of a different oil-exporting country with severe absorptive capacity problems and an imperfect public investment expenditure system (Indonesia), it appeared preferable not to raise domestic energy prices with world price increases; the allocative losses deriving from energy subsidies to the private sector were less than those resulting from the inefficient public investment that would otherwise result. And in one oil-importing country (Thailand), adjusting domestic energy prices so as to 'track' international prices also seemed unhelpful because of its indirect effects upon domestic savings rates and external borrowing. Similarly, "getting prices right" for rice seemed appropriate adjustment policy in rice-exporting Thailand but exacerbated adjustment difficulties in rice-importing Korea (where domestic rice prices were above world prices).

Inconclusive results were also found in the case of fiscal policy: "Is fiscal austerity a good structural adjustment policy? It depends."[17] In one case where real/financial interactions were analyzed and the distinction between "curb" and regulated financial markets was explicitly provided for—the case of Korea—the modeling of monetary and interest-rate policies generated "unconventional" results. In combination, higher (regulated) interest rates and monetary restraint led to a serious slowdown in investment and growth, the effects of which exceeded any positive effects for household savings.

How much improved economic performance—measured in terms of growth or broader measures of development—can reasonably be expected from policy reforms alone, assuming that they are in the right direction? Much of the international rhetoric and recent World Bank writing suggests that it would be great.[18] In fact, there is very little evidence to support such a presumption. A recent study of thirty-one developing countries found that growth experience in the recent past can be significantly related to only two major categories of price "distortion"—exchange rates and real wages—with some limited further relationship to the degree of protection of manufacturing.[19] No association was found between growth and the degree of taxation (or protection) of agriculture, the pricing of capital (interest rates), the rate of price inflation, or energy pricing.[20] Evidently not all pricing-policy changes are likely to be equally productive. Wages are self-evidently among the most "political" of prices, and policies relating to them are likely to be part of a broader political-economic strategy. In short, "the correctness of the prices must be decided by reference to a comprehensive development strategy, and not independently of it. . . . Getting policies right is more than a matter of getting prices right."[21]

In its recent emphasis on improved policies for efficiency, the Bank has noticeably downgraded its previous concern for equity and the alleviation of poverty, as Sheldon Annis shows in this volume. Lip service is still paid to the social impact of adjustment programs, but in the Bank's own *ex post* country-level assessments of their effects, details have been conspicuously missing. Difficulties in agreeing upon appropriate approaches and finding reliable data may explain some of the failures in this area; but if there had been more will, more progress undoubtedly would have been made. UNICEF has expressed serious concern about these issues; in only one case—that of Ghana, and then only to a limited extent—has the Bank thus far availed itself of UNICEF offers of assistance, in association with interested governments, in the development of adjustment programs emphasizing both growth and a more "human face."

John P. Lewis's recent survey of the state of development economics notes that there is a "new orthodoxy" about, composed of what is probably a minority of "mainstream" development economists "headquartered at the World Bank." Lewis notes that "Their 'orthodoxy' is, as to economics, neoclassical. It carries forward with redoubled vigor the liberalizing, pro-market strains of the thinking of the 1960s and 1970s. It is very mindful of the limits of governments. It is emphatic in advocating export-oriented growth to virtually all comers. And it places heavier-than-ever reliance on policy dialoguing, especially between aid donors and recipients."[22] Members of the more eclectic majority are typically much more concerned to differentiate approaches between different countries and circumstances; many retain interest in distributional equity and the alleviation of poverty as important conscious policy objectives; most are also more interested in and concerned with political processes and constraints on policy action.[23]

A "pragmatic neo-structuralism" (the phrase is Albert Fishlow's[24]) seems to be gaining ascendancy not only in Latin America, but also in Sub-Saharan Africa. Recognition of the inadequacy of overly aggregative approaches to macro-economic analysis is coupled with that of the need to differentiate carefully among countries with different structural characteristics. The important role of markets and incentives is accepted; and there is a new skepticism about the capabilities and interests of governments. At the same time, however, the potential for a productive—if more carefully selective—role for the state is recognized. Simplistic recommendations for reliance upon the 'magic of the marketplace' are seen as ideology rather than analysis.

There are no 'quick-fixes' or easy answers to the current debt and financial problems of Latin America and Africa. To play to the gallery that suggests that there are quick solutions would risk later disillusion and discredit. The World Bank must foster an image and role of continuing and flexible support for economic development in whatever ways are appropriate and politically acceptable in particular countries, periods, and circumstances. Increased program lending should be directed to countries making serious efforts to restructure their production for the purpose of medium-term external balance—*regardless* of whether their overall development strategies accord closely with the professionally controversial preferences of some of the Bank's major member governments and some of its staff.

Institutional Aspects of Policy-Based Lending

Development-oriented conditions are not only more complex and more intrusive than IMF-style demand management conditions; they are also much more time-consuming to develop, achieve agreement on, and eventually monitor. It is in the nature of the funds at present available from the Bank in the form of program loans that they cannot be disbursed as quickly as IMF funds. (Table 1 shows the fall in the share of program loans in Bank lending in 1985, despite the obviously increased need for them.) Nor can performance be monitored as effectively and quickly. The data required for reliable assessment of real development performance typically take much longer to assemble than do the Fund's financial variables, if they are available at all; and tradeoffs among the various elements of developmental performance must somehow be considered in an agreed manner. Consequently Bank-style (SAL) conditionality has often engendered more delay and controversy than IMF conditionality, both at the outset of a Bank-backed adjustment program and subsequently. Therefore, conditioning the disbursement of installments on structural adjustment and sector adjustment loans ("tranching") would normally be most efficient if based upon a relatively few indicators—ones relating, above all, to balance-of-payments management and/or sector-specific objectives rather than to controversial overall objectives on matters such as the size of government or market liberalization.

Developing countries have long argued for longer-term and more supply-oriented approaches to current adjustment problems—and hence, implicitly, for a greater role for the World Bank relative to the IMF—but many are now having second thoughts. Concern about the Bank's inappropriate mixing together of *temporary* adjustment issues with more controversial matters of *long-term* development strategy have led to nervousness about an expanded Bank role in program lending. IMF conditionality, however imperfect and inappropriate, may be seen as less intrusive and less potentially damaging to development than that imposed by a World Bank with convictions of its own as to a universal recipe for growth. IMF conditionality also tends to be more consistent and predictable in its country-level application.

A significant Bank shift from project to program lending raises fundamental questions about the appropriate relationship between the IMF and the World Bank. The Bank's developmental concern obviously involves a longer time horizon than does the Fund's stabilization mandate; on the other hand, there is bound to be some overlap—and therefore some potential for mutually inconsistent approaches. At present, country-level consistency is achieved on an ad hoc basis. The World Bank is being brought into the picture more centrally in those cases where the Fund's relatively short-term approach has failed to restore balance; in such countries, the Bank is perceived as "bailing out" the Fund, and it is not clear what the continuing role of the Fund may be. In general, it would seem important to agree, on a country-by-country basis, as to which of the two should be the "lead institution" during a medium-term adjustment period.[25] The presumption must be that the Bank should "lead" in Sub-Saharan Africa and in the "Baker 15" (of the Baker plan) for at least the next five years. Whether or not such formal "lead" arrangements can be agreed, the Bank and the Fund must effectively synchronize their independent approaches to the same countries. "Cross-conditionality" is particularly counterproductive and annoying when its details are inconsistent and unpredictable. The evident incapacity of the Fund and Bank to work out joint approaches that are satisfactory both to the major shareholders and to borrowers suggests the potential usefulness of an independent high-level review of the appropriate mode for future Fund-Bank relationships. Such a review might also consider the best means of developing a single authoritative forum for the integrated consideration of the medium-term balance-of-payments prospects and financing requirements of individual developing countries.

The one point on which virtually all those with experience in the attempt to impose policy conditions in IMF and Bank lending agree is that the required policies do not hold if there is not serious commitment to them on the part of borrowers. If the relevant policies are not fully understood and supported by the government—or if they cannot carry domestic political support (or if opposition cannot be repressed)—agreement will only be transitory and the adjustment programs ineffectual. There can be external education and persuasion concerning appropriate policies. But there cannot be effective external imposition. When all is said and done, borrowing governments must, above all, pursue their own interests. Policy-based program lending is therefore best seen as a device for encouraging overall policy dialogue, as Joan Nelson argues in this volume.

Within the Bank, just as outside it, there is probably a majority who advocate support for step-by-step changes in the appropriate direction, avoidance of unproductive confrontation over less important issues, and attempts to influence only a few major policies at a time rather than more dramatic reforms. Even those who might be expected to give vigorous support to orthodox Bank policies advocate lower expectations and longer time horizons.[26] The qualities of the Bank personnel most directly involved in the negotiation and monitoring of policy-based loans are therefore likely to be more important than generalized prescriptive proclamations. Knowledge of the details of country-level practices and experience, and sensitivity to them, are crucial in the elaboration of appropriate and credible policy packages.

Tensions between the Bank and debtor governments may by eased by expanding the practice of involving 'neutrals' in bilateral dialogue. Outside experts have been involved in controversial cases from time to time in the past (for example, in India in the 1960s, and in Tanzania in the 1980s[27]), and they have been liberally drawn upon in Bank research and other consultancies. The Bank's traditions in this respect have involved far greater openness to independent assessments and utilization of external research and opinion than has been typical of the Fund. These traditions should now be drawn on, both for overall assessment of Bank policies and, in individual country cases, for the assessment of adjustment programs and external resource requirements. An outside review panel has recently been suggested to examine the appropriateness of the conditionality attached to SALs[28]; such a panel could be more useful if it addressed the broader issue of policy-based program lending of all kinds in conjunction with a review of Bank-Fund relations such as that suggested above. At the country level, resort to knowledgeable authorities not in the employ of the Fund or Bank to produce 'neutral' background papers for consultative groups and debtor-creditor mediation efforts could also prove valuable.[29]

Implications for the Bank's Research Programs

Outward orientation, the use of markets, and a limited role for the state are constant themes in Bank conditionality. It is perhaps surprising that neither the Bank nor the economics profession knows any more than it does about the differential circumstances in which these approaches are conducive to development. But these matters are theoretically complex—as is the reality posed by over one hundred different sovereign entities.

The uncertainties and disagreements in these spheres suggest room for productive theoretical and empirical research. The Bank's research activities, which deserve more funding than they have received, have been imperfectly integrated with the Bank's own internal evaluations of its lending programs or with emerging developing-country needs. In recent years, the Bank's research has also gained a reputation for reduced diversity of approach and increased predictability of results. It has devoted quite disproportionate effort to the documentation of the errors of governments and the advantages of reliance upon markets. Predictably, in these activities, the Bank's research has altered few opinions but annoyed many. Part of the renewed assault upon adjustment and development on the part of the Bank should be a research effort that is both more balanced and more integrated with the rest of the Bank's activity.

The most striking imbalance in recent Bank research effort is the scarcity of positive analysis of the costs of imperfections and failures of markets relative to the host of projects seeking to measure the costs of governmental interventions and mistakes. Rationalization of this as rectification of reverse imbalance in the professional literature of development economics is unpersuasive. Balanced and parallel efforts on both tracks would improve credibility in the professional community.

In current circumstances, research efforts within the Bank would benefit from considerable redirection—toward analysis of alternative adjustment-policy packages and the complexities of alternative sequencing of policies. The Bank's research on policy sequencing has thus far devoted disproportionate attention to trade liberalization. Analysis of overall distributional effects of alternative development policies has recently been resurrected; these issues should be addressed in the context of medium-term adjustment programs, and greater resources should be devoted to them. As has been argued, the analytical framework for the Bank's policy-based lending is not as developed as that for the Bank's project lending—or for IMF lending, for that matter, however controversial it may be.[30] Efforts to intensify Bank research on adjustment processes deserve strong support. Further research is needed on the following subjects among others: interrelationships between real and financial variables, determinants of savings and the efficacy of different savings-investment processes, the role of expectations, the relative efficacy of sharp and gradual policy changes, the size of capital flight and measures to harness it, potential for increased utilization of capacity, the role of selective as opposed to "blunt" policy instruments, and improved understanding of differential supply elasticities and their determinants.

In donor agencies and the World Bank, as well as in developing countries themselves, too much attention has been devoted to project evaluation and not enough to overall policy frameworks and strategic planning. The redirection of Bank concerns toward the appropriateness of overall country-level policies suggests the relevance of further research on governmental economic decision-making systems. The development and sustainability of appropriate overall policies require sound systems for the provision of relevant and up-to-date information, both for daily decision making and for longer-term policy planning. Bank research might contribute to the development of such systems.

The Bank's current research program appropriately provides for investigation of the interaction between developing countries and industrialized countries within the world economy. Under this rubric, immediately relevant research effort could be directed toward balanced analysis of global requirements in support of successful adjustment and publicization of individual industrial-country performance in meeting these requirements. It is now conventional wisdom that adjustment success is significantly affected by such external circumstances as OECD growth, interest rates, market access, and adequate continuing capital flows. Adjustment of the dimensions now required in the developing world places obligations upon the industrialized countries. Large current-account surpluses can only be earned by major debtor nations if others permit or encourage their own deficits. Yet nowhere is the performance of individual industrialized countries vis-à-vis the requirements for successful developing-country adjustment set out against the background of either their own promises or of overall requirements. The Bank could play a useful role by documenting protectionist measures, new policies affecting the quality of aid and other capital flows, and other relevant policy changes—both positive and negative—undertaken by the industrialized countries— and in estimating their impacts on developing countries attempting adjustment. Such an effort by the Bank could usefully draw on other sources (Development Assistance Committee of the OECD, IMF, GATT, UNCTAD) to produce an integrated and comprehensive assessment of creditor as well as debtor performance in global adjustment. This material could be made available for country-level consultations between debtors and creditors and for consultative group meetings, and, on a more global basis, in the annual *World*

Development Report. Such an initiative might begin to restore the currently somewhat tarnished image of the Bank as an advocate of global development—rather than merely a disciplinarian for Northern banks and other interests.

Conclusions

An expanded role for the World Bank in policy-based program lending involves far more than structural adjustment lending. Sector adjustment loans are already more important than SALs, and greater flexibility in the use of other instruments may also be significant in the support of adjustment. Current Bank projections of program lending at 15–20 per cent of total lending do not appear to allow sufficiently for the expanded need for program lending over the next five to ten years. Program-lending decisions should be coordinated with those concerning debt restructuring and relief, and holistic approaches should be pursued to individual developing-country financing needs. If expansion of policy-based program lending is intended or likely to redistribute the overall flow of Bank lending among its member countries, this should be embarked upon explicitly rather than achieved as a by-product of the new policy.

There is general professional agreement on the need for supply-side restructuring toward tradables through appropriate realignment of real incentives, responsible fiscal and monetary policies, and expanded savings and investment. Disagreements remain, however, concerning the timing and sequencing of the required policies and such matters as the role of non-price constraints, links between real and financial variables, the role of interest rates, and the role and timing of import or financial liberalization. More fundamentally, there are profound political and professional disagreements concerning appropriate longer-run development strategies—including differences as to the degree of openness and the role of export expansion, the role of markets versus governments, the role of foreign investment, and the distribution of income.

Generalizations across countries are unlikely to be helpful; in fact, they are likely to arouse suspicions about the Bank's motivations. The Bank's conditions for program lending are therefore best confined to those relating to agreed medium-term balance-of-payments adjustment needs or, in some cases, to sector-specific issues, rather than to more controversial aspects of overall developmental strategy. Efforts should nevertheless be made to protect the welfare of the most vulnerable groups in overall adjustment programs.

Longer-term and development-oriented conditions are inherently more intrusive and more difficult to agree upon and monitor than are the traditional IMF conditions. There is concern that the Bank may be illegitimately mixing its own preferred brand of development policies with medium-term balance-of-payments adjustment policies. There is risk that agreed approaches to medium-term adjustment and necessary capital flows may be impaired by Bank efforts to pressure unwilling and unpersuaded borrowers.

Bank and Fund approaches must in any case be consistent. It would be helpful to assign one institution or the other a "lead" role at the individual country level—presumably the Bank in the major debtor countries and Sub-Saharan Africa for at least the next five years. An independent review of IMF-Bank interrelationships and policy-based lending might be highly productive.

Adjustment policies cannot be successful without both understanding and commitment at the country level. Dialogue rather than arm-twisting is the appropriate mode for Bank-member interaction. Knowledge of, and sensitivity to, country-level details are both critical to the development of appropriate adjustment programs. Step-by-step changes in the appropriate direction should be supported. 'Neutral' commentary on issues between the international financial institutions and borrowing members could be helpful in smoothing their relationships. The Bank has more of a tradition of using outside expertise than does the Fund, and it could now usefully draw on it.

The Bank's research program has been imperfectly integrated both with its own internal evaluation processes and with current developing-country needs. It has recently acquired a reputation for consistently pro-market approaches and would benefit from a more eclectic program. Much positive analysis remains to be done on adjustment processes and policies as well as their effects upon growth and distribution. The Bank might also develop an expanded role as monitor of policies and performances of industrialized countries as these relate to adjustment in developing countries.

Notes

Note: I am grateful to Richard Feinberg, Tony Killick, Joan Nelson, John Williamson, and numerous officials in the International Monetary Fund and the World Bank, none of whom is responsible for the content of this chapter, for discussions that have helped to clarify my own thought, and to Sidney Dell, Richard Feinberg, and John Williamson for comments on an earlier draft.

[1] Manuel Guitian, "Economic Management and International Monetary Fund Conditionality," in Tony Killick, ed., *Adjustment and Financing in the Developing World, The Role of the International Monetary Fund* (Washington, D.C.: IMF, 1982), p. 93.

[2] J. de Larosière, "The Debt Problem and the Challenges Facing the World Economy," *IMF Survey*, November 25, 1985, p. 358.

[3] IMF/World Bank, *Joint Press Release*, No. 85/37, December 2, 1985.

[4] Stephan Haggard, "The Politics of Adjustment: Lessons from the IMF's Extended Fund Facility," *International Organization*, Vol. 39, No. 3 (Summer, 1985), pp. 505–34; and Tony Killick, *The Quest for Economic Stabilization: The IMF and the Third World* (London: Heinemann, 1984).

[5] Lars Calmfors, ed., *Long-run Effects of Short-run Stabilization Policy* (London: Macmillan, 1983).

[6] World Bank, *World Development Report, 1985* (New York: Oxford University Press, 1985), pp. 50–51.

[7] Fahrettin Yagci et al., "Structural Adjustment Lending, An Evaluation of Program Design," *World Bank Staff Working Paper*, No. 735 (Washington, D.C.: World Bank, 1985).

[8] Stanley Please, *The Hobbled Giant, Essays on the World Bank* (Boulder, Colo. and London: Westview Press, 1984), pp. 297–98.

[9] John W. Mellor, "Agricultural Change and Rural Poverty," International Food Policy Research Institute, Food Policy Statement, No. 3 (Washington, D.C.: IFPRI, 1985).

[10] Mohsin S. Kahn and Malcolm D. Knight, "Fund-Supported Adjustment Programs and Economic Growth," *IMF Occasional Paper,* No. 41 (Washington, D.C.: International Monetary Fund, 1985).

[11] Carlos F. Diaz-Alejandro, "Goodbye Financial Repression, Hello Financial Crash," *Journal of Development Economics*, Vol. 19, No. ½, 1985, pp. 1–24.

[12] G.K. Helleiner, "Outward Orientation, Import Stability and Economic Growth: An Empirical Investigation," in Sanjaya Lall and Frances Stewart, eds., *Theory and Reality in Development* (London: Macmillan, 1986), pp. 139–53.

[13] Albert Fishlow, "The State of Latin American Economics," in *Economic and Social Progress in Latin America, External Debt: Crisis and Adjustment* (Washington, D.C.: Inter-American Development Bank, 1985), pp. 139–40.

[14] Theodore H. Moran, "The Future of Foreign Direct Investment in the Third World," in Theodore H. Moran and contributors, *Investing in Development: New Roles for Private Capital?* (New Brunswick, N.J.: Transaction Books, for the Overseas Development Council, 1986).

[15] Rati Ram, "Government Size and Economic Growth: A New Framework and Some Evidence from Cross-Section and Time-Series Data," *American Economic Review*, Vol. 76, No. 1 (March 1986), pp. 191–203.

[16] Warren C. Sanderson and Jeffrey G. Williamson, "How Should Developing Countries Adjust to External Shocks in the 1980s? An Examination of Some World Bank Macroeconomic Models," *World Bank Staff Working Paper*, No. 708 (Washington, D.C.: The World Bank, 1985).

[17] Ibid., p. 91.

[18] World Bank, *World Development Report, 1983* (New York: Oxford University Press, 1983); and R. Agarwala, "Price Distortions and Growth in Developing Countries," *World Bank Staff Working Paper*, No. 575 (Washington, D.C.: The World Bank, 1983).

[19] Esmail Aghazadeh and David Evans, "Price Distortions, Efficiency and Growth," *World Development*, forthcoming 1986.

[20] See also Albert Fishlow, "The State of Latin American Economics," op. cit., pp. 140–41.

[21] Ibid., p. 141.

[22] John P. Lewis, "Development Promotion: A Time for Regrouping," in John P. Lewis and Valeriana Kallab, eds., *Development Strategies Reconsidered* (New Brunswick, N.J.: Transaction Books, for the Overseas Development Council, 1986), p. 9.

[23] Ibid., p. 10.

[24] Albert Fishlow, "The State of Latin American Economics," op. cit.

[25] Stanley Please, *The Hobbled Giant*, op. cit., pp. 72–73.

[26] Elliot Berg and Alan Batchelder, "Structural Adjustment Lending, A Critical View," mimeographed, 1985.

[27] Stanley Please, *The Hobbled Giant*, op. cit., pp. 78, 93–94.

[28] Edmar L. Bacha and Richard E. Feinberg, "The World Bank and Structural Adjustment in Latin America," mimeographed, 1985.

[29] Gustav Ranis, "Debt, Adjustment and Development: The Lingering Crisis," in Khadija Haq, ed., *The Lingering Debt Crisis* (Islamabad, Pakistan: North South Roundtable, 1985), pp. 207–16; and G.K. Helleiner, "The Question of Conditionality," in Carol Lancaster and John Williamson, eds., *African Debt and Financing* (Washington, D.C.: Institute for International Economics, 1986).

[30] Fahrettin Yagci et al., "Structural Adjustment Lending, An Evaluation of Program Design," op. cit., p.2.

Chapter 2

The Diplomacy of Policy-Based Lending

Joan M. Nelson

In 1986, in the wake of the worst international depression in fifty years, two propositions are widely accepted: Most developing countries must make major changes in their policies and institutions to adjust to changed economic circumstances and resume growth. And most need substantially increased net capital inflows in order to adjust and grow. The spotlight therefore is on policy-based loans: stand-by lending by the International Monetary Fund, World Bank structural adjustment and sector adjustment loans, and similar multilateral and bilateral aid programs. These are the instruments best suited to transferring needed resources in flexible and fast-disbursing form. And these are also the instruments that give donors and creditors the greatest scope for influencing recipients' policies.

The World Bank has greatly expanded its policy-based lending since 1980, and it is contemplating further sharp increases over the next several years. This prospect raises two issues:

1. How can the Bank most effectively encourage policy reform? The 'get tough' rhetoric of some recent statements, mainly from official and non-official U.S. sources, seems to emphasize sharply increased conditionality as the means to speed reform. However, some informed observers and practitioners are deeply skeptical that conditionality can bring about reforms that recipient governments are not already prepared to undertake.

2. The call for more policy-based lending implicitly assumes that increased aid and increased influence go hand in hand. Do they? Or do the dual goals of resource transfer and policy influence under some circumstances interfere with each other?

Greater understanding of these issues should contribute to more effective influence on recipients' policies. Equally important, sustainable international support for an expanded Bank role demands realism regarding the Bank's ability to promote reform as well as sensitivity to the nature of the policy-influencing process. Expectations about the Bank's ability to promote reform are crucial to building support for increased funding for the Bank within the wealthy nations (through IDA VIII and a General Capital Increase) and for encouraging other agencies and the commercial banks to participate more generously in funding efforts. If expectations about the Bank's ability to promote reform are unrealistic, the results—within a year or two—will be disillusionment, the undermining of fragile and painfully constructed support and cooperation from other funding sources, and damage to the Bank's relationships with the countries it seeks to aid.

G.K. Helleiner's chapter in this volume focuses on the *content* of Bank policy-based lending—that is, on the kinds of policies that countries are being urged to adopt. In contrast, this chapter concentrates on the *process and techniques* of policy-based lending as conducted by the Bank and on the scope and limits of its likely influence.

The Process of Policy-Based Lending: Contrasts Between the Fund and the Bank

Historically, creditor and donor nations have linked financing in many ways to what they viewed as improved recipient policies. The various approaches range along a scale, according to the extent and specificity of involvement in the recipient's decision-making process. At the least invasive end of the scale is *ex post* allocation of funds to countries where, in the donor's judgment, the policy framework is generally valid. At the opposite end of the scale one might place, for example, the virtual receiverships imposed on the Ottoman Empire and some other chronic debtor nations in the nineteenth and early twentieth centuries, when agents of the creditors essentially moved in and took over the financial administration of governments. IMF stand-by agreements and World Bank structural adjustment loans (SALs) and sector adjustment loans obviously fall along the spectrum between these extremes.

Some analysts and practitioners argue that the *ex post* approach is the most effective way to encourage sound policies. The approach offers incentives while avoiding the risk of being wrong about what will promote adjustment and growth in a country's specific circumstances. It also avoids the charge of intervention. Governments that pursue irresponsible or corrupt policies would simply receive little or no aid. The international financial community in fact has largely withheld aid from some countries on these grounds, sometimes for years—as in the case of Haiti in the 1960s, or Ghana in the 1970s.

But there are strong arguments for a more active, interventionist approach. The least developed countries often have only a handful of officials trained to assess complex economic issues and design appropriate reforms. Even nations with extensive analytical capabilities often can benefit from experienced outside perspectives. Second, governments are not monoliths; those favoring reforms usually confront unconvinced colleagues and opposed vested interests. Intervention in the policy formulation process itself can provide the support of respected outsiders and suggest designs or phasing of policies that may reduce opposition. Third, many policy reforms have initial economic costs that hard-pressed governments cannot afford without bridging finance. For example, heavy export taxes may be suffocating a country's largest foreign-exchange earners. However, if those taxes comprise the major share of government revenue, and if alternative sources will take time to develop, the government may not be able to afford to remove the taxes without temporary compensatory financial support. Fourth, where economic deterioration has eroded public confidence in the government, quick-disbursing funds for imported production and incentive goods provide both an economic boost and political breathing space for implementing reform.

Post-World War II history provides a number of examples of bilateral and multilateral efforts to link sizable non-project aid to macro-economic policy reforms. The Marshall Plan called on European governments to stabilize their economies, establish investment priorities, and adopt basic changes in their trade policies. U.S. Economic Cooperation Administration missions in European capitals discussed these matters intensively with their host governments. Sometimes they went beyond dialogue and sought to exert pressure, particularly with respect to stabilization measures, usually through their control over counterpart funds.[1] During the 1960s, the U.S. Agency for International Development (AID) not only discussed governments' macro-economic policies, bilaterally and through the multilateral machinery of the Alliance for Progress, but also experimented with attaching conditions, as in the ill-fated Bell-Dantas agreement with Brazil in 1963. During the 1970s, however, AID narrowed its focus and concentrated on agriculture, health, and education, with little attention to macroeconomic policies. The World Bank from the outset almost exclusively funded *projects*—although it engaged in dialogue on macro-economic policies in the course of its periodic country economic studies, and although its project loans often carried policy conditions somewhat broader than the scope of the projects themselves. Thus, in the 1970s, the International Monetary Fund was the sole major institution engaged in extensive policy-based lending.

By 1980, two major factors converged to propel the Bank into much more extensive policy-based lending: the growing conviction within and outside the Bank that poor policies were a basic cause of problems in many developing countries, and a sharp escalation in the urgency of reform as a result of the post-1979 global economic crisis. The Bank had also expanded its policy analysis activities and capabilities during the 1970s, and many of its staff welcomed a vehicle that would use these capacities more fully. Structural adjustment loans, introduced at the end of 1979, provided such a vehicle. Starting in 1983, the Bank also sharply increased the number of sector adjustment loans, which, like SALs, generally provided quick-disbursing resources in support of policy and institutional change but focused on more sector-specific issues. By conservative count, structural and sector adjustment lending together accounted for roughly 17 per cent of the Bank's commitments by 1984—up from a bit over 2 per cent in 1980.[2]

Superficially, Bank SALs resemble IMF stand-by agreements in several ways. Both kinds of loans are formally initiated by the borrowing government's statement of the measures it plans to undertake: for stand-bys, a Letter of Intent, and for SALs, a Letter of Development Policy. These reflect extensive discussion and negotiation. Both stand-by agreements and SALs are typically designed to disburse over twelve to eighteen months. Both instruments are designed within analytical frameworks that attempt to look several years into the future. In principle, the Fund uses a three-to-five-year framework and the Bank a somewhat longer perspective, but the difficulty of anticipating most key trends for more than a few years probably makes the contrast more apparent than real. And both Fund and Bank policy-based loans seek as their ultimate goals medium-term balance-of-payments viability consistent with resumed growth.

Despite these apparent similarities, the real timeframe and the content of SALs are quite different from those of stand-bys. Fund stand-bys are designed to be single-shot, as signaled by their comparatively short repayment periods. Since the late 1970s, many developing countries have entered into a semi-continuous series of such arrangements with the IMF, but these have generally been responses to ongoing difficulties rather than an explicit design for cumulative reform. In contrast, SALs and sector adjustment loans are designed as ongoing programs. Up to five SALs may be extended to any one country. The interval between successive SALs has averaged twenty months. The process can also be extended by interspersing or following SALs with sector adjustment loans. Thus a SAL or sector loan is designed and handled as part of a process of adjustment stretching over as much as a decade.

The content of SALs and stand-bys also differs substantially. The contrasts are only partly captured in the conventional notions that the Fund emphasizes demand restraint while the Bank concentrates on supply-side measures, or that the Fund deals with macroeconomic policies while the Bank operates at a more "micro" level. Fund stand-bys focus on a few key, primarily monetary, targets: ceilings on expansion of credit, restrictions on new external debt, minimum levels of foreign-exchange reserves, and reduction in current arrears. Devaluation is often but not always a condition or pre-condition.[3] Letters of Intent attached to stand-bys often spell out the specific measures the government is contemplating, such as price changes, wage freezes, or interest-rate adjustments. These are often a focus of discussion between Fund staff and government officials, but they are rarely binding parts of the agreement.[4]

SALs address a much broader spectrum of policy reforms. In contrast to the financial targets in IMF stand-bys, which usually leave the choice of precise actions to the governments, SALs specify a sizable list of precise actions to be taken. Some measures, such as tax changes and interest-rate adjustments, are designed to mobilize resources. Other measures seek better resource use—for example, intensive reviews of public-sector investment programs, measures to improve the financial performance of state-managed enterprises, and pricing-policy reforms. Still other reforms are aimed at encouraging exports and, often, at liberalizing imports. Sector adjustment loans vary in scope: Some are nearly as broad as SALs, while others focus fairly sharply on a specific sector or sub-sector. Both SALs and sector loans often seek not merely a specific action, but the initiation of ongoing adjustment processes by the government itself. For example, a loan may require a government not only to increase producer prices for key crops, but also to establish a procedure for periodic price adjustments as conditions change.

Many of the reforms required in SALs or sector loans have quite different political and administrative characteristics than the key measures typically implied by Fund stand-by agreements. The latter often are swift, 'stroke of the pen' actions—such as devaluation, wage freezes, or across-the-board budget cuts—that can be taken by a few central economic officials. In contrast, the kinds of measures involves in SALs—institutional reforms, improved public-enterprise efficiency, revision of public-sector investment programs, tariff revision, and import liberalization—all entail a protracted series of decisions and choices involving a wide circle of public and often private agencies and groups.

Politically, IMF-supported austerity measures are typically viewed as highly risky. They usually impose immediate and highly visible losses on broad swathes of the public, particularly the vocal and volatile urban public. Yet major aspects of a stabilization program, particularly budget and wage restraints, can be presented (and are sometimes accepted) as temporary sacrifices to pave the way for restored balance that will eventually benefit all. In contrast, many of the measures central to Bank policy-based loans entail long-term realignments of institutions, incentives, and relationships—that is, shifts of power and privilege. The politics of medium-term adjustment are different, but even more difficult than the politics of short-run stabilization. Bank policy-based lending is less likely to provoke street riots than are Fund stand-bys—but it is more likely to generate intense resistance within bureaucracies and from varied interest groups.

Bank and Fund policy lending differ, then, in timeframe, in content, and in the administrative and political character of many of the reforms sought. These contrasts in turn cause differences in the pace and style of interaction with national governments and in techniques used to encourage reform. The popular image of the Fund probably exaggerates the role of conditionality in its overall relations with governments. In reality, the Fund maintains a fairly continuous lower-key exchange of views through annual consultations in each country, the Bank-Fund joint annual meetings, the work of IMF resident representatives in many countries, and the missions sent to evaluate requests for low-conditionality credit facilities.[5] But stand-bys, which are arranged under crisis conditions and with short timeframes, often do impose stringent conditions to elicit desired government action.

Because SALs and sector adjustment loans focus on 'real economic' processes (rather than financial targets) and because they go into considerable detail, they often require more protracted analysis and negotiations. Fund negotiations seldom involve officials outside the "central economic team"—the Ministry of Finance, the Central Bank, and often the Planning Ministry. In contrast, Bank analysis and negotiations involve much wider circles.

Since only genuine commitment can prevail against the protracted and dispersed resistance generated by medium-term adjustment measures, *the core task of policy-based lending in support of such adjustment is to create and sustain commitment rather than to press for specific measures at a particular moment.* Building commitment takes time. Occasionally, a new regime will take power that is already committed to reform. In such a situation, it may be possible to move very quickly—but the original process of generating commitment may well have taken years, even decades, as aspiring political leaders have formulated their ideas of what is wrong with the economy and what reforms are necessary.

Bank SALs and sector adjustment loans vary more among countries—with respect to content and style—than do Fund standbys. The Fund's Articles of Agreement require uniform treatment of members. The Bank has no similar legal constraint. Moreover, most stabilization crises demand similar short-run corrective measures precisely because a short timeframe offers little scope for taking into account the individual features of each economy. But these individual features are often crucial to the success of *medium-term* adjustment efforts, and Bank programs therefore are and should be more differentiated to reflect different situations. The Bank also has a wider range of instruments than the Fund, permitting more flexible responses to country differences. As the Bank has gained experience with policy-based lending, it has found it useful to shift from sector adjustment loans to SALs, or from SALs to sector loans, and to integrate both with project lending and technical assistance.

As a result, the style and nature of the policy dialogue—and, more broadly, the Bank's efforts to influence policy—vary dramatically among countries. In some countries, generally the smaller ones with comparatively limited local analytical capabilities, Bank involvement has been extremely detailed and continuous. Countries like Chile and Korea, with more extensive analytical abilities, have also welcomed SALs, but the Bank's role in these cases has been less tutorial and more collegial. In Colombia, the Bank has worked closely with the government to develop a sector adjustment loan focused on trade policy and export diversification but entailing key macro-economic measures; the Bank simultaneously took a direct and vigorous role in encouraging commercial banks to maintain credit and resume longer-term lending. In Brazil and Mexico, the Bank has played a much lower-profile role, and its policy loans have focused more narrowly on sectoral issues.

Bank Experience with Policy-Based Lending

From 1980 through 1985, the World Bank approved thirty-one SALs in eighteen countries. It also entered into thirty-two sector adjustment loans in twenty-five countries, including seven where SALs were also conducted at the same or different times. What can

Table 1. World Bank/IDA Adjustment Loans by Recipient Country FY1979–1985 ($ millions)

	Structural Adjustment Loans	Sector Adjustment Loans	Total Adjustment Loans
Latin America	**653.6**	**1,488.8**	2,142.4
Brazil	—	655.0	655.0
Mexico	—	350.0	350.0
Colombia	—	300.0	300.0
Jamaica	191.4	98.6	290.0
Chile	250.0	—	250.0
Costa Rica	80.0	25.2	105.2
Panama	60.2	—	60.2
Uruguay	—	60.0	60.0
Bolivia	50.0	—	50.0
Guyana	22.0	—	22.0
Africa	**841.6**	**938.2**	**1,779.8**
Ivory Coast	400.7	—	400.7
Nigeria	—	250.0	250.0
Kenya	185.9	—	185.9
Ghana	—	176.0	176.0
Sudan	—	115.0	115.0
Malawi	100.0	5.0	105.0
Zambia	—	100.0	100.0
Zimbabwe	—	70.6	70.6
Uganda	—	70.0	70.0
Senegal	60.0	—	60.0
Mauritius	55.0	—	55.0
Tanzania	—	50.0	50.0
Madagascar	—	40.0	40.0
Togo	40.0	—	40.0
Sierra Leone	—	21.5	21.5
Mauritania	—	16.4	16.4
Burkina Faso	—	13.7	13.7
Guinea-Bissau	—	10.0	10.0
Asia	**1,517.8**	**600.0**	2,117.8
Korea	550.0	222.0	772.0
Philippines	502.3	150.0	652.3
Pakistan	140.0	228.0	368.0
Thailand	325.5	—	325.5
Europe/North Africa	**1,831.3**	**640.4**	2,471.7
Turkey	1,556.3	300.0	1,856.3
Yugoslavia	275.0	90.0	365.0
Morocco	—	250.4	250.4
Total	**4,844.3**	**3,667.4**	8,511.7

Note: Structural adjustment loans approved as of November 1985.
Sector adjustment loans approved through June 1985.
Source: World Bank.

be learned from this substantial experience regarding the Bank's capacity to influence broad economic policies?

Legal Compliance with Loan Conditions

Legal compliance with specific conditions is the most concrete and immediate criterion of whether government policies have conformed with Bank requirements. But it is a seriously flawed gauge. Governments can technically comply with many conditions without the supplementary action necessary to make the measures effective or durable. Bank management and staff, concerned to transfer resources or preserve ongoing relations, may tailor specific conditions to what they believe the government is already prepared to do. And the kinds of performance targets used by the Bank permit considerably more staff discretion in determining compliance than do IMF stand-by performance criteria.

Of the thirty-one SALs approved through the end of 1985, only one—in Senegal—was cancelled due to the borrower's failure to take agreed actions. Roughly half of second loan-installment ("tranche") disbursements have been delayed for periods of a few weeks to many months—the average delay is five and a half months. Sometimes these delays reflect disputes between the Bank and the government as to whether agreements have been fulfilled. In other cases the government does not request release of the second tranche as originally scheduled—a tacit admission that conditions have not been met. Both situations, of course, indicate some failure to influence government action. However, serious delay or even cancellation do not always signal failure. For example, although the first SAL in Senegal was discontinued, the government did eventually address the problems that had caused cancellation. A new SAL has recently been approved for Senegal.

There are a number of cases where a first SAL was not followed by a second. In the cases of Bolivia and Guyana, this reflected the Bank's judgment that prospects for a viable adjustment effort were too slim to warrant a continued effort at that time. In Pakistan, in contrast, the Bank's decision not to follow an early SAL with a second one was a result of the considerable adjustment achieved, the fact that sizable aid was available from other sources, and the government's preference for less broad-gauged and intrusive sector lending.

'Real' Changes in Government Policies and Action

The formal record of compliance with loan conditions tells us little about real influence, but more direct assessments are also far from satisfactory. Gauging influence means trying to guess what the government would have done in the absence of Bank persuasion and pressure, and such judgments are inevitably subjective. Nevertheless, the Bank's evaluation studies and discussion with its staff support a few generalizations about the process of policy-based lending:

- Without question, policy-based lending has permitted *greatly expanded dialogue* on macro-economic and sectoral policies. The entire process of preparing, negotiating, and monitoring SALs or sector adjustment loans, especially where these have constituted an ongoing series, permits much more continuous and intensive discussion of a wide range of macro-economic policies.
- The process has often influenced the *agenda* of key economic decision makers. That is, it has shifted the relative priority of issues, altered and/or sharpened the definition of some of those issues, and brought some issues from the margin (or beyond the boundaries) of official debate into the center.
- The process has clearly affected the *design of solutions* to policy problems.
- In many cases, the *pace* of decisions or actions has been accelerated.

Bank advice, support, and pressure have been more effective in initiating actions than in guaranteeing their full implementation. The Bank's own assessments repeatedly note that follow-up measures have moved more slowly than originally anticipated. In some cases, Bank staff chose a deliberate strategy of setting ambitious targets in order to stretch government efforts. But often Bank staff appear not to have fully appreciated the limits on governmental capacity—above all, lack of staff with appropriate training and experience—as well as problems of bureaucratic and political resistance.

The discussion so far has focused on the Bank's ability to affect government actions in a direct and immediate way. Policy reforms can also be influenced indirectly—via improvements in governments' decision-making capabilities and changes in leaders' perceptions of the nature of economic problems and the range of potential solutions. The policy results of institutional and individual learning are often hard to attribute directly to Bank efforts. Yet, in contrast to direct influence, such indirectly catalyzed learning potentially can improve a wide range of policies and decisions. For this reason, especially in the least developed countries, influence on decision-making processes and attitudes is more important than direct and immediate impact on specific government actions.

Most Bank policy-based lending seeks to improve the economic management capabilities of governments. Roughly two-thirds of all SALs and sector adjustment loans include or are accompanied by separate technical assistance focused on institutional change.[6] Moreover, the whole process of policy-based lending, including analysis, discussion, negotiation, and evaluation constitutes an incentive and provides a focus for governments to improve their own analytical staff and coordinating mechanisms.

Policy reforms depend not only on governmental capabilities, but also on the attitudes and assumptions of key decision makers. In many developing countries over the past half-dozen years, there has been a reassessment of basic assumptions, particularly with respect to the roles of the state and private markets in promoting growth and equity. Gerald Helleiner, in his chapter in this volume, calls the new attitudes that are emerging "pragmatic neo-structuralism." The intensive analysis and discussions associated with Bank policy-based lending have undoubtedly contributed to this shift in attitudes.

The learning process should be, and often is, two-way. Intense and detailed involvement in a range of policy issues and programs in specific countries may lead Bank staff to modify their own views regarding, for example, the extent to which pricing changes alone can bring about desired production responses. More broadly, real economic processes are a product not only of economic principles and technology, but also of interlacing social and cultural, political, and bureaucratic forces. These linkages must be understood by those designing effective reforms.

The Role of Formal Conditions

What role have formal conditions played in the broader process of attempted policy influence? Calls for the Bank to take the lead in encouraging and supporting adjustment include proposals that the Bank "get tough"—presumably meaning that it insist on fundamental reforms as conditions for financing. Yet some experienced Bank staff and outside observers argue that conditions add little to the influence flowing from analysis, dialogue, and financial support. Actions taken primarily because of imposed conditions, rather than conviction, are usually counterbalanced or eroded in short order.

In principle, the conditions, targets, and tranching incorporated in Fund stand-by agreements, Bank SALs, and sector adjustment loans serve several functions. They sharply identify those measures without which additional finance can provide only fleeting relief. They anticipate difficulties, setbacks, and growing opposition. Provision of the first tranche of funding may itself erode commitment by seeming to lessen the need for further painful measures. To combat such tendencies, specific conditions set up monitorable performance targets and attach concrete incentives to meeting the targets.[7]

It would appear that such conditions would be most effective in IMF stand-bys. The Fund is usually lender of last resort, and other funding sources often link their support to the Fund's approval of a government's stabilization program. As noted earlier, short-run demand restraint, while painful, can be partly implemented by highly centralized economic decisions. Yet in reality the Fund has a spotty record of influencing policy. Many stand-bys are discontinued—sometimes because exogenous factors such as weather or international prices prevented targets from being met, but often because governments did not take agreed actions. The most frequent failed target, interestingly, is restrictions on government expenditures—a goal that usually demands decentralized and ongoing implementation.[8] Even where agreed actions are taken, governments often fail to take the follow-up measures necessary for more than a brief improvement. Thus an IMF study of exchange-rate adjustment in eleven African nations concludes that the effects of the devaluations were vitiated within one to two years.[9]

Bank SALs and some sector loans incorporate a long list of specific actions—often fifteen to twenty—that the government agrees to take prior to release of the second tranche. (Some sector adjustment loans do not use tranches, or have only a few conditions.) What have these conditions really accomplished? Some conditions have probably been 'window dressing'—in the sense that Bank staff were certain all along that the government would take the specified actions, with or without conditions. Much more often, however, specific conditions seem to have served to 'lean on an open door.' That is, key decision makers were persuaded that the measures were desirable, or at least worth trying, but their commitment was tentative or faced important opposition. Linking release of the first or second tranche of a loan to action on agreed measures served to bolster reformers, who could point to the concrete costs of backtracking and, if necessary, use the Bank as a scapegoat to deflect criticism.

Sometimes officials have even asked to include in a SAL or sector loan specific conditions that the Bank viewed as marginal or unrelated to the program's main thrust. The authorities sought to protect reforms to which they were committed by incorporating them into the package of measures labeled as crucial to national economic adjustment. Thus, for instance, reforms in the public housing program in the Ivory Coast were included as conditions in a SAL at the housing authorities' request.

But if specific conditionality has helped to prevent open doors from swinging shut, the obvious question arises of whether the same technique has not opened doors that were initially closed. There are certainly instances where specific conditionality in Bank loans pressed a government to adopt a measure in which it had little confidence. If the action has fairly prompt and desirable results, it may create conviction after the fact—a sort of learning by doing. In Ghana, for instance, many high officials were deeply skeptical about the reforms promoted by the Bank and the Fund in 1983 and 1984, but they modified earlier assumptions as they saw the first real progress in two decades, not all of which could be attributed to favorable weather. The reverse side of that coin is, of course, that if the action fails to be followed by economic improvement (whether or not such improvement could reasonably be expected as a result of that action alone) then the government and the public are likely to learn the 'wrong' lesson, further discrediting that line of action.

In sum, the conditions in Bank policy loans have focused the attention and maintained the resolve of governments, and they almost surely have accelerated some decisions and led to others that otherwise would not have been taken. Thus conditionality is not illusory, although its real impact is more modest than a simple listing of conditions and compliance would suggest. In assessing the value of conditionality, however, not only benefits, but also the costs must be considered: If conditionality is taken seriously, it makes the entire program hostage to the issue least likely to be implemented—either because it is genuinely difficult politically, or perhaps because it is relatively unimportant and may not receive enough high-level attention to ensure compliance. The early SALs tended to include very long lists of specific conditions, including progress on a great many studies by target dates. The Bank has backed off from that approach to some extent, but the tendency is still marked.

Conditions make most sense where they focus on a few key issues essential to the entire program. Only those circumstances justify jeopardizing the entire policy dialogue. The point dovetails with Helleiner's argument that Bank conditionality be focused on key, well-understood measures relating to balance-of-payments management and/or sectoral objectives.

A different, subtler risk may well be associated with extensive use of specific conditions: The process may tempt Bank staff to become increasingly interventionist, especially in small and poor countries. These are the cases where additional analytical expertise is most needed and where capacity to implement reforms may also be most limited. Just as many developing-country governments, eager to promote progress and frustrated by the complexities and difficulties of development, often seek solutions by devising even tighter controls, so Bank staff may be tempted to cope with frustrations and disappointments by seeking increasingly detailed agreements. At the very least, the relationship entails a heavy burden of moral responsibility for matters that would normally be the clear responsiblity of the government. Moreover, especially if there is a change of government, the relationship may backfire.

Finally, implicit political considerations affect the Bank's use of conditions in different countries. The Bank is less likely to insist on very stringent conditions in large countries with considerable importance in international affairs than in small countries that are less important to the Bank's largest shareholders. The larger Latin American countries have not been willing to request SALs. Even the sector adjustment loans in these countries use specific conditionality sparingly or rely on semi-tacit pre-conditions. That is, loans are made available in support of reforms already under way; often the loans are not tranched. For example, Bank staff working with Brazil are at best skeptical about the use of multiple conditions and tranching. In such countries, where commercial bank finance is also very important, the Bank's influence may result less from conditions attached to its loans than from its role as broker vis-à-vis the commercial banks. Extensive conditions play a much greater role in loans to many smaller and less advanced nations, especially in Africa, and many Bank staff working with these countries are convinced that the approach is helpful.

This poses a paradox. In terms of the flexibility and diversity of their economies, the heavily indebted newly industrialized countries (NICs) are probably capable of more rapid adjustment than the least developed nations. But in many NICs, extensive conditions are not politically feasible. In the smaller, less advanced nations, most of which are also much less confident and self-assertive on the international scene, the Bank can be much freer in using conditionality. But in most of these countries, effective structural adjustment is likely to be a much longer process. These are also the countries where it is most important to develop analytical capability and administrative skills. Extensive use of formal conditionality in these countries externalizes responsibility and may undermine the longer-run learning process so crucial for sustained reform. In short, in those countries where formal conditionality is easiest for the Bank, it should be used with restraint.

Policy Influence and Increased Resources: How Do They Interact?

The Bank is contemplating increasing its lending to about $21.5 billion by 1990—roughly 50 per cent above its 1985 lending level. Policy-based lending is expected to rise as a proportion of this increased total, implying a very rapid increase in SALs and sector adjustment loans. It is hoped that the Bank will also act as a catalyst to encourage considerably greater lending by commercial banks—at least to the more advanced developing nations.

Increased resources and increased policy influence usually are presumed to go hand in hand. The prospect of larger resources should in principle improve the Bank's access to the policy process, permit more ample bridging of short-run economic costs and political strains associated with particular reforms, and provide a stronger incentive for change. More adequate resources should help restore confidence and reverse the vicious circle of skepticism, hedging and disinvestment, and alienation that has stalled recovery or hastened decline in many countries. Many Sub-Saharan African nations and some others are currently so starved for imports and capital that policy reforms alone, without much greater aid, can do little to improve the economic situation.

But more resources cannot always buy more reform. The precise design of sound measures often depends on data that are not available and must be gathered, or on analysis of little-examined issues. And once technical staff, at the Bank and in the country, are satisfied that they know what needs to be done, there remains the task of education and persuasion of key decision makers. Increased resources cannot much accelerate these processes.

Even given substantial commitment by the government, there are administrative and political limits on the speed and scope of reform. Many of the Bank's evaluation and end-of-project reports for early SALs note the crucial role of top political leaders' attention in carrying through key reforms (or the failure of such reforms due to lack of such attention). Building political coalitions to support reform also takes time—especially where the costs of reform are prompt and concentrated on a few vocal groups, whereas the benefits are delayed and diffused among poorly organized sectors of society.

Sometimes increased resources, or pressure to provide increases, can actually undermine or conflict with policy influence. If the Bank is perceived to be under pressure to "move money," staff ability to exert influence on policy reforms is diminished. More broadly, where governments are confident that adequate alternative financing is available, incentive for reform—or at least willingness to enter into agreements contingent on reform—dwindles for all but the most dedicated. Availability of funds from other sources seems to have constrained Bank policy-based lending in Thailand and in Pakistan after the conclusion of the first SALs, and perhaps in Colombia as a result of rising coffee prices. Recent dramatic drops in oil prices may similarly undercut Bank influence in some other countries, while possibly increasing it in some oil-exporting countries. Finally, the Bank, and the donor community in general, may fear the chaos that could result if reforms are not accepted and aid not given.

With some exceptions, Bank policy-based loans have not been large relative to the scale of the economies assisted. Despite the points just noted, substantially larger stakes might prompt more response—perhaps especially from governments of some of the larger, heavily indebted countries (such as Brazil or Nigeria) that thus far have not been willing to enter into broad-gauged, policy-based agreements with the World Bank. In many cases, though, the main argument for accelerated transfer of resources in flexible, fast-disbursing form is not that this will directly or immediately buy more rapid or extensive policy reform, but that imports are urgently needed to break out of stagnation or a cycle of decline within only modestly altered policy frameworks.

Looking ahead, however, there is a stronger link between increased resources and accelerated reform. Unless some economic *growth* is combined with stabilization measures, a strong political backlash against measures already taken is likely. Conversely, where living standards have fallen for several or many years, a modest economic upturn (which in many cases is the best that can be hoped for) will strengthen confidence in the government's economic management and improve the political climate for further reforms.

Looking Toward the Future

While the international community has seen a good deal of policy-based lending since the Marshall Plan was launched, the next five years are likely to bring an effort by the World Bank that is unprecedented with respect to the number of countries involved and the range of policy change attempted. The endeavor will challenge the Bank's formidable analytical capabilities and will test still more severely its diplomacy, sensitivity, and judgment. The Bank's efforts will be both facilitated, and in some ways complicated, by its leadership role as envisioned in the Baker plan and in the new Structural Adjustment Facility of the IMF: It will be under strong simultaneous pressure to transfer resources quickly and to influence recipient-country policies. As the Bank enters this challenging new phase, the following points may be helpful to keep in mind—both within the Bank and on the part of its observers and critics.

1. *Sustained commitment, not only short-run acquiescence, is crucial to effective medium-term policy reform,* since such reforms provoke even more formidable political and bureaucratic resistance than short-run stabilization measures.

2. *Generating commitment is inherently slow: It is a learning process.* The process is not likely to be much accelerated either by the carrot of increased resources, or by the stick of conditionality. Where commitment is lacking, the example of progress in other countries in similar circumstances is likely to carry more weight than anything that the Bank can do directly.

3. *Less detailed (not softer) conditionality may accelerate the process of reaching agreement.* At first glance, this is a tradeoff of less reform for faster resource transfer. But if some of the finer points are of lower priority and/or likely to prove 'soft' in any case, not much reform will actually be lost. And if accelerated resource transfer helps restore confidence and paves the way for more reform in later rounds, the end result may be increased reform.

4. *In the smaller and least developed countries, particularly in Sub-Saharan Africa, the Bank must pursue policy-based lending with special self-restraint and sensitivity.* These countries have the greatest need for detailed intervention to analyze complex problems, devise solutions, and implement reforms. They also are often superficially compliant. Bank staff, with the best of intentions, are drawn into increasingly detailed intervention. But the truth is that a few dozen Bank staff cannot begin to control the intricate and often hidden processes of governance. By relying on detailed conditions, the Bank may bring about desirable specific actions, but at the cost of externalizing responsibility and generating deep resentment. These reactions may block the more durable and basic learning that is crucial for sustained reform. The current pressures on the Bank may make its staff less sensitive than they should be to the tradeoffs between short-run reform and lasting influence.

5. *In all countries, the style and content of Bank policy discussions with governments must evolve toward genuine dialogue.* Structural adjustment loans (SALs)—and, less clearly, sector adjustment

loans—were originally adopted as temporary expedients to cope with a transitory crisis. But they are likely to prove useful well into the 1990s and possibly longer. There is a consensus that adjustment in the least developed countries, primarily in Sub-Saharan Africa, will be a long, slow process. For quite different reasons, it may be realistic to expect only halting progress in some of the NICs burdened simultaneously with high inflation, heavy debt, and a need for liberalization. Each set of problems exacerbates the others, and little in past experience suggests that countries can cope effectively with all three simultaneously.

Although the need for ongoing adjustment will not evaporate as international economic conditions improve, the commitment of politicians may well wane. Instruments that help to keep attention focused on reform will become, if anything, more valuable. But as crisis pressures lessen, and as governments gain in technical abilities and confidence, the style and content of Bank discussions with governments will need to become more of a genuine dialogue.[10] Fewer and more selective conditions would facilitate such dialogue.

6. *The Bank now has sufficient experience with policy-based lending to gain from a probing assessment of its own tactics and strategies.* The evolution of policy-based lending in the Bank has inevitably, and probably usefully, taken the form of decentralized experimentation. Thus far, efforts to distill experience have been limited. The Operations Evaluation Department has done case studies of completed SALs, but these become available only a year or more after the loans are completed. Annual progress reports have assembled basic information, and there have been a few seminars for the exchange of experience. The time may be ripe for a more probing comparative analysis of various tactics and strategies and the circumstances under which these work well or poorly. For example: What are the costs and benefits of large numbers of conditions? Is it useful to design programs to 'over-stretch' government capacity? Is it useful to put a government on notice, initially, that the Bank anticipates ongoing support but at a dwindling level (as in the case of Jamaica)? Some deliberate strategizing, perhaps conducted jointly by Bank staff and outsiders, could provide the perspective that is difficult to gain while Bank staff are immersed in the details of current operations. Central staff can and should take a more vigorous and imaginative role in helping the Bank learn from its experience.

7. *The Bank should actively and creatively promote exchange and analysis of experience among top technical staff and decision makers in different countries.* Policy dialogue between the Bank and individual governments is one important channel for learning about policy options, but it is not the only channel available to the

Bank. The Economic Development Institute, the Bank's teaching arm, has in the past few years greatly expanded its training programs focused on policy issues. The Bank (and the Fund) have also sponsored or assisted some conferences and workshops for high-level officials. But most such officials still have very little knowledge of experience in other nations. Such knowledge might stretch their perceptions of options and accelerate the process of interpretation and learning that must underlie reform.

8. *The Bank needs to further adjust staffing patterns to support policy-based lending.* Since project divisions are usually responsible for sector loans, one high-priority need is for staff who can analyze links between macro-economic policies and trends, and sector or sub-sector issues. Field staff in countries with ongoing SALs or major sector loans should also be strengthened and given more authority. Policy design and adjustment are continuous and highly country-specific tasks, and the benefits of having staff on the spot are even greater than in the cases of project design and oversight.

In all its varied forms and styles, the World Bank's policy-based lending can make an important contribution to adjustment in the next few years. The prospects that it will do so are enhanced by the Bank's now considerable experience with the approach and by the growing economic sophistication and pragmatism in many developing countries. Policy-based lending combines learning—on both sides—and bargaining. But if the goal is lasting influence, the learning mode is much more fundamental than the bargaining.

Notes

[1] Imanuel Wexler, *The Marshall Plan Revisited: The European Recovery Program in Economic Perspective* (Westport, Conn.: Greenwood Press, 1983), Part II, especially pp. 100 ff.

[2] Some Bank non-project loans are similar to sector adjustment loans but are less clearly conditioned on policy reforms and are not classified as "policy-based lending." Therefore the statistics on the extent of policy-based lending are not entirely clearcut. Note also that sector adjustment loans vary widely in scope and duration. Roughly a quarter entail conditions affecting economy-wide policies; this is particularly true of trade-oriented "sector" loans, which cut across productive sectors. Such loans are not very different from SALs. (World Bank, "Sector Adjustment Lending: Progress Report," Washington, D.C., 1986, Table 2).

[3] Tony Killick concludes that devaluation was associated with roughly half the stand-bys between 1973 and 1981. Tony Killick, ed., *The Quest for Economic Stabilization: The IMF and the Third World* (London: Overseas Development Institute, 1984), pp. 192–95.

[4] Ibid., loc. cit.

[5] Ibid., p. 189; and Richard N. Cooper, "Panel Discussion," in John Williamson, ed., *IMF Conditionality* (Washington, D.C.: Institute of International Economics, 1983), p. 577.

[6] World Bank, "Sector Adjustment Lending," op. cit., Table 2, pp. 22–23.

[7] For further discussion, see Jeffrey Sachs, "Conditionality and Structural Adjustment: Some Comments for the World Bank," Draft manuscript written at Harvard University, February 1986.

[8] T.M. Reichmann and R. Stillson, "Experience with Programs of Balance of Payments Adjustment: Stand-By Arrangement in the Higher Credit Tranches," *IMF Staff Papers*, 25:2 (Washington, D.C.: 1978); W.A. Beveridge and Margaret R. Kelly, "Fiscal Content of Financial Programs Supported by Stand-By Arrangements in the Upper Credit Tranches, 1969–78), *IMF Staff Papers*, 27:2 (Washington, D.C.: 1980).

[9] Tun Wai and Paul Acquah, "IMF Experience with Exchange Rate Adjustment in African Countries," unpublished manuscript c. 1982.

[10] Philip Daniel, "Structural Adjustment and Policy Dialogue" (Brighton, England: Institute of Development Studies, University of Sussex, 1985).

Chapter 3

The Shifting Grounds of Poverty Lending at the World Bank

Sheldon Annis

It is ironic that poverty alleviation—once perceived as the World Bank's softest and least bank-like activity—has in many respects turned out to be what the Bank does best. And similarly, the supposed comparative advantage of the Bank—large-scale finance and economic forecasting—has in many respects turned out to be what it does not do particularly well.

The Bank of the 1980s is being thrust into the role of manager of the global economy—a role in which it has little actual experience and little reason to think it can succeed. At the same time, it is moving away from what it was learning to do and could certainly do much better: financing the alleviation of poverty.

Debt and recession are harsh realities. The argument here is not that the Bank can or should ignore the need for adjustment and economic growth. It can't and shouldn't. The question is what is the Bank's strongest suit in contributing to adjustment and growth. One idea is to stabilize the financial environment for commercial banks and hope for massive new private investment. Another is to punish governments that pursue economic or political policies that the U.S. government does not like. And another is to focus investment so that it builds upon the productive capacities of the poor majority—to stimulate economic growth from the ground up.

This chapter argues that the latter approach is not only right for humanitarian reasons (though that in itself is an excellent reason), but also is safer, more reliable, and what the Bank can do

87

well. Other strategies belong in other kinds of institutions, e.g., the IMF or the State Department. As the pre-eminent development institution, the World Bank is unique. It should exercise its leadership by marshalling its resources, technical capacity, and political clout to do something that no other institution can do so well: Lay the groundwork for economic growth on a world scale by investing in the poor.

In the long run, it may turn out that the most significant innovation of the mid-1980s' Bank is the idea of policy-based lending. But which policies and in whose interests? Looking to the future, the key issue now is whether the Bank will have the courage, independence, and imagination to couple this powerful new instrument with a crystal-clear commitment to the interests of the poor.

The Bank must make a set of decisions. From the point of view of this chapter, the first is to refuse to marginalize the poverty issue from the debt and adjustment issue. The Bank should renew its commitment not only to poverty alleviation, but more profoundly, to a kind of development in which growth starts with the poor. The Bank should reject failed poverty approaches by *correcting* rather than just learning from past mistakes. And as the Bank begins to explore more fully the realm of policy-based lending, it should not lose the opportunity to promote policies that are not only fiscally sound but socially just.

A Thumbnail Sketch of the Bank as a Poverty Lender

The Bank's experience with poverty alleviation was formed to a great degree during the period prior to 1973–74, which for the industrialized and most of the developing world was marked by relatively sustained growth, stable commodity prices, and cheap money. Yet that growth was selective; it bypassed most of the world's population, and everywhere the starkness of poverty stood out. Within and outside the Bank, it was widely accepted that import substitution, infrastructure, and industrialization projects either had not worked, were not enough, or had expanded the gap between the rich and the poor. Professionals generally accepted the need for small-farm development, preventive health services, and low-cost primary education.

Robert McNamara's speech on rural development at the Bank's annual Bank/Fund meeting in Nairobi in 1973 is generally regarded as the public launching of the World Bank's poverty orientation.[1]

"Absolute poverty," McNamara told the Bank's governors, "is a condition of life so degrading as to insult human dignity. . . . The fact is that very little has been done over the past two decades. It is time for all of us to confront this issue head-on."[2]

To do so, McNamara did substantially reorient the Bank. In retrospect, three milestones of his head-on confrontation with poverty stand out:

• First, the Bank redefined its main target to be the rural poor and directed significant new resources accordingly.[3] Between 1961 and 1965, 77 per cent of all Bank lending had been allocated for electric power or transportation, with only 6 per cent for agricultural development, and less than 1 per cent for social services.[4] In 1968, the outset of the McNamara term, Bank lending for agriculture and rural development amounted to only $172.5 *million*. Thirteen years later, it amounted to $3.8 *billion*—a 22-fold increase, coming to nearly a third of the Bank's total annual portfolio of nearly $12 billion.[5]

• Second, the Bank's research wing, under Hollis Chenery, focused its principal energies on poverty issues. Chenery's landmark 1974 volume, *Redistribution with Growth*,[6] argued that income redistribution could take place without slowing developing nations' rates of growth. This idea became, in a sense, the Bank's intellectual centerpiece and its marching order through the 1970s.

• Third, Bank research provided evidence that productivity gains from outlays in education, food and nutrition, drinking water, family planning, shelter, and health care made these worthwhile economic investments.[7] The concept of human capital became accepted within the Bank, then operationalized under the rubric of "basic human needs." By the end of the decade, such investment amounted to approximately $2 billion per year, or roughly 15 per cent of lending.

With poverty alleviation as its mandate, the Bank grew dramatically. In 1968, the year McNamara took over the presidency, lending amounted to less than $1 billion a year. By the end of the 1970s, it had risen to just under $12 billion. In 1968, the Bank employed 1,574 staff members; by 1981, the staff had grown to 5,201.[8] That is to say, until recently, the overwhelming majority of all loans ever made and all staff ever hired occurred within an institution that was guided, conceptually at least, by the idea of poverty alleviation.

The world's largest official financial institution and the world's poor may have seemed unlikely bedfellows. In the early years, many Bank old-liners saw poverty alleviation as a sop, not the real business of a Bank. Yet what they may have anticipated did not necessarily happen. Indeed, looking back over actual experience, what stands out is what might be called the *nonlessons* in poverty lending[9]—that is, what might have been expected but didn't turn out to be so about investing in the poor.

Nonlessons in Poverty Lending

First, the Bank did *not* find that the poor are less reliable borrowers than the nonpoor. On the contrary, studies generally showed better recuperation rates among small farmers than among medium and large farmers.[10] Similarly, loans to urban micro-entrepreneurs generally showed repayment rates at or better than those of wealthier entrepreneurs.[11] Where massive default occurred—even in crisis-ridden economies—analysis generally pointed to weakness in lending institutions and program design rather than to the borrowing characteristics of the poor.

Second, the Bank did *not* find that poverty projects have a higher failure rate than non-poverty projects. On the contrary, reviews of lending in agriculture and rural development consistently showed better performance for poverty than non-poverty projects.[12] (For an illustration of comparative performance of 78 evaluated agriculture and rural development projects, see Table 1.[13]) The Bank did indeed find that poverty projects may initially require more staff investment in design and a slower pace in implementation; but in the long run, poverty projects are not necessarily harder to plan, appraise, or evaluate than non-poverty projects.

Third, the Bank did *not* find investments in poverty alleviation and human capital formation to be less productive than investments in infrastructure, energy, or industry. On the contrary, empirical research sustained the human capital thesis that satisfying basic human needs yields high rates of economic return. One recent Bank survey of education projects in forty-four countries, for example, confirmed that the return to investment in *any* level of education in developing countries generally exceeds normal investment expectations of the Bank. The highest rates of return take place at the lowest levels of education in the poorest countries. (In the lowest income countries, return to investments in primary education averaged 27 per cent.[14] Similarly, the Bank found that a significant portion of a country's growth in GNP per capita can be attributed to its investments in human capital—all the more so in the poorest countries.[15]

In short, *from a banking point of view*, the Bank found that poverty alleviation was a fully bank-like activity that required no

Table 1. Comparison of Performance of 78 Completed Projects: Poverty-Oriented and Non-Poverty Projects

	Poverty-Oriented (Rural Development) Projects	Non-Poverty (Agricultural) Projects
Number of Projects	33	45
Total Project Costs	$1.611 million	$3.902 million
Bank/IDA Lending	$ 547 million	$1.374 million
1. Per cent that achieved increments in production greater than that estimated at time of appraisal	30% ($n = 10$)	22% ($n = 13$)
2. Per cent that reached the number of beneficiaries estimated at time of appraisal	54% (18)	29% (13)
3. Per cent with cost overruns	51% (17)	62% (28)
4. Per cent that achieved an economic rate of return (ERR) greater than rate estimated at time of appraisal	30% (3)	29% (13)
5. Per cent that achieved an economic rate of return (ERR) greater than the opportunity cost of capital (OCC)	76% (30)	53% (29)
6. Per cent cancelled or undisbursed	15% (5)	20% (9)

Source: "Annual Report on FY83 Lending for the Agricultural and Rural Development Department" (Washington, D.C.: The World Bank).

special justification on humanitarian grounds. In contrast, the Bank generally did less well in those "harder" areas in which it supposedly had a comparative advantage. In the 1960s, glamour "modernization" schemes, large-scale commercial agriculture, and capital-intensive industrialization plans often proved to be economic as well as cultural disasters. Massive infrastructure projects opened up expensive roads to nowhere. The cost overruns of Bank-financed hydroelectric projects made the "excesses" of social service ministries seem paltry by comparison. By the early 1980s, Bank-supported development finance institutions (DFIs), which channel investment capital into industrial development, had generally ended broke amid the shambles of larger financial systems. Oil prices caught the Bank by surprise in 1973, 1979, and 1985, each time with devastating results. The Bank was consistently over-optimistic about world commodity prices, which gravely undercut the massive gambles it made in agro-export. And perhaps most remarkably, the world's largest public lender—and largest concentration of world-class economists—failed to predict or adequately prepare for the debt crisis of the early 1980s.

Simply, the Bank did better in poverty than it did in "banking." Indeed, it is rather as if one looked back at MIT and found that the humanities and performing arts departments had performed better than engineering and astronomy.

Weaknesses of the Bank as Poverty Lender

Yet to say that the Bank reorganized itself around poverty alleviation—that it focused, thought about, learned about, or did better than expected—is not to say that it always did well or that it could not do much better. And certainly it is not to say that the Bank's past is the best model for its future.

An army of critics have taken their whacks at the Bank's performance in poverty alleviation, ranging from those who argue that it is a massive giveaway to those who argue that its net impact has been to make the poor poorer (implying in both cases that the less Bank, the better).

Among those who believe that the Bank on balance is or can be a positive force on behalf of the poor, the following criticisms are often raised to explain why the Bank does not do better.

1. *Although 'hardware' is easier for the Bank to plan and finance, the performance of projects and needs of the poor depend more on investments in 'software.'* In the Bank's terms, 'hardware' generally suggests physical expansion—for example, the construction of schools, health posts, or the laying of water pipes. 'Software' generally refers to investments that determine the quality and character of services—for example, investments in textbooks, school curricula, nurses' training, or the operation and maintenance of water systems. Often the Bank prefers hardware projects in part because they involve spending large amounts of money quickly. Borrowing governments also often prefer hardware projects because they tend to reinforce political authority and produce visible products. And donor countries often prefer hardware projects because they provide generous procurement opportunities for the sale of their turbines, bulldozers, computerware, and technical services. Yet the Bank has accumulated much experience with irrigation systems that are abandoned, clinics that are not visited,

schools that are not attended, and roads that are not traveled. Generally, empty infrastructure signals the need for greater attention to the human inputs, for slower pace and scale in project implementation, for labor- rather than capital-intensive construction techniques, for more village-level procurement and contracting, and for far greater emphasis on institution-building at the grassroots levels.[16]

2. *The long-term "sustainability" of projects is linked to participation by the poor.* The Bank knows by now that the long-term sustainability[17] of projects depends on the active involvement of the poor themselves. This is particularly true in hardware projects where infrastructure requires maintenance or where the poor are expected to assume an expanding share of recurring costs. Yet the Bank is on far more familiar ground dealing with *targets* than with *participants.* Many of its rural development projects limp along weakly or disappear when external subsidies end because the projects are unable to mesh with complementary grassroots organizations that allow the poor to invest in and fully benefit from the project. One corrective is for the Bank to collaborate far more actively with non-governmental organizations—or, more subtly, for the Bank to use its influence with governments to create public frameworks under which non-governmental organizations thrive and prosper.

3. *Even if aimed at groups of poor people, projects can be regressive in terms of overall equity objectives.* Until recently, the Bank's principal instrument was simply "the project." Projects are place- and time-specific. Their strengths are also weaknesses, as Michael Cernea points out:

> Projects concentrate resources on selected priorities, focus on circumscribed geographic areas, and can address specific population groups and constraints on development. . . . [they] are only segmented units of intervention; they often bypass overall structures, develop atypically, and are subject to the hothouse syndrome. Projects are also criticized because they tend to create enclaves, siphon resources from parallel nonproject activities, and may not generate sustainable development beyond their limited time frame.[18]

That is to say, assistance to the lucky few—even though they are very poor—can be given at the expense of the many. It can be argued, for example, that in overcrowded Third World cities no realistically conceivable Bank investment in site-specific housing (even assuming lowest cost self-help techniques) could keep pace with the absolute expansion of slums and need. Therefore, interventions that are not neighborhood-specific but affect factors such as the titling of squatter-held land, building codes, the placement of trunk highways and rail lines, taxes, the availability of rental housing, finance for building, the supply of low-cost construction materials, rates for water and electricity, or the responsiveness of municipal service agencies are not inherently less "poverty-oriented" than sites-and-services housing projects. The point is that projects have to be considered not so much in terms of their benefits to the few as in terms of their opportunity cost to the unassisted majority.

4. *Some "good ideas," generally the grandiose ones, simply do not work well in practice.* Certain schemes from the 1970s that were carried out with the nominal aim of helping the poor (for example, integrated area development in Tanzania) and certain technologies (for example, livestock raising and large-scale irrigation in the Sahel) generally have been expensive failures in economic, social, and environmental terms. One thing that these and many of the World Bank's better-known white elephants (various colonization schemes, the Polonoroeste program in Brazil's Amazonia, the Chico dam in the Philippines) have in common is the hubris of overextended reach. They underestimate complexity and overestimate the number of variables that a centrally directed project can understand and control. What is needed is for the Bank to learn how to operate at a small scale . . . on a large scale—that is, to create large umbrellas under which local efforts thrive and decisions rest in the hands of those who must bear their consequences.

5. *The distinction between poverty and non-poverty sectors, projects, and policies is, really, a false one; segmenting poverty can be counterproductive to alleviating poverty.* In order to create standards according to which its work could be measured, the Bank for many years distinguished rigorously between poverty sectors (e.g., health, education, and rural development) and non-poverty sectors (e.g., energy, industry, transportation). But in practice what affects the rich affects the poor, and vice versa. Equity must be a driving principle in *all* sectors. Power projects, for example, are not technically classified as poverty-oriented, yet they are important to the poor—when shortages of electricity reduce employment by cutting into industrial production or slowing water-pumping in agriculture; when kickbacks to military officials lead to cutbacks in social services; when dam construction displaces tribal minorities; when watershed damage undercuts the productivity of small farmers.

How to design a poverty-oriented hydroelectric project? To be sure, governments cannot build power stations that provide electricity to the working poor but not to the air conditioners of the rich. The equity issue here is anchored in larger public policy questions, such as how to design cross-subsidies through electricity rate structures; what the social implications are of various cost-recovery options; where facilities are built; how the long-term costs of exploitation of non-renewable energy resources will be shared; and how power development is balanced against other priorities in the national budget. Ultimately, these kinds of decisions can be far more significant to the poor than, say, a nominal increase to the ministry of education's budget or a new infant feeding program in a backwater province.

6. *Adjustment is generally painful to the poor, but unfortunately so is non-adjustment; the issue is the distribution of pain and the social basis for renewed growth.* After the oil shocks of the 1970s and the world recession of the early 1980s, the principal causes of poverty arguably became the vast income losses associated with the reversal of earlier growth. This reversal pushed millions below the subsistence level—all the more so because governments failed to take progressive measures to adjust, let alone offset the pain with targeted programs to alleviate the burden on the poor. Ironically, though the poor bore the pain and paid most of the price, it is certain that they were not the cause. Debt and recession hardly came about from extravagant spending on the poor, though it can be argued that it was seriously aggravated by economic policies that generally favored the short-term interests of national elites. In industry, for example, incestuous relations between the financial and productive sectors, combined with the easy availability of foreign funds, often allowed upper-class entrepreneurs to divert investment from productive enterprise to non-productive business activities (such as currency speculation), which ultimately led to capital flight, inflation, and devaluation. In agriculture, dependence on agro-exports produced corresponding subsidies to large landholders, which eventually made governments and national economies hostage to international commodity prices. Now, virtually all governments are trying to diversify their range of crops—but they are not necessarily trying to diversify their range of producers. In industrial lending, the Bank insists on positive real interest rates, non-oligopolistic competition within financial systems, and—to the extent that it can—assuring the separateness of private borrowers from state-supported lenders. But in the meantime, the larger, more difficult, and more pressing question is who is to bear the immediate and medium-term pain of adjustment? Even more important, as economies recover and re-gear for production, a social groundwork must be laid to support future growth.

Will Bank-inspired policy reform and adjustment programs simply rehabilitate the same horses that did so poorly in the last race, or will they work to redistribute opportunity? Will the poor emerge from adjustment only with the memory of pain and the certainty of a new phase of poverty, or will they emerge as producers?

Has the Bank Moved Away from Poverty?

If experience with poverty alleviation taught the Bank that, basically, poverty alleviation is a responsible, bank-like activity, where is the Bank heading today? Is it imaginatively addressing the challenges cited above, or is it diverging onto a different and riskier path?

At the outset of the 1980s, debt, recession, and a new administration in Washington changed the way the Bank thought about and responded to poverty. With the departure of Robert McNamara and the arrival of A.W. Clausen, the Bank shifted its explicit "focus on poverty" to what Clausen called a "balanced strategy," i.e., one of "faster economic growth combined with pragmatic measures to reduce absolute poverty."[19] In practice, that meant greater emphasis on free market economics, pressure to privatize many functions assumed by the public sector, and the promotion of "efficient" policies that would act as incentives for commercial banks to cooperate in debt restructuring and to significantly increase their capital flows to de-capitalized economies.

Has this shift acted at odds with the needs of the poor?

Officially, the Bank answers that it hasn't—that growth helps the poor as much as it helps anyone, and that softening of the poverty focus is largely a matter of rhetoric and the juggling of numbers. Extensive interviews at the Bank, however, lead one to the conclusion that the shift is deeper than that. There is much to suggest that, fundamentally, the direction of the Bank is changing.

Relative Decline in Lending to the 'Poverty Sectors'

As argued above, the distinction between poverty and non-poverty sectors is artificial, and in itself a highly imperfect measure of the degree of the Bank's commitment (much less the seriousness of a borrowing country's determination to eradicate poverty). Nevertheless, the Bank's own categories do reflect broad institutional priorities and signal where stars are rising and where they are falling.

Using the Bank's poverty/non-poverty breakdown, sectoral lending from 1975 through 1985 is shown in Table 2. Several points are to be noted:

• Between *1975 and 1980*, lending to the poverty sectors rose by $2 billion (135 per cent). Then, *from 1980 to 1985*, poverty lending rose only another $0.8 billion. Between *1975 and 1980*, lending to the non-poverty sectors rose by $3.5 billion (81 per cent). But then, *from 1980 to 1985*, it rose another $2.0 billion.

• Lending in most poverty sectors has generally stayed roughly constant or has increased by about $100 to $200 million per year. In contrast, lending in the major non-poverty sectors increased dramatically between 1980 and 1985: in agriculture, from $1.7 billion to $2.2 billion; in natural energy, from $457 million to $1.3 billion; in power, from $1.4 billion (FY1979) to $2.3 billion; in transportation, from $1.4 billion to $2.1 billion. The *increase* in these four sectors alone over these years ($2.9 billion) equals more than 60 per cent of the poverty total for 1985. And a safe guess is that the *content* of these increases in large-scale agriculture, power, energy, and transportation (which theoretically could be poverty-oriented) is not so notably reoriented to the poor as to offset the benefits that would be obtained by targeted investment.

• Within the poverty sectors, the major decline was in rural development, which dropped from a record high of $2.2 billion in 1981 (17.8 per cent of total Bank lending for that year) to $1.2 billion in 1984 (and rose again to $1.6 billion in 1985). Had rural development maintained a steady proportion of the total portfolio, it would have amounted to $2.8 billion in 1984. It is worth noting that $1.6 billion—the difference between what rural development lending was and what it would have been had its relative share remained constant—represents approximately *twice* the total assistance that the U.S. Agency for International Development extends to all the poorest IDA countries (not counting Economic Support Fund assistance).[20]

On the other hand, it should also be pointed out that Bank lending to poor countries (as opposed to lending to sectors or to poor people) has generally increased in recent years, especially to Africa and more recently to China. Lending to the very poorest IDA countries now constitutes 57 per cent of the IBRD/IDA total (see Table 3).

Such numbers suggest priorities. But still, if it is not evident that sectoral expenditures on, say, health are necessarily more beneficial to the poor than power plants or SALs, what indicators are *more* revealing of where the Bank is heading?

Table 2. World Bank Sector Lending (\$ millions)[a]

POVERTY SECTORS		FY 1975	FY 1976	FY 1977	FY 1978
Rural Development[b]		$1,013.0 (17.2%)	$722.0 (10.9%)	$1,235.0 (17.5%)	$1,722.0 (20.4%)
Education[c]		223.8 (3.8%)	321.3 (4.8%)	288.6 (4.1%)	351.9 (4.2%)
Population, Health, and Nutrition		40.0 (0.7%)	25.8 (0.4%)	47.3 (0.7%)	58.1 (0.7%)
Small-scale Enterprises		— —	— —	— —	— —
Urban Development		93.0 (1.6%)	79.6 (1.2%)	158.2 (2.2%)	368.6 (4.4%)
Water and Sewage		145.1 (2.5%)	334.6 (5.0%)	300.7 (4.3%)	375.2 (4.5%)
	Subtotal	1,514.9 (25.7%)	1,483.3 (22.4%)	2,029.8 (28.7%)	2,875.8 (34.2%)
OTHER SECTORS					
Agriculture[b]		845.0 (14.3%)	906.0 (13.7%)	1,073 (15.2%)	1,548.0 (18.4%)
Energy Natural		—	—	—	—
Electric Power		503.7 (8.5%)	949.3 (14.3%)	951.5 (13.5%)	1,146.2 (13.6%)
Industry		790.3 (13.4%)	606.0 (9.1%)	736.8 (10.4%)	391.8 (4.7%)
DFC's, IDF		504.0 (8.5%)	761.1 (11.5%)	756.2 (10.7%)	909.9 (10.8%)
Non-Project		520.0 (8.8%)	429.0 (6.5%)	216.5 (3.1%)	155.0 (1.8%)
Technical Assistance		— —	32.0 (0.5%)	16.9 (0.2%)	20.3 (0.2%)
Telecommunications		199.0 (3.4%)	64.2 (1.0%)	140.0 (2.0%)	221.1 (2.6%)
Transportation		988.7 (16.8%)	1,370.9 (20.7%)	1,047.6 (14.8%)	1,092.9 (13.0%)
Tourism		30.7 (0.5%)	31.0 (0.5%)	98.6 (1.4%)	50.0 (0.6%)
	Subtotal	4,382.1 (74.3%)	5,149.5 (77.6%)	5,037.1 (71.3%)	5,535.2 (65.8%)
	Total Lending	**$5,895.8**	**6,632.8**	**7,066.9**	**8,410.7**

[a]Figures in parentheses indicate percentage of total lending.
[b]Figures for agricultural and rural development are estimated from *Focus on Poverty Reports* (Washington, D.C.: The World Bank, 1983).
[c]Only primary education is considered a poverty sector; thus these figures overestimate actual resources devoted to the poor.

FY 1979	FY 1980	FY 1981	FY 1982	FY 1983	FY 1984	FY 1985
$ 1,272.0	$1,742.5	$2,202.0	$2,173.4	$1,438.0	$1,237.2	$1,571.8
(12.7%)	(15.1%)	(17.8%)	(16.7%)	(9.9%)	(8.0%)	(10.9%)
496.0	440.1	735.3	526.4	547.9	693.8	927.8
(4.9%)	(3.8%)	(5.9%)	(4.0%)	(3.8%)	(4.5%)	(6.4%)
114.0	143.0	12.5	36.0	118.4	243.0	191.0
(1.1%)	(1.2%)	(0.1%)	(0.3%)	(0.8%)	(1.6%)	(1.3%)
85.6	260.0	229.0	285.7	531.1	672.6	560.6
(0.9%)	(2.3%)	(1.8%)	(2.2%)	(3.7%)	(4.3%)	(3.9%)
309.5	348.8	501.0	374.8	554.3	500.0	384.6
(3.1%)	(3.0%)	(4.0%)	(2.9%)	(3.8%)	(3.2%)	(2.7%)
1,018.8	631.1	534.6	441.2	810.9	640.8	780.8
(10.2%)	(5.5%)	(4.3%)	(3.4%)	(5.6%)	(4.1%)	(5.4%)
3,295.9	3,565.5	4,214.4	3,837.2	4,006.6	3,987.4	4,416.6
(32.9%)	31.0%)	(34.0%)	(29.4%)	(27.6%)	(25.7%)	(30.7%)
1,275.0	1,742.6	1,660.9	934.2	2,260.3	2,226.9	2,177.5
(12.7%)	(15.1%)	(13.4%)	(7.2%)	(15.6%)	(14.4%)	(15.1%)
112.4	457.0	659.5	766.3	1,049.9	864.4	1,331.4
1,354.9	2,392.3	1,323.0	2,131.2	1,768.2	2,651.3	2,250.3
(14.6%)	(24.8%)	(16.0%)	(22.2%)	(19.5%)	(22.7%)	(24.9%)
842.5	422.5	885.5	959.4	691.8	554.6	644.0
(8.4%)	(3.7%)	(7.1%)	(7.4%)	(4.8%)	(3.6%)	(4.5%)
591.2	817.5	1,112.5	1,093.3	1,238.2	963.3	565.3
(5.9%)	(7.1%)	(9.0%)	(8.4%)	(8.6%)	(6.2%)	(3.9%)
406.5	522.5	1,012.0	1,240.7	1,434.7	1,377.9	629.2
(4.1%)	(4.5%)	(8.2%)	(9.5%)	(10.0%)	(8.6%)	(4.4%)
29.7	13.0	131.1	72.5	52.7	135.0	111.7
(0.3%)	(0.1%)	(1.1%)	(0.6%)	(0.4%)	(0.9%)	(0.8%)
110.0	131.0	329.2	395.8	57.0	166.5	121.6
(1.1%)	(1.1%)	(2.7%)	(3.0%)	(0.4%)	(1.1%)	(0.8%)
1,904.4	1,444.5	1,062.8	1,614.2	1,923.3	2,596.9	2,138.7
(19.0%)	(12.6%)	(8.6%)	(12.4%)	(13.3%)	(16.7%)	(14.9%)
113.2	—	—	—	—	—	—
(1.1%)	—	—	—	—	—	—
6,736.8	7,942.3	8,176.5	9,207.6	1,047.6	11,536.8	9,969.7
(67.1%)	(69.0%)	(66.0%)	(70.6%)	(72.4%)	(74.3%)	(69.3%)
10,032.7	11,507.8	12,391.0	13,045.9	14,476.7	15,524.2	14,386.3

Source: World Bank Annual Reports (various years).

Table 3. IBRD/IDA Lending to Groups of Low-Income Countries as a Proportion of Total Lending (in percentages)

Country Income Groups	through FY 1968	FY69–73	FY74–78	FY79–83	FY84–85
Per capita income up to $400[a]					
IBRD	19	11	16	10	24
IDA	80	80	86	87	94
Total	**27**	**31**	**33**	**31**	**40**
Per capita income of $401–$790[a]					
IBRD	10	12	19	17	21
IDA	6	10	12	6	6
Total	**10**	**12**	**17**	**15**	**18**
Total of both Income Groups					
IBRD[a]	29	23	35	27	45
IDA	86	90	98	93	100
Total	**37**	**43**	**50**	**46**	**58**

Source: World Bank
[a]Income levels in 1983 $US

Non-Poverty Orientation Reflected in Use of Staff Resources

Staff members frequently point out that the Bank moves not so much to the rhythms of its public positions and explicit policies as to more subtle "cues and signals." Internally, *the* Bank is many banks. It is smart, argumentative, intellectually heterogeneous, and politically factionalized (so that interviews are invariably punctuated with, "Well, off the record. . ."). Externally, the Bank is also many banks: It feels vulnerable to the U.S. administration, the Congress, and the press. Not surprisingly, it often sends mixed signals—one set to conservatives in the Treasury Department and another to liberals in Congress;[21] one set to the press, and another to its staff.

Which is the face and which the mask?

Answered one young staff member: "The best way to tell what the Bank is serious about is by watching which loans are going through easily, how staff resources are allocated, and who's getting promoted."

Which loans are going through easily. Structural adjustment packages and large policy-based sector adjustment loans are obviously more glamorous these days than standard poverty projects (though old-line projects still account for the statistical majority of Bank lending). The relative newness of these instruments requires intensive staff work (all the more so if they address equity concerns, which, if addressed at all, tend to be marginalized as "monitoring" problems).

Unfortunately, a characteristic of standard poverty projects is that they are *also* staff-intensive—at least they should be. To be successful (much less innovative), they require field visits, consultation with potential participants, and patient institution-building at the grassroots level. Such projects generally work better if they are planned slowly and implemented in phase with the evolution of public institutions and organizations of the poor.

In contrast, the new loans are *supposed to* move and disburse quickly, since, in large measure their purpose is to bridge shortfalls in foreign currency. The Bank is confronted on the one hand by central banks and planning ministries that are howling for cash, and on the other, by criticisms that it is bureaucratically inept and sitting on piles of money while the Third World is starved for currency. Under these circumstances, staff members are under intense internal pressures to massage what goes through the system easily. In terms of the quality and character of lending, these pressures exacerbate tendencies to:

(1) Shortchange the complexities of figuring out how sectoral adjustment and policy reforms can be targeted to the poor and then negotiating these complexities with impatient or reluctant governments;

(2) Back off from innovativeness in old-line poverty lending— particularly in projects that require unusual planning, local participation, or slow-paced implementation; and

(3) Succumb to temptations to re-tool standard poverty loans into de facto adjustment loans by revising criteria for currency fungibility, which has the effect of moving money without necessarily retaining the real strengths of either kind of loan.

How staff resources are allocated. For an institution that regularly announces the need to deal with the social, humanistic, and ecological dimensions of development, the Bank remains as much as ever dominated by economists, engineers, lawyers, and financial analysts.

Among *more than 3,000* professionals, the Bank employs:

—One sociological advisor, who has responsibility for reviewing *all* agricultural and rural development projects (i.e., $3.6 billion a year in new commitments).

—A handful of non-economist social scientists (several of whom are now functioning as economists or as project managers)—even though the social impact of all projects is supposed to be analyzed.

—One full-time professional ecologist—even though all projects are supposed to be assessed for environmental soundness.

—One full-time staff member whose responsibility is to encourage linkages with non-governmental organizations—even though the Bank has made repeated declarations of its willingness to broaden its interaction with non-governmental organizations.

—One full-time specialist in women in development (and very few professional women on the staff).

—One full-time consultant who specializes in non-quantitative participatory approaches to evaluation, i.e., spends extended periods of time in the field discussing projects directly with their beneficiaries.[22]

—One person who spends half-time encouraging attention to poverty issues.

In general, most upper-level decision makers are economists. Most non-economists who work at upper levels are "advisors." Of course, that is not to say that economists cannot be concerned about the non-economic dimensions of development or that the Bank's work should be measured by academic disciplines. Nevertheless, it does reflect the fact that perspectives that would seem to be most in demand are in short supply, and that vision tends to narrow rather than widen at the top.

Who is getting promoted. Unlike the heady days of staff expansion during the McNamara period, the present Bank is relatively stable in size; thus there are fewer opportunities for promotion. It is perhaps not surprising that those of the McNamara generation who advocated a targeted project approach to poverty alleviation have generally been moved aside, or, taking into account the political environment, that the hot questions these days are not how to put landless farmers to work building feeder roads but how to "get the prices right."

Looked at in terms of job advancement, "the rising stars around here are *not* those who are doing brilliant work on poverty alleviation," said one young staff member. By this he means not that poverty is no longer an issue, but that it is not the rewarded issue. In a tight, intensely competitive internal job market, poverty alleviation is not the hook upon which a savvy young professional is likely to hang his career ambitions.

A New Faith in the Fairness of Growth

Perhaps no single idea characterized the moral tone of the 1970s at the World Bank as much as the idea that the Bank needed to use its muscle to intervene on the side of the poor. The most basic idea was that the poor are no less efficient as producers, but simply have less to work with. Implicitly and explicitly, Bank projects attempted to equalize opportunity by targeting advantage to the poor.

In contrast, the catch-word logic often repeated in today's Bank is that "a rising tide lifts all ships." This is illustrated in Table 4, which shows hoped-for effects of selected agricultural policy reforms in Ecuador.

Unlike an older-style rural development loan—which typically would have financed feeder roads, extension service, or credit to small farmers—the $100-million Ecuadorian agricultural-sector adjustment loan will finance the general import of agricultural inputs on condition that Ecuador enact a series of policy reforms, including liberalization of commodity pricing and interest rates and the reduction of public-sector interventions in agriculture.

Table 4 (which, it should be noted, is an econometric model, not empirically determined effects of the proposed policy reforms) argues that everyone will benefit from the proposed loan, but that better-off people will benefit more—and by implication, that that's okay.

Assuming that the policy measures can actually be implemented and will then have the effects that are projected, the policy measures will have differential impact because they reinforce the existing advantage of the medium and large farmers—more land to fertilize, collateral and access to credit, knowledge of export markets, and readier access to roads, transport services, and storage

Table 4. Simulated Medium-Term Effects of Select Policy Reforms in an Ecuadorian Agricultural Sector Adjustment Loan[a] (projected rates of increases in the medium term)

	Simulated Effects on Incomes of:		
Policy Reforms	Small Farmers	Medium Farmers	Large Farmers
Removal of Fertilizer Constraint	−4%	7%	45%
Plus Liberalization of Prices	26%	26%	58%
Plus Import Tariff			
of 10%	48%	43%	70%
of 25%	74%	75%	91%

[a]Adapted from "Table 1: Simulated Effect of Policy Reforms," p. 21.World Bank Document P-4126-EC, "Agriculture Sector Loan."

facilities. (Landless farmers are, as they always have been, off the benefit chart altogether—excluded from calculation.)

This is not a simple matter. The Bank would argue that the rates of return to small farmers are in themselves as favorable as might be expected in a standard poverty loan, i.e., that the table only "looks bad" when one compares the column for small farmers to the columns for medium and large farmers. Similarly, because there are more small farmers than large farmers, total benefits to the small farmers may exceed those to large farmers.

The unknown is whether a $100-million incentive package to carry out reforms that theoretically could be enacted for free can and will be carried out. And if so, whether such broad-scale policy reforms really help the overall economy (and the poor) as much as tightly focused efforts that directly channel resources to build upon the productive capacities of the poor.

The Bank generally believes that they will. Elsewhere in this volume, Joan Nelson and Gerald Helleiner express caution that the Bank may know less and be capable of less than it wishes. So the issue is not simply the abstract question of the fairness of growth, but rather the cost to everyone if growth induced by structural adjustment and macro policy-based lending—whether or not it is fair to the poor and ignoring the fact that it is more than fair to the nonpoor—turns out to be wispier than the Bank imagines. By contrast, the Bank *knows* that it can stimulate growth—and moreover, growth that is fair—by direct investment in the capacities of poor majorities.

A Recrudescent Anti-Statist Bias

For an institution that works with governments, there is in the Bank today a surprising hostility toward the public sector and a general sense that governments (particularly leftish ones) are themselves the obstacles to development. When the Bank talks about public enterprises, it almost automatically tags them "*inefficient* public enterprises." When it talks about "public-sector interventions," it means *reductions* in public-sector interventions. When it refers to "government policies" it implies that they are *wrong* policies—that the consequence of these policies is not growth but "distortions."

With the Bank's new faith in the fairness of growth, today's Bank has much in common with the early period of Bank history when, as Mason and Asher noted, the Bank literature was ". . . full of references to 'sound' economic policies, 'sound' fiscal and monetary policies, and 'sound' policies of various other kinds, with the clear implication that the distinction between sound and unsound policies is as obvious as the distinction between day and night."[23]

Then as now, the situation is more complex. Actual Bank experience does not reveal that government agencies are necessarily fat, inept, and corrupt or that the private sector, in contrast, is lean, skilled, and honest. Or that what is tagged 'private sector' is necessarily sound and what is 'public' necessarily unsound. On the contrary, where governments have been receptive, many of the Bank's most successful experiences have dealt with building the effectiveness of social service ministries, while many of the Bank's worst experiences have had to do with attempts to pump resources into the private sector.

If the Bank allows itself to mask an ideological agenda as if it were a set of development principles, not only the poor will be hurt. No one, but least of all the poor, benefits from inept, overblown public bureaucracies. The issue is whether reasonable housecleaning of oversized public institutions and revision of policies that pointlessly discourage private investment are used to disguise a more fundamental attack on the role of the state, particularly its responsibility to equalize opportunity on behalf of the have-nots.

The Muffled Drum and Loss of Moral Vision

One Bank veteran—a "relic," to use his own term—looked back at the 1970s and described "his" Bank this way:

> During the 1970s, it was as if there were a big bass drum beating beneath the surface . . . boom . . . boom . . . boom [thumping the side of his desk slowly, loudly, and steadily]. The drum was the *idea* of poverty alleviation. It was as if the Bank were a galley that plowed through the water to the rhythm of that drum. When the galley got off course, which it did frequently, the drum brought it back and gave it direction. Now, the drumbeat is muffled and erratic. Well, perhaps I was merely younger then, but it seems to me that what the Bank has lost is the dynamism and direction that came through following a compelling idea and a moral vision.24

Perhaps more than any hard indicator, this notion of the muffled drumbeat characterizes what has happened to the idea of poverty lending at the World Bank. No one who knows the Bank would say that it is not concerned with poverty. And probably no one would claim that McNamara's was the ideal poverty vessel. Rather, the key is in a shift in commitment and how that is translated into institutional priorities that guide day-to-day decisions.

Why the Bank is Better Equipped Today to Focus on Poverty

Ironically, at the same time that the Bank is shifting away from poverty alleviation to take on the improbable task of managing the world's economy, the opportunity for effective poverty lending in many ways has never been better. This is so for several reasons.

First, after more than a decade of intensive experience, the Bank has become increasingly skilled and sophisticated in its understanding of poverty. It knows more, even if it doesn't necessarily know *how*. The weaknesses in its approach to poverty are all matters that the Bank understands and, in varying degrees, is experimenting to overcome.

Next, within the past five years, the Bank has significantly expanded the array of tools that it applies to poverty alleviation. Most important, it has linked lending with a new willingness to challenge policies that contribute to poverty. While the impetus for much policy-based lending may have initially been narrow (to unshackle presumed constraints upon economic growth in support of the adjustment process), the idea has taken on new shades and variations as it has been translated from sector to sector. For example, a recent education loan in Morocco not only finances classrooms, trains teachers, and provides textbooks, but also works to institutionalize a deeper shift in policy from higher to primary education. Urban lending has shifted from neighborhood-specific, low-cost shelter to issues of pricing and the overall fairness of housing programs (i.e., how to reduce frequent public subsidies to the middle class and target subsidies to the poor). Future energy loans could not only give more emphasis to renewables (particularly fuelwoods, charcoal, and crop residues) but also to establishing pricing policies that discourage wasteful harvesting of forests and give incentives to small farmers to participate in tree planting and conservation. Power projects that displace small farmers or indigenous minorities could go beyond compensation and more broadly establish the *rights* to compensation and resettlement. At the macro level, tax policies, land reform measures, land-titling provisions, pricing policies of state enterprises, credit policies, tariffs, utility rates, social security programs, agricultural commodity pricing, consumer food subsidies, and labor legislation all have enormous equity implications that can be addressed directly through policy-based lending. The door opened by policy-based lending leads into a very large and unexplored room. A vast array of powerful new tools is available—if the drum is beating for staff members to take them up.

Third, in several important respects, many countries—especially those in Latin America and East Asia—are themselves very different than they were in the early 1970s, and as a result they present better grassroots-oriented investment opportunities. New democracies, fragile though they may be, are politically more attuned to the poor; hopefully they will offer more honest public bureaucracies than did the military governments that generally prevailed when the Bank launched its poverty crusade ("Why did *our* Bank have to get the generals?" lamented one older Latin American economist).[25]

And finally, in most countries, the social characteristics of the mid-1980s poor are far different from those of the mid-1960s poor (with Sub-Saharan Africa a notable exception). Throughout the world, there is widened availability of primary education and basic literacy. In China, India, and Indonesia, food production has expanded dramatically over the last decade. In most countries, there is a generation of experience with institutionalized development, access to electronic media, penetration of core infrastructure, widening networks of grassroots organizations, interventions of private voluntary organizations, expanded political democracy, and at least the bare bones of social service bureaucracies installed.

None of this is to say that the poor are any less poor. They aren't. Debt and recession have taken care of that. But they probably *are* better organized and more responsive to public initiative—in a word, more "investable."

It is perhaps fortunate for the Bank that small farmers all over the world have turned out to be more reliable borrowers than their governments—and certainly more reliable than the commercial bankers and industrial entrepreneurs who live in their capital cities. In Sub-Saharan Africa, investments in the education of primary schoolchildren turned out to yield highly satisfactory rates of return while massive investments in large-scale agriculture turned to dust. Jobs created through investment in the industrial sector usually cost about $50,000 each; a family-planning acceptor, on the other hand, cost about $50. The Bank's investment in research on basic grain production may well turn out to have been its single most important and productive investment, not its research on wonder export crops like African palm.

What this suggests is the following: Looking forward as well as backward, for economic as well as humanitarian reasons, for growth as well as fairness, the Bank should resist the ideological and operational pressures to abandon poverty. Instead, it should refocus its energies upon financing growth that builds directly upon the needs, capacities, and productivity of those who have been and are still being bypassed.

Notes

[1] The history and evolution of the Bank's poverty focus is analyzed in Robert L. Ayres, *Banking on the Poor* (Cambridge, Mass.: MIT Press, 1984). See also Bettina S. Hurni, *The Lending Policy of the World Bank in the 1970s: Analysis and Evaluation* (Boulder, Colo.: Westview Press, 1980), and *Focus on Poverty* (Washington, D.C.: World Bank, revised edition, 1983).

[2] Robert S. McNamara, "Address to the Board of Governors," Nairobi, Kenya, September 24, 1973.

[3] See "Rural Development: Sector Policy Paper" (Washington, D.C.: World Bank, 1975).

[4] Edward S. Mason and Robert E. Asher, The World Bank Since Bretton Woods (Washington, D.C.: The Brookings Institution, 1973), in Ayres, op. cit., p. 3.

[5] As a kind of complement to the highly selective focus on rural poverty, McNamara also built an urban department, but similarly, with poverty alleviation as its principal objective. See Michael A. Cohen, *Learning by Doing: World Bank Lending for Urban Development, 1972–1982* (Washington, D.C.: World Bank, 1983).

[6] Hollis Chenery, Montek S. Ahluwalia, C.L.G. Bell, John H. Duloy, Richard Jolly, *Redistribution with Growth* (Oxford: Oxford University Press, for the World Bank and Institute of Development Studies of the University of Sussex, 1974).

[7] For a synthesis of the Bank's findings on the relationship between investments in basic human needs and economic growth, see especially, *World Development Report 1980* (Washington, D.C.: World Bank, 1980). Also, *Poverty and Basic Needs* (Washington, D.C.: World Bank, 1980), especially Paul Streeten, "From Growth to Basic Needs," pp. 5–8; and *First Things First: Meeting Basic Human Needs in Developing Countries*, Paul Streeten, with Shahid Javed Burki, Mahbub ul Haq, et al. (Oxford: Oxford University Press, for the World Bank, 1981).

8 Ayres, op. cit., p. 5.

9 The most cogent summary of Bank-learned lessons on poverty is in *Focus on Poverty* (Washington, D.C.: World Bank, revised edition, 1983). A more extensive overview of Bank learning from the 1970s and early 1980s is in Warren C. Baum and Stokes M. Tolbert, *Investing in Development: Lessons of World Bank Experience* (Oxford: Oxford University Press, for the World Bank, 1985).

10 Data on recuperation rates among small farmers are cited in several annual reports of the Bank's Agriculture and Rural Development Department and in a forthcoming review of rural development projects to be published by the Operations Evaluation Department.

11 See, for example, extensive documentation that is available on the Calcutta Small-Scale Entrepreneur Program, a component of the Bank-supported Calcutta Urban Development Project.

12 This is all the more striking if several very large failed African projects are excluded from the averages. For detailed analysis of performance of poverty/non-poverty agricultural projects, see "Analysis of Lending Operations for Agriculture and Rural Development Department," 1975 through 1986, the in-house annual report produced by the Agriculture and Rural Development Department, and more recently, the Operations Evaluation Department study (forthcoming).

13 The reader who is unfamiliar with Bank statistics—particularly Economic Rates of Return as measures of project performance—is cautioned to take these numbers (as well as the somewhat strained distinction between poverty/non-poverty projects) with a grain of salt. Though they are cited as measurements by the Bank, they are indicators (sometimes convenient myths) that often serve to formalize what staff members subjectively know or believe in response to institutional requirements for "the numbers."

14 S. P. Heyneman, "Investing in Education: A Quarter Century of Bank Experience," (World Bank) Economic Development Institute, Seminar Paper No. 30, 1985, p. 18.

15 In OECD countries, investments in education can be shown to account for about 1 per cent of growth in GNP per capita; but in contrast, in Sub-Saharan Africa, investments in education can account for as much as 25 per cent of growth in GNP. Cited in Heyneman, ibid., p. 18.

16 Among Bank units, the education divisions have most self-consciously made shifts from hardware to software (from "product" to "process"). See, for example, S.P. Heyneman, "Investing in Education," op. cit.

17 This point is well made in the Bank's largest and most systematic review of its project performance, the *Tenth Annual Review of Project Performance Audit Results.* See especially "Factors Bearing on Project Sustainability," Volume One, pp. 36–37. Bank thinking on participatory development is also well illustrated in Michael M. Cernea, ed., *Putting People First* (Washington, D.C.: World Bank and The Johns Hopkins University Press, 1985).

18 Michael M. Cernea, "Sociological Knowledge for Development Projects," in Michael M. Cernea, *Putting People First,* op. cit., p. 4.

19 A.W. Clausén, "Address to the Board of Governors," Toronto, Canada, September 6, 1982. Although less frequently, Clausen occasionally spoke out eloquently on the Bank's imperative to address world poverty, most notably in "Poverty in the Developing Countries," an address given at the Martin Luther King, Jr. Center, Atlanta, Georgia, January 11, 1985.

20 Analysis of AID economic support to poorest countries from Jonathan Sanford, "Status of the Poverty Alleviation Focus of the International Development Association," (Washington, D.C.: Congressional Research Service, No. 33, Foreign Affairs and National Defense Division, 1984), Table 3.

21 It is typical of the Bank's political dilemmas that at the same time that it is reassuring the Treasury Department that it is aggressively taking the lead on the Baker initiative (with administration support for IDA and a general capital increase hanging in balance), it is also reassuring a coalition of sixty-three Congressmen that it is not less devoted to rural development and poverty alleviation (with *approval* of IDA and the general capital increase hanging in the balance).

22 A report on this work is contained in Lawrence Salmon, *Listen to the People* (World Bank, forthcoming).

23 Edward S. Mason and Robert E. Asher, *The World Bank Since Bretton Woods,* op. cit., p. 186, cited in Ayres, op. cit., p. 3.

24 The author has taken some liberty here in paraphrasing somewhat lengthier remarks and in unscrambling a mixed metaphor.

25 For a discussion of the positive impact of democracy on economic development, see Atul Kohli, "Democracy and Development," in John P. Lewis and Valeriana Kallab, eds., *Development Strategies Reconsidered* (New Brunswick, N.J.: Transaction Books, for the Overseas Development Council, 1986), pp. 153–182.

Chapter 4

The World Bank and Private Capital

John F. H. Purcell and Michelle B. Miller

The 1980s have been a period of major global transition, reevaluation, and crisis in the established economic and financial institutions, both international and domestic. It is hardly surprising that the World Bank, the single most important international institution charged with furthering Third World development, should have come under pressure and been faced with criticism over its role in helping developing countries adjust to a new and more difficult environment.

In responding to such criticism, the World Bank is faced with an array of competing and often highly ideological demands. Old models of development are being challenged from political and economic standpoints in both the industrialized and the developing worlds. The contradictory demands are most intense with respect to the contribution of private capital to Third World development. Some of the demands on the Bank regarding the role of the private sector in its mission would imply such vast changes in the institution that they would make it almost unrecognizable. As the World Bank struggles to resolve whether simply to expand and adjust traditionally successful activities or whether to attempt radically new departures, it is useful to examine how the institution currently involves the private sector in its activities.

The overall theme of this chapter is that the World Bank is of necessity an institution that stands between the vast field of activities reserved primarily for governments and the equally large and varied set of economic and financial roles played by private capital. This means the Bank must constantly explore the interstices between the two, finding niches of opportunity where development can be promoted through constructive interaction between government initiative and resources, and between private capital and entrepreneurship.

As we shall argue below, the World Bank—consisting of the International Bank for Reconstruction and Development, the International Development Association, and the International Finance Corporation—is a unique mix of public and private sector orientations, goals, and programs. We shall suggest that the World Bank in its largest programs is quite properly and necessarily oriented toward the public sector; and we shall disagree with those critics who complain that the Bank and its programs do not sufficiently involve the private sector.

Before looking at the ways in which the World Bank interacts with the private sector, we briefly define what we mean by that term. The 'private sector' is not monolithic in either its structure or interests, and it includes actors of varying sizes and goals in both the industrialized and developing worlds. The major components of the private sector are: 1) commercial banks in the industrialized world that lend or have lent funds to developing countries; 2) individual and institutional investors in the industrialized world who, while they do not invest directly in the Third World, do buy World Bank bonds, thus enabling the Bank to fund its lending program; 3) corporations based in the industrialized world that are potential foreign investors in developing countries; and 4) the private sector within developing countries, which is itself made up of banks, financial institutions, and industrial groups large and small.

The World Bank currently involves, interacts with, and attempts to stimulate private sector investment and lending in a variety of ways:

- Through its treasury operations, the World Bank funds itself by *borrowing from private investors* on international capital markets. These risk-averse investors from the industrialized world provide their resources because the capital support of member governments and the Bank's extremely conservative financial policies make it a triple-A credit.

- Through World Bank *co-financing* arrangements, commercial banks in both the industrialized and the developing worlds participate in Bank loans to developing countries.

- Through the International Finance Corporation (IFC), the World Bank undertakes *joint ventures* with both foreign and domestic private sector investment.

- Through the soon-to-be-established Multilateral Investment Guarantee Agency (MIGA), the World Bank will provide *investment insurance* to potential foreign direct investors.

The World Bank itself tends to direct its loans toward projects and sectors that cannot alone attract foreign direct investment. However, a great deal of Bank lending supports development of the local private sector. Much of this is indirect lending to private enterprises through national agricultural or industrial development banks set up to on-lend World Bank funds. World Bank loans for public sector activities such as transportation, power, or education also have an impact on the local private sector. Finally, the Bank's policy adjustment lending aims to improve the environment in borrower countries to enable them to attract new levels of commercial bank lending and foreign direct investment; in doing so, the World Bank works with corporations and banks in the developed world to seek out interested investors and lenders.

The preceding list should make clear that both public and private actors play an important role in World Bank activities. Third World economic development is too large and complex a task to be viewed in terms of some inherent contradiction between the public and private sectors. In fact, there is a certain complementarity between the two (for example, public sector investments are often essential preconditions for profitable private investment opportunities). Nonetheless, there is a dominant orientation toward the public sector in the work of the Bank—an orientation that in our view should be regarded as necessary and appropriate. The World Bank was established by governments, is owned by governments, and lends to governments or with a government guarantee. The tremendous capital needs of the Third World and the more risky political and economic environment within which development lending takes place mean that the opportunities for massive, across-the-board private sector involvement are limited. We believe that Third World development will continue to require major governmental commitments, particularly on the part of developing-country governments, to the mobilization of resources for public and private investment, to public investment programs in economic and social infrastructure, and to policies that stimulate private sector growth. The Bank as an institution appears to recognize that it would be inappropriate and counterproductive to loosen the close ties with developing-country *governments* that allow for smooth working relationships not only with the Bank but often for private-sector foreign investors and lenders. We will argue, however, that there is room for the Bank to modify in certain ways the manner in which it interacts with various private actors without radically changing its current public sector orientation and approach.

We have characterized recent criticism of the World Bank as asking it to become in some fashion *more* private-sector-oriented. In the broadest sense, we believe this is a call for the Bank to become more active in creating opportunities for profitable investment (either equity or financial) that would not exist without its involvement, and to ensure that the realization of these opportunities contributes to Third World development—a very tall order. Possible schemes for carrying out such an expanded role might be described as falling somewhere between two poles. Some want the Bank to alter its orientation and mission so that these goals become its primary objective. Others, ourselves included, advocate a more modest approach, under which the Bank would incrementally expand and refine its current orientation to the private sector. The body of this chapter looks at the range of Bank programs in existence that involve private actors in various ways. In our conclusion, we address what we believe should and should not be done to refine and modify current approaches.

The Bank has confronted numerous challenges throughout its forty-year history and for the most part has met them successfully. The shift from its original mandate of participating in postwar reconstruction to exclusive involvement in development; tremendous growth in membership, staff, and capital; and evolution of the focus on project lending have all been accomplished with minimal changes in the Bank's Articles of Agreement. We believe the Bank will be able to assimilate the challenges outlined above in a similar manner.

In this chapter, we first trace the Bank's original formulation and its successful evolution in response to past challenges and assess the attributes of current pressures for change. We next examine four programs through which the World Bank and affiliate institutions incorporate the private sector into their lending activities, and then discuss the Bank's borrowing activities and loan participations program, which use private capital as a source of financing. Finally, we draw some conclusions about the range of possible private-sector-oriented responses to recent demands and offer recommendations about which of these the World Bank should pursue.

Challenge and Response: Institutional Adaptation by the World Bank

From Reconstruction to Development: 1946–1960

The World Bank was originally established to provide funds for European reconstruction, and to do so in part by guaranteeing private investment. This role rapidly shifted as the Bank became exclusively a development institution and an intermediary, borrowing funds from private investors and lending them to developing countries for economic infrastructure projects.

This shift in both means and ends holds important lessons for the Bank today. The task of European reconstruction was too big for the Bank's limited resources.[1] The Bank focused instead on the more clearly defined and attainable task of financing primarily Third World development through lending for infrastructure projects. The means for achieving these tasks also shifted early in the Bank's history. Instead of acting as a guarantor of private investment, the Bank became an intermediary between private actors (investors, corporations, and commercial banks in the developed world) and state-led development activities. It also assumed the role of identifying and formulating projects rather than responding to private sector plans and initiatives. While private capital remained crucial, the Bank worked primarily with governments in developing countries to create and implement lending programs.

During the 1950s, the Bank grew in staff size, membership, capital base, and borrowing while maintaining its focus on project finance of infrastructure. To complement this focus and expand the Bank's range of activities, the International Finance Corporation was established in 1956 as the private sector affiliate of the Bank. IFC's legal framework differed from that of the Bank to allow it to fulfill this complementary role. While the IBRD and IDA may lend only to governments or with a government guarantee, IFC is permitted to make equity investments and provide loans without government guarantees. Thus the IBRD and IDA as well as IFC can lend to the private sector, but under different rules with respect to sovereign risk. Yet IFC's small size and its autonomy within the World Bank reinforced the notion that the Bank is primarily a public sector-linked institution that relies heavily on private capital but de-emphasizes lending to private enterprise.

Evolution and Expansion: 1960–1973

The evolution of the Bank during this period further reinforced its separation from private actors in lending operations while increasing its dependence on the private sector as a source of funds. The appointment of Robert McNamara as Bank President in 1968 reinforced a shift already under way at the Bank toward lending for basic needs, particularly in the world's poorest countries, where the private sector, both foreign and domestic, often plays a less active role relative to that of governments. As social programs, education, agriculture, and tourism joined infrastructure development as targets of World Bank lending programs, technical assistance became a large part of Bank activities. These developments required a tremendous increase in the size of the Bank's staff and financial resources—an increase that was achieved through a series of general capital increases and significantly expanded borrowing. Outstanding borrowings grew from $2 billion to $9 billion between 1960 and 1973.

As in the 1946–1960 period, the Bank addressed shifting needs and obtained new funding without changing its basic mission or institutional formulation. A number of factors accounted for this: First, the United States continued to press the Bank to focus on the range of tasks that it had historically been assigned. Second, relatively high levels of bilateral aid and commercial bank lending provided development finance for areas outside the Bank's purview, allowing it to pursue its own agenda. Third, experimentation with the political/economic model of import-substituting development in much of the Third World as well as hostility in some quarters toward multinational corporations kept the focus on government-sponsored development. The congruence of these variables meant that, during the 1960s and into the 1970s, the Bank maintained its traditional public sector focus while expanding significantly through the membership of newly de-colonized states, capital increases, and the addition of new sectors to its lending programs.

The Current Dilemma and Its Roots

The dilemmas facing the Bank today—at what rate to expand its operations, how to take a broader role in coordinating international development activities, whether to spearhead a private-sector-led development effort—are not new, but they are being addressed with a new urgency. As Richard Feinberg points out in the overview chapter of this volume, these issues have intensified in the context of the international debt crisis, new interest in private-sector-led growth in many developing countries, and the recent emphasis on seeking the appropriate macro-economic environment and policy framework for development.

These challenges require that the World Bank evaluate its current approach to working with private sector actors to stimulate economic growth in developing countries. Several *constraints*, however, influence the Bank's choices on how best to proceed. First, a decision-making process that sometimes separates private-sector-oriented activities from Bank programs may impede new private sector initiatives. Second, the motivations of developing-country governments as well as the concerns of investors may be difficult to alter in the short to medium term. A third and fundamental question is whether Bank assistance can promote efficient domestic capital markets and generate private investment in countries that lack infrastructure and strong industrial bases.

Responses: Private Capital and World Bank Lending Programs

We base our evaluation of future prospects for the World Bank's relations with private sector actors primarily on an analysis of the World Bank's four programs and affiliates that focus on this component of economic development. The Bank's reliance on developed-country investors as a source of funds for its lending program will be treated in a later section. The Bank's private sector links are concentrated in:

—The *Energy and Industry Departments' work* with the country program units, which aims to bring commercial bank lending and foreign direct investment back into the borrower country and to improve conditions for the local private sector.

—The *co-financing program*, whereby commercial banks participate with the World Bank in lending activities.

—The *International Finance Corporation (IFC)*, which makes loans and equity investments without a government guarantee, and with private sector partners, to projects in the developing world.

—The soon-to-be-established *Multilateral Investment Guarantee Agency (MIGA)*, which will aim at improving the environment for foreign direct investment by issuing guarantees against non-commercial risk.

Before examining each of these areas of World Bank-private sector interaction more closely, it is useful to note that they share some common characteristics:

• They tend to be small relative to the overall scale of World Bank operations.

- They are specific and difficult to replicate, involving an effort by the Bank to locate niches of opportunity between the areas financed primarily by the public sector and those where the private sector is willing or allowed to invest.

- They therefore tend to be relatively labor-intensive, requiring Bank staff and management to locate and take advantage of opportunities as they present themselves.

- Liaison and coordination with major Bank programs is generally ad hoc and informal, depending more than most Bank activities upon personal contacts and relationships.

In sum, the programs discussed here tend to be both modest in scope and fairly concentrated within the Bank's organizational structure. We believe that these programs must necessarily remain modest, but that they can become less concentrated, and their goals more diffused throughout the Bank. The size, unique nature, and relative labor-intensiveness of these activities are necessary corollaries of their mandates, but there is room for a careful analysis of possible changes in the relationship between these programs and other areas of the Bank.

The Energy and Industry Departments

Through policy adjustment lending (discussed by Joan Nelson and Gerald Helleiner in this volume), the Bank and many member countries hope to create an economic, financial, and political environment in borrowing countries that will enable them to attract private capital in the form of both renewed commercial bank lending and foreign direct investment. The United States explicitly recognized the utility of this approach when it introduced the Baker plan in 1985. The adjustment loan packages conceived by the Bank and now supported by the United States work, for example, toward:

1. Stimulating exports, by reducing red tape, changing procurement requirements, and reforming trade policies that create a bias against exports.

2. Increasing the domestic savings rate by improving tax collection, reducing the monopoly position of national banks, and encouraging tax and interest rate reform.

3. Improving the performance of new and existing investments by encouraging countries to halt inefficient projects, establishing units to screen new investments, and developing a system of investment tax credits.

Policy loans, like project loans, are administered by the Bank's Regional Offices. Each Regional Office is divided into *country units*, responsible for individual countries, and *sector-specific units*, upon which the country units draw when assembling a loan package. Sector-specific units exist for agriculture, power and transportation, water supply, public sector management, and industrial development finance (IDF). For projects in the oil and gas, steel, mining, chemicals, telecommunications, and other technical sectors, expertise is located in the Energy and Industry Departments; these sectors are the lending areas most directly involved with potential foreign direct investors in the developed world. Because of the nature of the sectors involved, such projects tend to be highly technical, expensive, and at times risky, requiring the participation of industrial-country corporations large enough to absorb these costs and risks.

Among the "pockets" of private sector expertise within the Energy and Industry Departments are the industrial restructuring (INDRE) and industry development finance (INDFD) divisions. The INDRE and INDFD divisions serve as internal consulting groups for the country units—writing policy papers, participating in missions, generating ideas for loan packages, and evaluating their appropriateness. INDRE's objective is to help countries restructure their industries, which may lead to privatization of state-owned enterprises. INDFD is the central coordinating point for the activities of the industrial development finance units of the Regional Offices. The IDFs lend to the private sector through financial intermediaries in borrowing countries (central banks or national development banks) to help improve the performance of those countries' financial systems.

For each industrial development finance loan, there is a lead adviser in INDFD who is charged with bringing a 'private sector' perspective to the project, and advising the country team. In the event of a disagreement between the Regional Office and the Energy and Industry Departments, the position of the Regional Office will prevail. But this dual authority has a critical impact on the Bank's ability to move quickly on key issues. When consensus cannot be reached at the operational level, issue resolution must move up to higher levels of authority. Most major decisions are cleared with all levels of management, consuming a great deal of staff and management resources. The division between functional and geographic focuses and the lack of a strong coordinating mechanism between the two are stumbling blocks to Bank efforts to encourage change in the developing-country policies that could improve the climate for foreign as well as domestic private investment.

The Energy and Industry Departments are deeply involved in sector adjustment lending. Their officials point out that the need for adjustment goes beyond setting policies. In some cases, particularly where government monopolies control key sectors of the economy like oil and gas or steel, it is necessary to address the industrial structure of a country to create more room for the private sector to invest. Where government monopolies exist, Energy and Industry personnel encourage the country program units to use lending programs to help increase competition.

This discussion brings us to the central issue with respect to policy lending and both foreign and domestic private capital: Developing-country governments have widely varying attitudes toward the role of the private sector and widely varying political tolerance for 'privatization' of the economy. Of course, the Bank has considerable latitude over the nature of and means of imposing conditionality in the areas of sector and structural adjustment. In cases where a government is motivated to undertake steps to enhance the role of the private sector, the Bank should help develop, encourage, and monitor this process. Expansion of this approach, which is already under way, may have to involve some bureaucratic and structural changes, as well as changes in perception of the private sector, to make the IDFs and the Energy and Industry Departments more central to the work of the regional divisions.

Co-Financing Operations

We focus here only on that portion of the Bank's co-financing activities that involves private developed-country commercial banks; the Bank also co-finances with public-sector export credit agencies and bilateral aid institutions.[2] Co-financing with commercial banks takes place under the "B-loan" program, in which the Bank makes an "A-loan" independently of commercial banks and then participates with them in a B-loan.[3]

The goals of the B-loan program are to induce private sector lenders to lend more than they would otherwise, and to lend in places and at maturities that private sector lenders have avoided in the past. Most commercial bank co-financing loans have been extended to creditworthy countries (58 per cent), but a considerable number have gone to countries that have rescheduled commercial bank debt.[4] The program has been successful in several ways:

1. Over the last three years, a $500-million pilot program designed to leverage $2 billion in combined World Bank-commercial bank flows exceeded that target, generating $2.2 billion of loans with a $400-million World Bank commitment.

2. Creditworthy countries have received terms that would not have been obtainable without World Bank participation. For example, in its first B-loan, Thailand got the advantage of a substantially longer maturity—16.5 years compared to the maximum of 12 years that would otherwise have been permitted by Japanese regulations.

3. Co-financing loans have helped some countries avoid reschedulings. Hungary has had six B-loans, of which the initial ones were crucial in enabling the country to avoid seeking a rescheduling. According to one observer, an argument can be made that the two B-loans to Colombia helped that country avoid a rescheduling.[5]

4. In the case of Chile, a needed new money package was generated through co-financing. Chile was able to reach an agreement with its commercial bank creditors for $1.1 billion in new loans, partly because of a $150-million World Bank guarantee for the longest maturities of a $300-million commercial bank loan for the highway sector.

5. The program has increased the number and diversity of banks lending to the developing world. More than 350 banks (172 not including the Chile loan), most of them European, Arab, or Japanese, are participating in B-loans.

These are some of the reasons why the B-loan program has recently moved beyond its pilot phase to become a regular part of Bank activities. Commercial bank co-financing clearly has allowed some countries to borrow at incrementally better terms. Yet the program has not led to the vast mobilization of resources suggested by some of the rhetoric surrounding the program. A partial explanation is that the debt crisis occurred soon after the approval of the B-loan program and seriously reduced the scope for B-loans. But this is also a case where reality necessarily fell short of raised expectations. Commercial bank co-financing was intended to supplement or perhaps even replace government aid flows in a climate of declining levels of U.S. foreign assistance. In a somewhat defensive posture, the U.S. government played up the potential contribution of co-financing; only recently has it acknowledged that both supply of and demand for such financing are limited.

Those who urge expansion of co-financing as a means of easing the debt crisis offer the Chile loan as a possible prototype for future agreements. But the unique attributes of the Chile situation point out why this approach is not suitable for the other major debtors: Chile's payment problems persisted despite the country's strict adherence to an International Monetary Fund (IMF) adjustment pro-

Table 1. World Bank Co-Financing Operations, 1975–85, ($ billions)

Fiscal Years	Number of Projects with Co-Financing	Co-financiers' Contribution				Bank Contribution		Total Project Costs
		Commercial Banks	Export Credit Agencies	Other Official Sources	Total	IBRD	IDA	
1975	51	0.1	1.0	0.9	1.9	1.0	0.3	8.8
1976	67	0.3	0.9	1.1	2.2	1.6	0.4	9.6
1977	78	0.7	0.2	1.5	2.4	1.9	0.7	10.0
1978	79	0.2	0.5	1.8	2.5	1.7	0.8	11.4
1979	105	0.5	0.3	2.0	2.8	3.0	1.1	13.3
1980	86	1.7	1.6	2.6	5.9	3.0	1.6	20.3
1981	72	1.1	0.5	1.5	3.1	2.6	1.5	15.1
1982	98	1.2	1.8	2.2	5.3	4.1	1.2	20.0
1983	84	1.1	3.0	1.8	5.7	3.3	1.1	20.8
1984	98	1.1	0.9	2.0	4.0	4.6	1.3	21.7
1985	104	1.1	1.3	2.4	4.8	4.7	1.5	23.7

Source: *World Development Report 1980, World Bank Annual Report, 1985* (Washington, D.C., The World Bank).

Table 2. B-Loan Program, 1984–86, ($ millions)

Country	Sector	Amount of IBRD A-Loan	Amount of IBRD B-Loan	Form of B-Loan	Commercial Amount	B-Loan Total
FY 1984						
Thailand	Telecommunications	232.1	8.5	direct	25.5	34.0
Hungary I	Agriculture	130.4	30.0	direct	170.0	200.0
	Industry	109.0	9.0	direct	61.0	70.0
Brazil	Iron ore	304.5	7.7	guarantee	52.3	60.0
Colombia	Electric power	170.0	25.0	direct	150.0	175.0
			3.8	direct	21.2	25.0
FY 1985						
Hungary II	Industry	110.0	35.0	direct	350.0	385.0
	Petroleum	90.0	13.3	direct	88.7	102.0
Hungary III	Livestock	80.0	36.0	direct	264.0	300.0
	Chemicals	73.0				
	Transport	75.0	14.0	direct	106.0	120.0
Paraguay	Livestock	25.0	3.8	guarantee	15.0	15.0
			3.3	contingency		
FY 1986						
Ivory Coast	Highway sector	110.0	8.0	direct	32.0	40.0
Chile	Road sector	140.0	150.0	guarantee	300.0	300.0
Turkey	Electric power	200.0	50.0	direct	300.0	350.0
Uruguay[a]	Power sector	45.2	NA	guarantee	50.0	50.0
			397.8		1,985.7	2,222.6

[a]Not yet signed. Source: The World Bank.

gram; they were due largely to a fall in the price of copper—a factor well beyond the Chilean government's control. Commercial banks are far less confident that Argentina, Brazil, and/or Mexico would make the political sacrifices necessary to avoid a rescheduling at all costs, and they might well press for stronger forms of protection in loan agreements than they accepted in the case of Chile. In the event of a rescheduling, the World Bank has preferred creditor status. (A Bank guarantee of the late maturities of a loan protects against default, but rescheduling remains a possibility.) The commercial banks sought to deny this status to the Bank in the Chile loan by asking that the Bank subordinate its claims to theirs in the event the guarantee is called (a request the Bank and its member countries refused). The banks ultimately, and only after much debate, agreed to participatte in co-financing, and they did so only because they considered Chile likely to avoid a rescheduling if at all possible.

Co-financing is unlikely to generate large loan packages to the major debtors because of commercial bank reluctance to risk reschedulings without preferred creditor status. But Bank officials believe that co-financing could be expanded if the loans offered involved more reliable credits (i.e., Malaysia, Indonesia, India). These countries have direct access to capital markets and have been reluctant to co-finance, in part because they foresee some possible disadvantages of closer links between commercial banks and the World Bank. To attract these better borrowers and increase commercial bank participation, the Bank hopes to move toward the use of more innovative financing techniques, including securitized instruments like floating rate notes or notes issuance facilities.

In addition to constraints on demand for and supply of co-financing loans, the program's mission and structure inherently limit its size. It is neither politically acceptable nor particularly sensible for the Bank to compete directly for assets where private lenders are willing to go without guarantees. The Bank can offer only limited guarantees under this program, and the case of Chile and other instances show the highly specialized occurrence of situations where these guarantees stimulate new private lending. Commercial bank co-financing is located in the niche between private and public capital flows and tends to occur only in those special cases where the situation is right, the appropriate personnel are in place to encourage it, or where there is some sort of unique outside impetus.

The institutional arrangements of the Bank's co-financing group reflect but also somewhat reinforce this situation. Project loans are identified, planned, and administered by the country units of the regional divisions, and country officers are often not familiar with the perceptions and practices of commercial bank lenders. Contact between the regional areas (responsible for relations with borrower countries) and the co-financing division (responsible for relations with co-financiers) tends to be informal and ad hoc.

Maintaining even the current volume of B-loan lending will require a strong commitment by the Bank's leadership. This appears to exist, as senior management values the market sensitivity and exposure to commercial bank perceptions that its staff gains by running the B-loan program. The program fits in with the Bank's view of itself as a "catalytic agent"—one that starts the flow and helps it along, but is not the only, or even the primary, participant. But the purpose of the B-loan program is likely to remain that of "additionality," or broadening the base of borrowing countries and lending banks.

Commercial bank co-financing has proved to be an effective way of bringing certain marginal credit risk countries into the market in some instances and of involving smaller, developed-country regional banks in lending to these countries. Its perspective is longer-term, focused on developing the international financial system, not on assuming risk on behalf of commercial banks or resolving the debt crisis.

The International Finance Corporation

The IFC is essentially a provider of venture capital: it invests in the start-up phase of a project and sells off shares once the project is creditworthy. It makes both equity investments and loans. In fiscal 1985, IFC provided financing to seventy-five projects—93 per cent in the form of loans and 7 per cent in the form of equity or quasi-equity investment. In addition to providing its own funds for a project, IFC encourages banks and other financial institutions to participate in projects it has identified.[6] IFC also sells off portions of its equity investment in a project after the project's financial viability has been established. The contribution of IFC should not, however, be judged merely by the volume of projects or syndications. The projects it participates in or funds serve as models that foreign investors can emulate in their own activities. The importance of this catalytic role has increased as flows of foreign direct investment and commercial bank lending to the private sector in the developing world have slowed.

IFC's size—roughly one-tenth of the capital of the Bank—necessarily limits its impact. IFC programs are of course meant to have significant 'snowball' effects beyond the specific deals in which it is involved. But observers should not expect an institution with $1.3 billion in capital (after a doubling of capital was agreed to in December 1985) to reorient Third World economies or established patterns of investment. In addition, there are several factors at work that will keep IFC relatively small in comparison to the Bank:

1. IFC's mandate of funding projects that cannot get private financing on their own, but that will be profitable when completed, is a major and probably unresolvable limitation on the size of any such program.

2. The need for personnel who can identify markets, shape and craft joint ventures, and bring opportunities to investors makes IFC activities highly labor intensive and requires a staff with qualifications different from those required elsewhere in the Bank.

3. While IFC is more private-sector-oriented and less bureaucratic than much of the rest of the Bank, there nevertheless is something of a "culture gap" between IFC and developed-country private investors and lenders. Some bankers familiar with IFC are skeptical of its ability to foster and maintain an aggressive, entrepreneurial approach in putting together deals. Yet IFC certainly has impressed many firms that have elected to work with it: A recent independent survey found that 90 per cent of firms that had used IFC in the past would use it again.

A great deal of attention has focused recently on IFC's Capital Markets Department, through which IFC seeks to encourage private capital flows by funding the establishment or expansion of local capital markets and financial institutions. IFC acts as both adviser and investor, providing technical assistance and supplying equity, loans, and financial technology to countries developing their financial systems. As part of this program, IFC has introduced its Emerging Markets Growth Fund, intended to accelerate capital investment in selected developing countries by investing in their stock markets.[7]

While the program has received well-deserved applause, we should not have overly high expectations that the Emerging Markets Growth Fund—and the activities of the Capital Markets Department as a whole—will have a significant policy impact in the near term. Some observers, including some in IFC, question whether capital markets can be 'developed' as a means of generating investment, or whether their absence is an indication of fundamental weakness in the industrial structure of a given country. IFC explicitly recognizes that the removal of barriers within the financial sector is an important goal and a necessary precursor to investment, but that the development of capital markets must go hand-in-hand with the development of industry.

Finally, institutional separation from the World Bank and weak coordinating mechanisms between the two agencies both imply potential for improved diffusion of IFC experience throughout the Bank. While the above-mentioned decision to double IFC's capital is laudable, it also calls for attention to the possibility of encouraging further interaction and coordination between the Bank and the IFC.

The Multilateral Investment Guarantee Agency (MIGA)

As official development assistance stagnates in an environment of fiscal constraints and political uncertainty, foreign direct investment has come to be seen as one source of external finance that has the potential to increase significantly, given a clear improvement in the investment climate of developing countries. (More important, unlike the renewal of lending flows, such investment is not debt-producing.) But flows of direct investment to developing countries have been shrinking even as many governments have increased their efforts to attract them. There are strong indications that investors tend to avoid some of the existing investment opportunities in developing countries because of their concern about non-commercial or political risk.

The Multilateral Investment Guarantee Agency is intended to stimulate the flow of investment to its developing-country members by issuing long-term guarantees against non-commercial risks surrounding foreign investment.[8] MIGA will provide insurance against risk of currency transfer and inconvertibility, expropriation and nationalization, and breach of government contract coupled with denial of justice, war, and civil unrest. In addition, MIGA will work to promote investment in its member countries, providing information about investment opportunities to potential investors and assisting governments in developing their investment policies. For example, it might help a country set up its own insurance and investment guarantee agency, or aid in the drafting of foreign investment guidelines. Those designing MIGA hope that in the longer term, by setting precedents, the agency will help in the evolution of global investment standards. The preparatory process and ratification by member countries are not yet complete, so that MIGA's first guarantees are not likely to be issued until late 1987 at the earliest.

If MIGA is successful, how much money can it be expected to generate? Its authorized capitalization can ultimately support up to $5 billion in insurance guarantees. A recent independent study suggests that, at best, MIGA could have a portfolio of projects totaling $2 billion by the late 1980s, growing by roughly $500 million annually, of which about $200 million might constitute net new flows that would not take place in the absence of MIGA.[9] For these limited resources to have the greatest possible impact, MIGA's activities should be closely coordinated with other Bank programs that aim at improving the investment climate—and particularly with policy-based lending and the investment activities of IFC.

MIGA will complement the strengths of the World Bank. Its direct contact with the corporate investor in the developed world and its risk orientation can supplement IFC's financing ability. MIGA's contact with investors will allow it to track corporate demand for guarantees and private sector attitudes toward various investment opportunities and regulatory regimes, so that the agency can provide a major contribution to the Bank's understanding of the private sector as a partner in development.

But the formulation and likely evolution of MIGA once again underscore our general conclusions. MIGA was created to fill a niche in the provision of investment insurance, insuring those types of investments not covered by national export credit institutions, and increasing the level of coverage currently available. At the same time, it is under pressure to avoid treading on the toes of private sector insurance companies in the developed countries that are willing and able to offer such political risk insurance. MIGA will probably view itself as a 'service facility,' following private investors where they see emerging opportunities and assisting motivated host-country governments to attract new private sector investors. It is small and institutionally separate from the Bank, and will be most valuable if its activities are well coordinated with those of the Bank and IFC.

MIGA is still in its formative stages; here, we outline several suggestions for maximizing its effectiveness:

1. *U.S. Ratification.* Before MIGA becomes operational, the United States and/or other major OECD countries must ratify its Convention.[10] The United States is slated to contribute 20 per cent of MIGA's capital, which calls for an actual contribution of $22 million. This sum is not a major financial commitment, but any new program faces opposition in the current budget-cutting environment. The Reagan administration, which requested the funds for MIGA in its 1986–87 budget, is awaiting congressional support before it signs. MIGA's low cost and its concordance with broad U.S. policy goals ought to earn for it the support of Congress.

2. *A Collaborative Mechanism.* Although MIGA is envisioned as an autonomous institution with only symbolic ties to the World Bank, its small size means that it will need to collaborate with the Bank and IFC as much as possible. The preparatory committee should make one of its main priorities that of developing extensive formal and informal mechanisms for information-sharing and institutional coordination, particularly between the IFC and MIGA.

3. *Quasi-Equity Investment.* MIGA's charter should be kept flexible enough to allow it to guarantee quasi-equity as well as equity investments.[11] While MIGA will initially focus on equity interests and other forms of direct investment, it is authorized in its convention to expand coverage to any other medium- or long-term form of investment. In setting up the agency's operating procedures, the preparatory committee should build in coverage of quasi-equity arrangements and begin considering methods of promoting this type of investment.

Accessing Private Capital for Development

Through its borrowing on financial markets, the World Bank is the key international institution channeling private capital into areas and projects in the developing world where it would not otherwise go. Now that the Bank is confronting the demand that it lend significantly more, it is turning toward its borrowing operation, and to a lesser extent to a pilot loan participations program, to see whether additional funds can be leveraged.

The Treasury Department's sophisticated understanding of the capabilities of international capital markets and the credit concerns of investors has allowed the Bank to access a huge pool of global capital for the purpose of making loans to developing countries. The Bank's ability to obtain advantageous terms rests on two key factors: 1) the full faith and credit commitment of capital support by the major industrial-country governments of the world; and 2) conservative and clear policies, well understood by investors, that cover the circumstances of Bank lending, procedures for repayment, and the management of Bank liquidity and other financial transactions. There has been discussion for years about whether the Bank should change its "gearing ratio," or ratio of capital to assets, which is currently one-to-one; we concur with Charles Blitzer's discussion of this issue in this volume. Such a move would adversely affect investors' perceptions of the Bank, in that the Bank would have to pay more for its borrowings and might not be able to access adequate funds. Since Blitzer's chapter provides a detailed discussion of this issue, we will concentrate on another aspect of the Bank's use of private capital: its loan participations program.

To free up room on its balance sheet, the Bank has introduced a pilot program under which it sells loans already on its books to private investors. In cases where the Bank is approaching its internal country limit, selling loan participations is also a way of opening up new lending capacity in a country. Another key goal of the program is to create "additionality" in Bank funding by obtaining financing from institutions that do not otherwise contribute to Bank resources.

Under the current pilot program, the Bank sells participations in loans to countries that have not had to go through any debt restructuring and that have raised money on their own on the international syndicated loan markets. The loans involved are for projects well under way. At this early stage, the program has been successful, partly because of a major effort by the Bank to market the loans. The Bank recognizes that this is a slow and labor-intensive means of raising capital, particularly when compared to the ease with which it can borrow. While the financial results— interest rates, pricing, etc.—have been positive, the key consideration has become whether the program is accomplishing its goal of additionality. And the verdict on that will not be in until the pilot program is completed and evaluated.

The loan participations program may eventually include the packaging of portfolios of loan participations to be sold as securitized instruments. Such packaging would be likely to generate additionality, as the lenders who would participate are from different areas within financial institutions than those who currently underwrite or buy bank debt.

Loan participations are unlikely to become a true alternative to borrowing as long as the Bank is able to command low spreads and to borrow in the volume it currently does. Nonetheless, the loan participations program is a useful one, despite its labor-intensive nature. The Bank has the staff and technical expertise to package the loans, market them, and sell them as securitized instruments. Through its marketing effort to date, it has gained valuable insight into the conditions under which private sector financial institutions will and will not fund the Bank. Furthermore, a $5-billion pool of loans to the twenty countries has already been approved for the loan participations program currently on the World Bank's books. Even with a capital increase, it makes sense for the Bank to pass along its loans for well-established projects in creditworthy countries to the private sector, reserving its own lending capacity for those nations in deeper need.

Recommendations: An Appropriate Role for the World Bank

An underlying theme of this discussion has been that the historical and most appropriate role for the World Bank has been on the borderline between the broad range of development activities that the public sector directly carries out with public funds from governments and official agencies (including the Bank), and those commercially attractive activities that the private sector undertakes in the developing world. The niches of opportunity between these two realms—particularly those involving direct private sector lending or investment—are inherently limited, and the Bank's programs that utilize different forms of private capital are necessarily limited as well.

For reasons discussed above, we do not advocate a substantial transformation of the Bank's relationship to the mix of public and private actors who participate with it in the development process. As the Bank seeks to accommodate new demands within its existing institutional structure, it should keep in mind the lessons of the past. The task of solving the debt crisis is one that is clearly beyond the Bank's resources—as was that of European postwar reconstruction forty years ago. While the Bank can expand its lending in line with the Baker plan, and can continue its shift toward a more policy-oriented approach aimed at the resumption of growth, it cannot be expected to leverage the amounts needed to resolve the debt crisis, let alone lend those amounts on its own. The U.S. Treasury recognizes that the Bank cannot be called upon to do this, in large part because of the importance of maintaining investor perceptions. If the World Bank comes to be seen as a mechanism for "bailing out the banks," the Bank will find it difficult to issue the amounts of debt it needs to continue lending even at its current level.

The Bank should also avoid becoming the spearhead for an ideological emphasis on the private sector. Private capital can play a beneficial role in the development process only under certain conditions and not in all cases. While the size of capital flows is in itself an important variable, and while there is growing recognition that flows of private capital are essential to complement public sources, the more important question is where private capital goes and for what purposes it is used. There are plenty of bad examples of the role of private capital in developing countries (the formulation of monopolies, corruption in private sector enterprise management, capital flight). The Bank's foremost role should be to provide guidelines about what policies encourage beneficial private sector participation.

Policy-based lending should focus on project and sector-specific loans that aim to improve the environment within which the private sector operates. In implementing policy loans, however, the Bank should avoid exercising IMF-type conditionality or playing the role of policeman. By doing this, it would run the risk of alienating a large part of its constituency and damaging its credibility in the countries to which it lends. The assumption of an adversarial role would constrain the Bank's ability to impose the micro-level or sectoral conditionality needed to implement the kind of sector adjustment lending that can contribute to 'getting the environment right.'

Without changing its fundamental mission, the Bank can work to improve its ability to accommodate the concerns and approaches of private investors and lenders within its existing structure. Detailed knowledge of and experience with the operations, specific priorities, and goals of financial institutions and potential investors located in industrialized countries is concentrated in the areas of the World Bank discussed in this chapter. While a number of Bank programs effectively utilize this expertise, it is our conclusion that there is room for considerably more diffusion of this orientation into a wider variety of Bank programs. This may require some organizational and staffing changes and will necessitate the leadership of top-level management to modify some aspects of bureaucratic culture. Current mechanisms for coordinating operations across different areas of the Bank could be streamlined. At present, these mechanisms, such as special task forces, appear to be both ad hoc and unwieldy. The Bank could begin to examine ways of creating new methods of coordination and communication designed to create bridges between various parts of the institution.

With more effective diffusion of pockets of private sector expertise throughout the Bank, more cross-fertilization between programs that have a private sector orientation, and less dependence on ad hoc communication and collaboration, the Bank will be better able to judge the circumstances under which a loan helps create the conditions for renewed private sector lending and investment. Better methods of information-sharing and coordination, and increased inclusion in decision-making of individuals with expertise in financial markets and new instruments on the Bank's staff, will increase the Bank's collective knowledge and sensitivity to the potential contribution of private capital to development. The Bank can then be a more effective catalyst for productive relations involving public and private sector actors on a global scale.

Notes

Note: The authors would like to thank the World Bank for its cooperation, and Richard Feinberg, Elizabeth Goldstein, and William Drake for their assistance.

[1] European reconstruction became the job of governments through the Marshall Plan. As these countries became more creditworthy, they began to be funded through voluntary private sector capital flows.

[2] The types of partners involved in co-financing depend largely on the borrowers. For the poorest countries, lenders that can offer concessional terms are the main co-financing sources, whereas for creditworthy developing countries, the World Bank seeks commercial banks and official export credit agencies as co-financiers (see Table 1).

[3] B-loans take one or sometimes two of the following forms: a) *direct lending*, in which the World Bank takes a share of a syndicated loan concentrated in the longest maturities to ensure that a default on the loan would be a default against the World Bank; b) *a guarantee option*, under which the World Bank guarantees repayment of the longer maturities of a loan provided exclusively by the commercial banks; and c) *contingency liability financing*, under which the World Bank accepts a contingent obligation to finance an element of deferred principal at final maturity of a loan with level debt-service payments.

[4] Creditworthy countries are defined here as those which have not rescheduled commercial bank debt.

[5] Statement by John Williamson, Institute for International Economics, before the United States House of Representatives, Committee on Banking, Finance, and Urban Affairs, Subcommittee on International Development Institutions and Finance, July 9, 1985.

[6] Of the $937 million in investment approvals in 1985, $609 million was for IFC's own account while $328 million was expected to be syndicated, or sold, to other investors. During the past five fiscal years, IFC has signed participation agreements with banks totaling $1.3 billion and has under administration for the account of other financial institutions a portfolio of $1.2 billion.

[7] The closed-end investment fund started operations in spring 1986 with a capital base of about $50 million. It will invest in countries with relatively open and developed securities markets, including Malaysia, Thailand, Indonesia, Mexico, Brazil, and India. Initially, shares in the fund are being placed among a small group of institutional investors in a few capital-exporting countries who seek diversification in a 'high risk, high return' direction. But IFC hopes that the $50 million becomes the first tranche of perhaps a $500-million fund, with small and medium-size financial firms that want geographical distribution in emerging markets as its typical investors.

[8] MIGA's activities will complement the many local institutions that already provide risk insurance. As such, it will guarantee or co-guarantee investments with national or regional guarantee agencies, or with private companies that may not be fully covered by such agencies. It would also guarantee investments from countries that do not have national programs, investments not now eligible for national programs, and multinationally financed investments.

[9] See Theodore H. Moran, "The Future of Foreign Direct Investment in the Third World," in Theodore H. Moran and contributors, *Investing in Development: New Roles for Private Capital?*, ODC U.S.-Third World Policy Perspectives No. 6 (New Brunswick, N.J.: Transaction Books, for the Overseas Development Council, 1986), pp. 12–15.

[10] MIGA will come into being once five capital-exporting and fifteen capital-importing countries ratify its convention, provided the total subscriptions of these countries amount to at least one-third ($360 million) of MIGA's proposed initial capital of $1.08 billion.

[11] Quasi-equity forms of industrial cooperation such as management and service contracts, licensing and franchising agreements, and arrangements concerning technology transfer where the investor assumes a stake in the venture's performance are likely to become increasingly important sources of investment flows. For discussion of these new forms, see Charles P. Oman, *New Forms of Investment in Developing Countries*, in Theodore H. Moran and contributors, *Investing in Development: New Roles for Private Capital?*, op. cit., pp. 131–55; and *Financial Intermediation Since the Debt Crisis* (Washington, D.C.: Institute for International Economics, September 1985).

Chapter 5

Financing the World Bank

Charles R. Blitzer

During the past year, a consensus has emerged favoring an enhanced role for the World Bank in coordinating international efforts aimed at achieving higher growth rates in developing countries, particularly in Latin America and Sub-Saharan Africa, where per capita incomes have declined substantially since 1980. The basic ideas embodied in the Baker plan—a shift in objectives from stabilization toward growth, policy reforms aimed at improved economic efficiency, increased lending by both commercial banks and the World Bank, and a coordinative role for the latter—have been widely endorsed. Causing more debate has been the question of the necessary amounts of money forthcoming from different groups and the exact nature of the policy reform conditions to be placed on recipient countries.

The focus of this chapter is on the availability of World Bank financial resources to facilitate the recovery of self-sustaining economic growth in the developing countries, and alternative methods of raising the resources that may be needed to support the Bank's concessional and non-concessional lending operations.

The main argument presented here is that, precisely because the debt crisis has inhibited the supply of private capital, additional near-term World Bank lending is needed to facilitate a turnaround. To fulfill its role in the policy-reform process, the Bank needs to be given greater financial leverage. Policy reform and an improved investment climate are the conditions necessary to improve

135

resource-use efficiency and to re-establish *private* financial intermediation. Successful reforms therefore can be expected to diminish the need for *official* lending in the longer term.

To substantiate these conclusions, I first attempt to quantify a range of potential developing-country foreign financing needs over the first five years of a recovery process.[1] Projections are made for: a) developing countries in the aggregate, b) a group of seventeen major debtors, and c) the Sub-Saharan African countries. These projections indicate that foreign financing needs may be very large in terms of present levels of available funding even if significant gains are made in increasing productivity and in raising domestic savings.

No attempt is made to calculate the precise amount of additional resources that the World Bank will need, since both private capital flows and the rates of return on additional investment are impossible to project accurately. Nevertheless, the case for substantial increases in World Bank lending capacity seems compelling, particularly in the near term, when private flows remain constrained. Rough calculations do suggest, however, that if the World Bank's member countries are serious about achieving a restoration of growth in the hardest hit countries, Bank lending might have to double during the initial years of recovery. This cannot happen with the present capitalization and lending limits of the World Bank itself (IBRD) and without an increase in the funds available for concessional lending.

The issue of World Bank financing is especially urgent because of the coincidence of a perceived need for an enhanced Bank role and the current hesitancy of donor governments to contribute budgetary resources. This problem is most acute in the case of concessional lending through the International Development Association (IDA) because this agency accounts for the bulk of governmental appropriations to the World Bank. Formal discussions for the eighth replenishment of IDA are currently under way, and even the most optimistic projections do not forecast a sizable real increase in IDA funding.

In the United States, severe budget stringency will make it difficult even to maintain the existing level of IDA appropriations, regardless of the short-term potential of recipient countries to use additional sums productively. Moreover, it is widely assumed that the United States has hedged its position, largely on budgetary grounds, regarding a capital increase for the World Bank to support non-concessional lending. But, as discussed below, a strong case can be made for increased capitalization of the World Bank in the very near future.

Assuming both budgetary constraints and the desirability of

increased World Bank lending capacity, this chapter addresses the degree to which alternative financing mechanisms can be utilized to minimize direct budgetary costs to member governments while allowing the Bank to pursue a more upwardly flexible lending program.

In the case of non-concessional lending, the best option for increasing the Bank's capacity to lend is early agreement on a General Capital Increase (GCI). The recommendation offered here is that, for reason of the Bank's own creditworthiness and ability to borrow at low spreads, capital subscriptions should be increased and the one-to-one gearing ratio maintained. Changing this ratio would be a second-best means of increasing the Bank's lending capability because such a change could seriously compromise the World Bank's own standing in the credit markets and make its financial intermediation role more difficult. Furthermore, a GCI need not be costly in terms of government appropriations, because the paid-in portion can be reduced substantially from previous levels.

As to concessional lending, increased appropriation levels would be required for IDA to expand its operations. Even if terms were tightened, the benefits of faster repayments to IDA would be felt only after a lag of many years. One option that will be discussed at length below is replacement of the present IDA financing mechanism with an interest-subsidy facility. The attractive feature of this proposal is its use of leverage to achieve simultaneously both a reduction in required appropriations and a substantial increase in the Bank's capacity to lend to the present IDA countries. This advantage seems most appropriate as a way of overcoming the extraordinary budget stringency that exists in the United States and that makes larger IDA appropriations difficult to achieve regardless of their underlying justification.

Growth, Productivity, and Investment Requirements

Before discussing how World Bank lending should be funded, it is important to address, at least briefly, the reasons why additional capital flows may be required in the short run to stimulate economic growth in many developing countries. As a cautionary note, it is important to recognize that there can be no precise way to forecast the financing needs of a large set of countries. Aggregate needs will depend on such uncertain variables as world inflation, interest rates, policy changes in specific countries, perceptions of creditworthiness, banking regulations, growth in the industrialized countries, the openness of industrialized countries to exports from the developing countries, and changes in commodity prices. At best, analytical methods can reduce the range of uncertainty.

The international debt crisis has caused severe adjustment problems for many developing countries. In order to meet their debt-servicing obligations during a period of rising real interest rates and falling commodity prices, countries have had to drastically reduce their trade deficits. By 1985, the developing countries as a group succeeded in eliminating a trade deficit that had totaled about $78 billion in 1981.[2] Their aggregate current-account deficits fell by $67 billion in this period. This turnaround was made possible by macro-economic constraints on domestic spending that had the dual effects of stimulating a larger share of production to exports and reducing demand for imports. Investment spending in particular was cut substantially in many countries; this has had a demonstrably adverse impact on their economic growth.

Real growth rates in most developing countries deteriorated sharply after 1980. Excluding China and India, which stand out as special cases, the average rate of economic growth in the period 1973–80 was 5.5 per cent. During the past five years, that rate fell to 2.1 per cent. Per capita income in Latin America has fallen by 7–9 per cent since 1981, and per capita income in Sub-Saharan Africa is 15–18 per cent lower than five years ago. Although these are the most affected regions, growth rates have also fallen by about one-third in East Asia (excluding China) and by almost one-half in the developing countries of Southern Europe and North Africa.

The decrease in the investment/GDP ratio has been severe in those countries in which growth has declined most sharply. For example, the investment/GDP ratio has fallen by almost one-third in a group of seventeen major debtor countries, and by as much as 50 per cent in Sub-Saharan Africa.[3] These numbers indicate that substantial increases in the rate of investment spending in these groups of countries will be required as part of a growth-oriented strategy.

Additional investment can be financed by domestic or foreign savings. However, it appears likely that considerable additional foreign financing will be required, at least in the short run, to increase investment to the levels required for significant increases in economic growth. In some cases, domestic savings rates are already high enough, but a large fraction of the total is being used to service debt. For example, in the group of seventeen debtors, the investment/GDP ratio is only two-thirds the domestic savings/GDP ratio. In other cases, such as Sub-Saharan Africa, consumption levels are so low that it would not be appropriate to raise additional savings through higher taxation. In both types of situations, substantially higher domestic savings will have to come about as part of the growth process itself. In the longer run, as countries succeed in changing policies to make savings more attractive and investment more profitable, the need to rely on foreign financing can be expected to decline.

This is not meant to imply that increased investment spending alone will be sufficient to ensure self-sustaining growth. An equally crucial condition is that the developing countries use their resources more efficiently than has been the case in the past.[4] The lack of creditworthiness of many developing countries is, in large measure, a reflection of the low real rates of return on investments undertaken in the past.

At the same time, it is important to recognize the structural nature of the efficiency, or productivity, problem. The scope for changing the commodity composition of a nation's output, pursuing an export-oriented strategy, or increasing the labor-intensity of capital is limited in the short run. The greatest opportunities for increased efficiency can come only through structural changes arising from productive use of current and future investment. The developing countries themselves of course bear the principal responsibility for setting the macro and micro policies that create an appropriate environment for efficient resource use.

Both higher savings rates and greater productivity of investment can contribute to enhanced economic growth. A simple growth model developed to illustrate this point indicates, for instance, that for the group of seventeen major debtors, a 1-per cent increase in aggregate growth would require a 40-per cent productivity improvement if the investment rate did not increase, or a 7-per cent increase in the investment/GDP ratio if productivity did not change from existing levels.[5] The combination of both increasing at those rates together would yield an increase of almost 2.5 per cent in the growth rate. In the case of the Sub-Saharan African countries, even if the productivity of investment improved by 40 per cent immediately, the investment rate would also have to increase somewhat to achieve just a 1-per cent growth increase.

Figure 1 illustrates how foreign savings requirements vary depending on the desired future growth rate, the marginal domestic savings rate, and improved investment productivity. The depth of each bar below the baseline represents the implied average trade deficit, or foreign savings, during the initial five years of each scenario. The status quo scenario represents a continuation of present trends, with no productivity or savings improvements. The other three cases assume that growth will be two percentage points higher than present trends imply. Case 1 further assumes a 50-per cent increase in marginal savings rates and a 20-per cent improvement in investment productivity. In case 2, domestic savings rates

Figure 1. Projected Average Annual Trade Balances, 1987–91

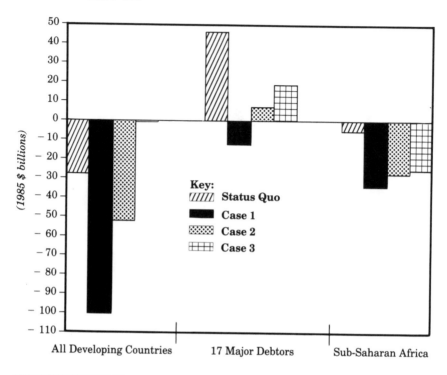

	Economic Growth Rate	Domestic Marginal Savings Rate	Increase in Productivity of Investments
		(percentages)	
Status Quo			
All Developing Countries	4.4	22	0
17 Major Debtors	2.5	23	0
Sub-Saharan Africa	1.5	15	0
Case 1			
All Developing Countries	6.4	35	20
17 Major Debtors	4.5	35	20
Sub-Saharan Africa	3.5	25	20
Case 2			
All Developing Countries	6.4	22	40
17 Major Debtors	4.5	23	40
Sub-Saharan Africa	3.5	15	40
Case 3			
All Developing Countries	6.4	35	40
17 Major Debtors	4.5	35	40
Sub-Saharan Africa	3.5	25	40

Source: Author's Projections.

do not increase, but productivity rises by 40 per cent. Case 3 assumes that the country groups are able to simultaneously raise marginal domestic savings rates by 50 per cent and productivity by 40 per cent.

For all three country groupings, moving from the status quo to cases 1 or 2 implies that additional foreign savings would be required to increase average growth rates by 2 per cent. In the most optimistic scenario, case 3, the growth target could be met with the trade-deficit picture actually improving because of the rapid rise in domestic savings relative to investment needs. As Figure 1 shows, however, the foreign financing problem is concentrated in the major debtor and Sub-Saharan African countries. In all cases, the combined deterioration in the trade balances of these country groups, in comparison with the status quo, exceeds that for the developing countries as a whole. For these most seriously affected countries, the net trade position would be likely to worsen in the short run with 2 per cent more rapid growth, even if they succeeded in immediately increasing their marginal savings rates by 50 per cent and the productivity of investment by 40 per cent (case 3)—admittedly a heroic and unprecedented jump.[6]

These projections are of course highly speculative. Projections made by others may be more or less optimistic about the need for additional reliance on foreign savings as a component of an enhanced growth strategy for either the major debtors or Sub-Saharan Africa. An additional point that does not appear in Figure 1 is that the need for foreign savings to supplement domestic savings declines rapidly as growth itself raises average domestic savings rates. For the major debtors, the trade surplus could return to present levels by 1992 in case 3. The process is slower for Sub-Saharan Africa because of lower growth and a smaller absolute change in the savings rate. This only underscores the essential pump-priming role that foreign savings can fill in restoring renewed, but sustainable, growth.

The Role of the World Bank

The preceding analysis does not in itself indicate the degree to which World Bank lending should expand. An approach used in the past has estimated the magnitude of private capital flows from various sources and then subtracted these flows from estimated current-account deficits. This approach is here rejected for several reasons. In the first place, it is nearly impossible to derive reliable estimates of private capital flows in the present circumstances. Uncertain changes in interest rates on foreign debts and oil prices will also have a substantial impact on the current account which, in turn, will affect creditworthiness and financial capital requirements. The impact of lower interest rates will certainly reduce the link between capital inflows and the changes in trade deficits that are likely to be associated with faster growth. And for most developing countries, lower oil prices will have the same effect.

However, it seems highly unlikely that net private capital flows will expand by very much in the short run under present conditions, among which looms the unresolved debt crisis. To keep the potential supply of private capital flows in perspective, it must be considered that in 1985 net private lending to developing countries was \$10.8 billion. The turnaround since 1980 has been dramatic. In that year, net private lending was \$61.1 billion.[7] While some reversal in lending might occur in the next few years, it is most unlikely that net lending (either in absolute volumes or as a fraction of GDP) will rapidly return to previous levels.

Exacerbating the problem is the fact that the countries in which growth has fallen most rapidly are those which currently appear least creditworthy: the major debtors in Latin America and Sub-Saharan Africa. Even if these countries were to begin undertaking the policy reforms necessary to increase the productivity of new investments, the resultant decline in debt/GDP and debt-service ratios would show up with a lag. Until these objective indicators of creditworthiness change, it is probable that private capital markets will be reluctant to increase their exposure by very much in these countries.

Tables 1, 2, and 3 summarize recent World Bank lending through IBRD and IDA. Commitments refer to the total size of *new* lending agreements. Disbursements are significantly lower because most loans are for specific projects that are completed over a period of many years. In some cases, disbursement rates have slowed in recent years because countries have been unable to budget or borrow sufficient sums to finance their share of total project costs.[8] Net disbursements are disbursements less repayments of previous loans, and net transfers are this amount less interest payments.

Examining Table 1, we see that despite lending in the \$12-billion range, net transfers have been much smaller—on the order of \$2.5 billion annually. This amounts to about 1 per cent of total investment in the borrowing countries. About half of IBRD net transfers were accounted for by the seventeen major debtors. Lending levels seem to have stagnated in recent years, perhaps due to difficulties in reaching agreements on the conditions to be attached to fast-disbursing, non-project lending in the form of structural adjustment loans (SALs). Another factor may be the World Bank's reluctance to finance much larger shares of total project costs in a period when many governments can increase neither their own spending nor foreign borrowing from private sources.

More worrisome is that, according to the projections of this study, net transfers—the crucial indicator of how much the Bank is adding to aggregate investment in borrowing countries—are likely to be less in the 1986–90 period than in 1981–85. Although the World Bank has indicated in various statements that anticipated commitments could rise by 50–60 per cent and disbursements by even more in 1986–90, increased amortization interest payments on past IBRD loans will rise even more rapidly after several years.[9] Reversing this trend would require a combination of greater commitments, increased disbursement rates from existing loans, and faster disbursement on new lending that could be brought about by greater reliance on non-project lending. These steps would be justified for countries where it appeared that additional net transfers would be used productively.

Table 2 illustrates the stagnation of concessional IDA lending in recent years. IDA has not increased in terms of commitments, disbursements, or net transfers. And because of inflation, the purchasing power of IDA flows has declined. Although annual IDA commitments are only 26 per cent of IBRD commitments, IDA and IBRD net transfers to the borrowing countries are of a similar magnitude. This is because of IDA's extended repayment periods (fifty years, with a ten-year grace period) and very low interest rates (0.75 per cent a year). Net transfers to the Sub-Saharan African countries, accounting for approximately 30 per cent of the IDA total, represent about 5 per cent of the total investment of these countries. When large countries such as China and India are included, the relative contribution of IDA to total investment is much smaller. Future trends in IDA operations depend on the appropriations of donors. In present circumstances, it would be unrealistic to expect large increases.

These trends point to the serious dilemma that is the focus of this chapter: The World Bank should be increasing its financial support for developing countries as a necessary condition for enhanced growth and better policy leverage, but the trends indicate at best stagnation in lending capacity and at worst real declines. Juxtaposing the projections discussed in the previous section (and summarized in Figure 1) with present lending levels underscores the importance of finding appropriate means for the World Bank to increase its concessional and non-concessional lending, the subject we now turn to in detail.

Table 1. World Bank Non-Concessional (IBRD) Lending, 1981–85, ($ billions and percentages)

Global Totals	1981	1982	1983	1984	1985	1981–85 Total
Lending Commitments	8.8	10.3	11.1	11.9	11.4	53.5
Gross Disbursements	5.2	6.4	6.9	8.7	8.9	36.1
Repayments	1.4	1.7	2.1	2.5	3.0	10.7
Net Disbursements	3.8	4.7	4.8	6.2	5.9	25.4
Interest	2.1	2.4	2.8	3.2	3.5	14.0
Net Transfers	1.7	2.3	2.0	3.0	2.4	11.4
15 Major Debtors[a]						
Gross Disbursements	2.3	2.7	3.6	4.3	4.5	17.4
Repayments	0.7	0.9	1.1	1.4	1.7	5.8
Net Disbursements	1.6	1.8	2.5	2.9	2.8	11.6
Share of IBRD total	42%	38%	52%	47%	47%	46%
Interest	0.9	1.0	1.1	1.4	1.6	6.0
Net Transfers	0.7	0.8	1.4	1.5	1.2	5.6
Share of IBRD total	41%	35%	70%	50%	50%	49%
Sub-Saharan Africa						
Gross Disbursements	0.3	0.3	0.3	0.4		1.2
Repayments	0.1	0.1	0.1	0.1		0.4
Net Disbursements	0.2	0.2	0.2	0.2		0.8
Share of IBRD total	6%	3%	4%	3%		4%
Interest	0.1	0.1	0.2	0.2		0.6
Net Transfers	0.1	.0	.0	.0		0.2
Share of IBRD total	5%	1%	2%	1%		2%

Source: World Bank.

[a]These countries are those in the original Baker plan: Argentina, Bolivia, Brazil, Chile, Colombia, Ecuador, Ivory Coast, Mexico, Morocco, Nigeria, Peru, Philippines, Uruguay, Venezuela, and Yugoslavia

Table 2. World Bank Concessional (IDA) Lending, 1981–85 ($ billions, millions, and percentages)

Global Totals	1981	1982	1983	1984	1985	1981–85 Total
		($ billions)				
Lending Commitments	3.5	2.7	3.3	3.6	3.0	16.1
Gross Disbursements	1.9	2.1	2.6	2.5	2.5	11.6
Repayments	<$100 mil.	<$100 mil.	0.1	0.1	0.1	0.3
Net Disbursements	1.9	2.1	2.5	2.4	2.4	11.3
Interest	0.1	0.1	0.1	0.2	0.2	0.7
Net Transfers	1.8	2.0	2.4	2.2	2.2	10.6

15 Major Debtors[a]

			($ millions)			
Gross Disbursements	23	21	17	14		75
Repayments	2	3	3	4		12
Net Disbursements	21	18	14	10		63
Share of IDA total	1.1%	0.9%	0.6%	0.4%		0.7%
Interest	2	2	2	2		9
Net Transfers	19	16	12	8		55
Share of IDA total	1.1%	0.7%	0.6%	0.3%		0.6%

Sub-Saharan Africa

			($ millions)			
Gross Disbursements	554	695	666	783		2,697
Repayments	36	27	20	22		106
Net Disbursements	518	667	645	761		2,591
Share of IDA total	27.2%	31.8%	25.8%	31.7%		29.1%
Interest	19	24	69	37		149
Net Transfers	498	643	576	724		2,442
Share of IDA total	27.7%	32.2%	24.0%	32.9%		29.1%

Source: World Bank.
[a]These countries are those in the original Baker plan: Argentina, Bolivia, Brazil, Chile, Colombia, Ecuador, Ivory Coast, Mexico, Morocco, Nigeria, Peru, Philippines, Uruguay, Venezuela, and Yugoslavia

Table 3. Regional Distribution of Total World Bank Lending (IBRD and IDA) ($ millions and percentages)

	South Asia		East Asia and Pacific		Europe, Mideast, and North Africa		Latin America		East Africa		West Africa	
	1985	1981–85	1985	1981–85	1985	1981–85	1985	1981–85	1985	1981–85	1985	1981–85
Commitments	3,559	15,894	3,101	15,193	2,429	12,906	3,700	16,318	786	4,691	811	4,696
Gross Disbursements	1,611	8,383	2,343	10,261	2,388	9,759	3,242	11,893	763	3,277	721	3,077
Repayments	171	746	560	1,928	718	2,464	1,120	3,752	113	481	129	462
Net Disbursements	1,441	7,638	1,783	8,333	1,670	7,295	2,123	8,141	650	2,796	591	2,615
Share of Total	17%	21%	22%	23%	20%	20%	26%	22%	8%	8%	7%	7%
Interest	294	1,082	862	3,250	767	3,038	1,013	4,108	167	728	220	804
Net Transfer	1,147	6,556	920	5,082	904	4,257	1,109	4,033	484	2,068	372	1,811
Share of Total	23%	28%	19%	21%	18%	18%	22%	17%	10%	9%	8%	8%

Source: *World Bank Annual Report, 1985.*

Financing World Bank Non-Concessional Lending

Before discussing how the World Bank might fund additional lending, it is important to describe how the present system operates. In many respects the World Bank functions in the same way as other financial intermediaries. IBRD lending to developing countries is financed by borrowings (mainly in the form of long-term bonds) in world capital markets. As of June 30, 1985, these borrowings amounted to $50.2 billion. Outstanding and disbursed loans to developing countries were $41.4 billion, while an additional $40.2 billion awaited disbursement.[10] The interest rate charged on new loans depends on the World Bank's borrowing costs, to which is added a 0.5-per cent spread and a commitment fee of 0.75 per cent on undisbursed balances. This rate is adjusted every six months. In this sense, World Bank lending is non-concessional.[11]

The subscribed capital of the World Bank is currently $58.8 billion. Of this total, the member countries have paid in, or deposited with the Bank, $5.1 billion, or almost 9 per cent of the total. The remaining $53.7 billion is callable in case the Bank needs it to service its borrowing obligations. It is the size of this combined capital base that limits total lending. The Articles of Agreement limit disbursed loans to no more than the sum of total capital subscriptions (paid-in and callable) plus retained earnings. This limitation is often referred to as the one-to-one gearing ratio. Since retained earnings total about $5.2 billion, current lending capacity is $64 billion. The authorized capital of the World Bank now is $78.5 billion which, if fully subscribed, would increase the lending limit by about $20 billion.

Without additional capitalization or a change in the gearing ratio, net disbursements will be able to grow only modestly in future years because outstanding loans will approach total capital subscriptions and retained earnings. As the Bank nears its limits on disbursed loans, net transfers by necessity become negative, even though gross lending can continue to be substantial. Consider the implications of currently anticipated lending over the 1986–90 period: If commitments were in the $85-billion range, likely gross disbursements would be $55–70 billion and net disbursements $30–45 billion, depending on the relative reliance on non-project lending. Net disbursements at the $37-billion level would imply that the Bank's capital subscriptions would have to increase by $12 billion (to about $71 billion), assuming that annual retained earnings are in the $500-million range for this period.[12] Since authorized capital is $78.5 billion, this increase in lending would not require a new General Capital Increase (GCI). If all authorized capital rather than only $12 billion were subscribed by then, total disbursements could increase even faster, but at the cost of slowing down later unless the level of authorized capital were increased.

This chapter has emphasized that the World Bank should not necessarily attempt to meet any specific lending targets. Instead, the Bank should be in a position to increase its operations substantially if warranted by circumstances such as successful policy reform by borrowing countries or the current case of temporarily constrained supplies of private capital.

It is useful, nevertheless, to look at the Bank's financing issues with some tentative upper bounds in mind. For example, if we assume the World Bank were able to increase net disbursements to $65 billion over the next five years—for instance, via expanded fast-disbursing loans with appropriate policy conditionality—it is the estimate of this study that the level of net transfers would average about $7 billion, or about $4.5 billion more than the recent average. These magnitudes would require an increase in subscribed capital of $40 billion and in authorized capital of $20 billion. Although an additional $4.5 billion annually may appear small relative to some of the magnitudes shown in Figure 1, it could be extremely important if properly directed both as a contribution toward structural adjustment and as a catalyst for larger private flows.

After 1990, it would be reasonable to plan for a gradual decline in net disbursements in line with this study's earlier conclusion that higher levels of World Bank lending in the short run would be part of a successful growth-oriented program leading to restored creditworthiness and private capital flows. If net disbursements after 1990 were to decline gradually, for instance by 12 per cent annually, total subscribed capital in the year 2000 would have to be about $175 billion, which would imply an increase in authorized capital of about $100 billion and of subscribed capital of $120 billion.

While these projections are meant to be illustrative only, let us assume that member countries wish to increase the authorized lending limit of the IBRD by an additional $100 billion. The straightforward way to increase the lending capacity is to increase the capital base through a General Capital Increase (GCI). This involves a vote by the Board of Governors to increase authorized capital, followed by subscription commitments by the member countries. The subscription process can take place gradually, as disbursed loans increase. The principal advantage of financing the IBRD with a General Capital Increase is that this approach maximizes the creditworthiness of the World Bank's own obligations.

With a one-to-one gearing ratio, bond purchasers know that the Bank's assets are either in the form of government securities or loans to developing countries that are secured by the Bank's capitalization and retained earnings. This is the single most important factor accounting for the low spreads over government securities paid by the Bank on its borrowings.[13]

From the perspective of a legal limit on disbursed loans, even if lending were accelerated by 50 per cent over the next five years, capitalization through a GCI might be postponed for several years, if some additional capital were subscribed under the presently authorized GCI. But the need for a GCI well before the net lending limit is reached may be critical from the perspective of the Bank's borrowing costs. We have argued that in valuing World Bank bonds, the credit markets treat very seriously the guarantee provided by subscribed capital. The fact that the spreads paid by the Bank did not increase in the wake of the debt crisis—in fact they actually fell—is one indication of the importance of this guarantee.[14] However, it is unlikely that bond purchasers give much weight to the capital subscriptions of the developing countries in determining the credibility of the guarantee. Rather, the effective guarantee in terms of the marketplace probably includes only the capital subscriptions provided by the industrialized countries and retained earnings.

The industrialized countries account for about two-thirds of total subscribed capital, which now amounts to some $37.8 billion. The effective guarantee would include this amount plus the Bank's $5.2 billion in retained earnings—or a total of $43 billion. The difference between disbursed loans and this number represents lending to developing countries that is implicitly guaranteed only by the developing countries. At the end of the Bank's last fiscal year, outstanding and disbursed loans stood at $41.4 billion, nearly the total of industrialized-country subscribed capital and the Bank's retained earnings, which means that in 1986 the ultimate guarantee of the marginal bondholder will be the callable capital of the developing countries themselves.

As soon as the markets realize this, the riskiness of the Bank's loans can be expected to become a larger factor in determining the spreads. Not only would this be unfortunate in terms of the interest rates charged borrowing countries, but, perhaps more important, it would reduce the flexibility of the World Bank in making productive loans when private credit markets consider them too risky; this would undermine one of the basic purposes of the institution. This line of argument suggests that it would be desirable to negotiate a GCI at the earliest possible date. Certainly the timing of increased subscription should be moved up so that the ratio of World Bank-disbursed loans to the sum of retained earnings and subscribed capital of the industrialized countries remains below one.

Under the pressure of the Gramm-Rudman-Hollings legislation, it will be difficult to obtain a GCI in the United States. Nor is the environment for budgetary increases promising in other industrialized countries. But a new GCI need not involve large budgetary outlays. There is no technical reason why the paid-in portion could not be reduced from the present 7.5 per cent to as low as zero. If the U.S. share of a $100-billion capital authorization were 20 per cent and the subscriptions were made over a ten-year period, the annual budgetary cost to the United States would be only $50 million if 2.5 per cent were paid in. From the viewpoint of the Bank's ability to borrow, there is, however, no compelling reason for any paid-in portion at all—other than demonstrating member governments' commitment to the institution. Zero paid-in capital is possibly preferable to a difficult political fight over a small paid-in portion.

The other way to increase the World Bank's net lending authority would be to relax the present one-to-one gearing ratio—in other words, to allow disbursed loans to exceed the capital base. This type of approach has been suggested frequently in the past as an alternative to capital increases. The obvious advantage is that it avoids the political problem of authorizing subscriptions and appropriating paid-in capital. Those who argue for increasing the gearing ratio point out that other financial institutions operate with loan/equity ratios far larger, and that since there have been no defaults on World Bank loans, there would be little additional risk to bondholders or the Bank's creditworthiness.

The key issue is what is meant by "little additional risk." Even supporters of a changed gearing ratio concede that a GCI yielding equally increased lending capacity would be preferable if it could be obtained. The argument here is that a change in the gearing ratio would, at best, result in substantial worsening of the Bank's credit rating. This would yield increased borrowing costs, and would inevitably change the World Bank's relationship with borrowing countries. The increased spreads that would result from a changed gearing ratio would force the Bank to face continually the dilemma of larger borrowing costs or avoiding increased country exposure in specific risky cases. Moreover, if spreads were to rise as a result of the difficulties of some developing countries, the cost would be passed on to all borrowing countries.

This discussion indicates that a comparison with the gearing ratios of other financial institutions is not appropriate, since the World Bank is not just another financial institution. It is a multilateral agency that maintains a special relationship with the borrowing countries. Therefore it makes sense to preserve the present system, which uses the capital base to separate the funding of operations from the management of those operations. If the United States and the other industrialized countries are serious about using the World Bank to promote enhanced growth in the developing countries, there simply is no satisfactory alternative to demonstrating that commitment by 'biting the political bullet' and subscribing more capital.

Financing World Bank Concessional Lending

The International Development Association is the window through which the World Bank provides concessional loans to the poorest developing countries. IDA operates very differently from the World Bank itself (the IBRD) in terms of its funding arrangements. The funds to cover disbursements and administrative costs come predominantly from government contributions, with small additional amounts provided by repayments, interest charges, and transfers out of World Bank income.[15] Contributions in 1985 were $2.6 billion.

One measure of the degree of concessionality in IDA lending is the grant element, a measure that varies from zero to one. If the grant element is zero, there is no concessionality, while if it is one, the loan is the equivalent of a gift or grant. The grant element depends on interest rate charged, maturity, grace period, and opportunity cost of funds. For instance, if the opportunity cost (or discount rate) of the funds is 10 per cent, then the grant element in IDA loans is about 85 per cent.[16] Clearly, borrowing on these terms is highly desirable for any developing country.

Periodically, the Bank organizes negotiations to replenish IDA, since it is not self-financing. With each round of replenishment since the early 1970s, negotiations have become more difficult regarding total size, appropriate burden sharing, and country allocations. One result of this, which reflects the deeper political problems with foreign aid in the United States, is that IDA lending has failed to keep up with inflation. The seventh replenishment provided a total of $9 billion over a three-year period, with the United States contributing one-quarter of the total. Discussions on the eighth replenishment are now under way. Although some donor countries have expressed a willingness to increase their contributions to IDA substantially, the U.S. administration has indicated that it would consider a replenishment in the $9–12-billion range—reflecting the amount that it is willing to pay.

This method of capitalization has turned the process of lending to poor countries on its head. Instead of basing the size of a lending program on how much resources can be used productively in conjunction with policies stimulating private capital flows—including equity capital—IDA's capacity to lend has become dependent on the political process and the current budget situations of donor countries. In the case of the United States, annual appropriations of $750 million to support a $9-billion IDA (over three years), or $1 billion if a $12-billion replenishment is approved, seems unrealistically high in the current budget climate. Moreover, the need to appropriate such large amounts for IDA further jeopardizes the prospects for a large GCI that is considered as part of the same budgetary process. However, under the present arrangements, there is simply no way to increase IDA lending substantially in the short run without recourse to the budgetary process in the donor countries.

A number of donor countries have suggested that IDA's terms be hardened as a way of increasing lending levels. This could be accomplished by raising the interest rate, reducing the grace period, and reducing the repayment period. These types of changes would increase payments into IDA by the borrowing countries, allowing lending levels in excess of the amounts contributed by the donors. In addition, it is sometimes argued that in present circumstances it would be politically easier to obtain appropriations for IDA if the grant element were lower and the money provided by IDA looked less like a gift and more like a loan. Another argument for reducing the grant element is that borrowing countries might be more careful in using the proceeds if the opportunity cost to them were greater.

While this approach has considerable merit, its effects on IDA's lending capacity would build up slowly. Quantitatively, hardening the terms of new lending would have virtually no impact until at least the mid-1990s. Similarly, increasing the share of World Bank profits transferred to IDA could increase lending by 10 per cent at most. But such transfers imply a one-to-one reduction in the World Bank's own lending capacity.

Simply stated, the dilemma is that there is an immediate need for increased (productive) investment financing in many IDA countries, at the same time that severe budget stringency (especially in the United States) makes larger replenishments virtually impossible. In this context, it is here proposed that serious attention be given to an alternative financing mechanism—replacing present IDA arrangements—aimed at increasing the World Bank's capacity to lend to poor countries in the near future while diminishing required appropriations from donor governments.

The suggested alternative is to replace the existing IDA funding mechanism with an interest-subsidy facility, at least for the present period of extreme budgetary stringency. This would involve raising the funds to be lent to IDA countries by resorting to the same method used in the case of non-concessional lending: through the sale of bonds that offer the same types of guarantees as World Bank bonds. In addition, the interest costs of servicing these obligations would be shared by the borrowing countries and donor governments.[17] The required appropriations from the donors would be the difference between the interest rate paid to the bondholders and the interest rate charged the borrowing countries, plus the paid-in portion of the capital subscriptions required to provide the bondholders with the standard World Bank guarantee.[18] The obvious advantage of this type of arrangement is that much higher lending limits could be set with much lower required appropriations. This outcome is possible because government appropriations would be heavily levered in the same way as non-concessional lending.

For instance, let us compare the budgetary implications of the current IDA with an interest subsidy. Consider first a series of IDA replenishments that permit net lending of $3.5 billion annually during a nine-year period. This represents the midpoint of the range being considered for the eighth replenishment of IDA. Nearly the entire amount would have to come from donor appropriations, assuming that the transfer to IDA from World Bank profits remains in the $100-million range. The associated annual appropriation from the United States would be $875 million if its share in the replenishments remained at 25 per cent. In the context of the Gramm-Rudman-Hollings legislation, these levels may not be feasible even if the Administration agrees to propose them.

Alternatively, suppose that an interest-subsidy facility were set up permitting lending levels consistent with annual net transfers of $7 billion, or twice what is implied by IDA operating at the $3.5 billion level.[19] In addition, assume that the interest cost of borrowing the principal for these loans averages 9 per cent a year and that the borrowing countries pay only 4.5 per cent, the rest being made up by donor contributions.[20] Further, assume that the maturity of the loan is reduced to twenty-five years with no grace period, and that 2.5 per cent of capital is paid in. In this case, donor contribution during the nine-year period would total $14.5 billion—or 46 per cent of what was needed to fund an IDA of half the size in terms of net transfers. Of this total, $12.6 billion would be for interest-subsidy payments and the remainder would be the paid-in portion of the subscribed capital amount of $75 billion.

For the United States, the required appropriations would average $125 million in the first three years (only 14 per cent of the appropriations needed in this period for a $10.5-billion IDA-VIII!) and $215 million for the first five years. This is exactly when

Figure 2. Comparison of U.S. Appropriations, IDA versus Interest-Subsidy Facility

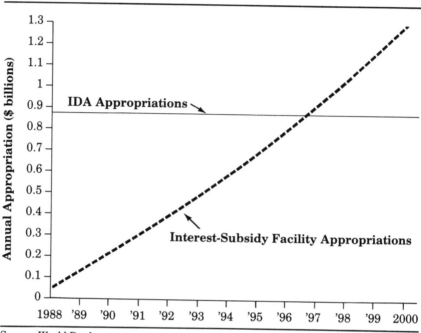

Source: World Bank

budget stringency is likely to be most severe. Appropriations would get larger over time, as the base on which the interest subsidy is paid increases. But annual appropriations would reach $875 million only after ten years of operation at this level. These trends are illustrated in Figure 2, which assumes such a facility beginning operations in fiscal year 1988.

Clearly, this type of approach represents something of a compromise between the essential interests of borrowing and donor countries. The borrowing countries are asked to give up some concessionality in return for greater net flows. If additional resources can be put to productive use, and if the additional net lending is sufficiently large, this is a profitable tradeoff. In return for substantial reductions in appropriations, the donor countries are asked to increase the guarantees they provide World Bank borrowing (through larger capital subscriptions) and to promise to subsidize future interest payments.

Various versions of interest-subsidy schemes have been proposed periodically, and there are several standard objections. One argument is that the World Bank would be unable to sell bonds to support this type of lending because the proceeds would be lent to countries that are not creditworthy. As stressed earlier in this chapter, the most important single consideration for bondholders is the reliability of the guarantee, not the riskiness of the loan portfolio itself. As long as lending is limited by a one-to-one gearing ratio, the commitment to subsidize interest is credible, and the borrowing countries are seen to be using the funds productively, there is no reason to doubt that such bonds could be marketed. That is not to say that the financial markets would price these bonds and conventional World Bank bonds identically. There may be added risks of either default or donor failure to keep up appropriations that would discount the price of such bonds. The above calculations were made assuming that these bonds would be priced with yields 1.5 per cent above non-concessional World Bank bonds.

However, the issue of the creditworthiness of the borrowing countries deserves additional comment. It might be argued that many of the countries borrowing from an interest-subsidy facility would be unable to service new debts to the World Bank that had harder terms than present IDA arrangements. This would imply a high probability that subscribed capital would have to be used to meet obligations to bondholders. In such circumstances, this alternative would not be viable.

Several rebuttals can be offered: In the first place, the World Bank should not be lending on either non-concessional or concessional terms unless the loans are expected to contribute to more productive use of resources. Income maintenance and debt relief should not be the Bank's responsibility. As long as the new investments financed by IDA have rates of return above the interest rates charged in these countries, they will generate profits to the country that services the debt and leave a residual that can add to future domestic savings and investment. This is contingent upon the existence of proper policies to ensure that not all benefits leak into current consumption. The World Bank has consistently appraised its operations on this basis.[21] Thus, productive lending contributes to creditworthiness even when positive interest rates are charged.

In the cases of countries whose foreign-exchange receipts are not expected to grow substantially in the short run or whose debt-servicing burdens are especially severe, the returns may be entirely in the form of non-tradable goods and services. In this situation, even servicing loans with subsidized interest rates may be very difficult. Several modifications could be introduced to handle such cases. The interest rate for this subset of borrowing countries could be reduced until they become more creditworthy. A grace period could be added, or repayments could be extended. Alternatively, a much smaller IDA could be maintained specifically for such special situations, with most concessional lending conducted under the interest-subsidy facility. As with all increases in the grant element, these modifications would add somewhat to donor costs but would still leave total appropriations well below what they would be under present IDA arrangements.

Recently, interest-subsidy accounts and hardened IDA terms have been viewed as alternative options for changing IDA's structure in order to stretch donor contributions further. Hardening the terms would have the effect of speeding up the replenishment of IDA by the borrowing countries, thus in the long run reducing the need for appropriations to achieve the same level of gross lending. But as discussed previously, hardening the terms does little to increase lending in the short run and does not affect net transfer levels even in the long run. If the objective is the near-term goal of increasing capacity to lend when donor budgets are severely constrained, the alternatives are not competitive or mutually exclusive.

Another objection is that, in the long run, required appropriations continue to increase under an interest-subsidy facility. The reason is that the base on which the interest subsidy is paid increases steadily with net disbursements. This objection requires consideration of several factors. It would be many years before the accumulated appropriations in an interest-subsidy arrangement exceeded what would be required under present IDA arrangements. In the case of a facility that operated to support net transfers of $7 billion annually, it would be eighteen years before accumulated donor contributions exceeded what would be needed to fund an IDA operating at $3.5 billion annually, leaving aside any discounting of future appropriations.

Moreover, if it is reasonable to suppose that the need of the developing countries for official lending is immediate, and that this lending can succeed in fostering self-sustaining growth, then net disbursements need not continue to grow forever; growth would allow appropriations first to level off and then to decline. Another factor to consider is that it is in the next few years that donor budgets are likely to be most constrained. This is particularly obvious in the United States, where there is considerable consensus that the budget-balancing process should be completed during the next five years, if not sooner.

As a practical matter, decision makers in the donor countries will have to decide whether the risks inherent in a potential increase in future appropriations under an interest-subsidy facility are worth the gains in budget savings and the benefits of increased lending to those poorer developing countries that are willing to take on the policy reforms necessary to enhance growth. Decision makers in the countries that now borrow from IDA will have to weigh the relative loss in degree of concessionality against the benefits of having access to larger amounts of resources available to increase investment and growth rates.

Conclusions

The following points summarize the main conclusions and recommendations made in this chapter.

1. Increasing economic growth rates in most developing countries—in particular the group of major debtors and the Sub-Saharan African countries highlighted in this chapter—will require foreign financing beyond that which is available to them through either commercial markets or existing development bank lending. With a growth increase of 2 per cent, the net trade position of the most seriously affected countries would be likely to worsen in the short run even if they were to succeed immediately in increasing marginal savings rates and the productivity of investment by large amounts.

2. The need for large inflows of foreign capital is concentrated in the near term. If developing countries succeed in changing their economic policies to promote greater efficiency, and if they can obtain the foreign financing to begin accelerating the growth process, they can increase domestic savings sufficiently to support further growth, and they can begin to repay prior loans or accelerate growth even more. These types of changes can also be expected to increase their creditworthiness and their capacity to tap private capital markets. It is under these conditions that larger foreign financing from official agencies such as the World Bank would be justified as part of a pump-priming strategy.

3. If the developing countries are to attain efficient and self-sustaining economic growth, the World Bank should be given an enhanced role both in its capacity as a financial intermediary for development and in its policy-advisory role. In addition to possible changes in operational policy, the World Bank in all likelihood will

need greater lending capacity to fulfill these roles. Given the current mood of budgetary restraint, especially in the United States, alternative capitalization methods must be sought.

4. *A substantial General Capital Increase*—perhaps on the order of $100 billion—is the method recommended here for the expansion of World Bank non-concessional lending. This would allow the World Bank the flexibility to increase net disbursements in the next five to six years, if conditions warrant, to $65 billion over currently anticipated levels. The advantages of increased capital subscriptions in comparison with an increase in the gearing ratio are substantial. Early agreement on a GCI is also desirable due to the decline in the ratio of industrialized subscribed capital plus retained earnings to disbursed loans. The budget impact of a GCI need not be large since the paid-in portion can be reduced.

5. A more fundamental change may be necessary in the case of concessional lending. Because the need for expanded lending is immediate and coincides with a period of extreme budgetary stringency, serious consideration should be given, at least as a temporary measure, to *replacement of the present IDA arrangement with an interest-subsidy facility.* The principal of loans made under this facility would be raised by the sale of bonds, with a one-to-one gearing ratio to insure investors; the interest costs on these obligations would be shared by the donors and the borrowing countries. Assuming a 4.5-per cent annual interest subsidy, if such a facility were organized with the capacity to provide net transfers of $7 billion annually in the initial years, the average budgetary cost to the United States over the next five years would be $215 million. By comparison, the U.S. budgetary costs of IDA operating at $3.5 billion annually would be $875 million over the next five years. Although the developing countries would lose concessionality under this proposal, they would gain through the increased investment financing that this scheme would permit.

Notes

Note: The author wishes to express thanks to the numerous persons in the public and private sectors who have offered information, ideas, and guidance, while emphasizing that responsibility for the analysis, conclusions, and recommendations are his alone. The author also is most appreciative of the very able research assistance provided by Mary Sheehan.

[1] It is emphasized throughout this chapter that potential needs must be related to the ability of borrowers to use additional resources productively as well as to the availability of other private and public capital.

[2] The economic data reported in this section are from the World Bank's Economic Analysis and Projections Department. All projections are the author's.

[3] The set of seventeen debtor countries includes Costa Rica and Jamaica in addition to the fifteen countries specified in the "Baker plan": Argentina, Bolivia, Brazil, Chile,

Colombia, Ecuador, Ivory Coast, Mexico, Morocco, Nigeria, Peru, Philippines, Uruguay, Venezuela, and Yugoslavia.

4 Lack of "efficiency" is here used, in its broadest sense, to include inappropriate choices of technologies within sectors, failure to take full advantage of comparative advantages in world trade, poor pricing strategies, discrimination against the private sector, etc. At the macro-economic level, these shortcomings are reflected in the average rate of return to capital. Comparison of the average productivity of capital during the past decade provides a compelling explanation of the fact that some countries are faced with a debt crisis while other countries continue to be creditworthy despite high debt/GDP ratios.

5 The model determines required investment as a function of desired growth and marginal productivity. Domestic savings depend on marginal savings rates and income growth. Foreign savings requirements are estimated as the difference between total investment and domestic savings. Projections were calculated for a five-year period covering 1987–91. Country-specific data are from the World Bank's Economic Analysis and Projections Department. Similar stylized growth models have been developed recently at the World Bank and elsewhere, although with somewhat different purposes in mind.

6 In the case of the major debtor countries, the projections do not necessarily imply that direct use of foreign savings (trade deficit) would be required. These countries now run substantial trade surpluses, meaning that large amounts of domestic savings are used for debt servicing rather than to finance domestic investment. Figure 1 indicates that moving away from the status quo is possible only if the fraction of domestic savings allocated to investment increases.

7 *World Economic Outlook* (Washington, D.C.: International Monetary Fund, 1986).

8 The Bank's Special Action Program was aimed, in part, at alleviating this problem.

9 Net transfers depend on disbursements, amortization, and interest rates. Perhaps because of interest rate uncertainty, the World Bank has not publicly discussed its own forecasts. If net disbursements in 1986–90 were $37 billion and the interest rate on floating World Bank debt averaged 8 per cent, net transfers would be about $2 billion annually, in comparison with $2.8 billion in 1981–85. Net transfers in 1987–88 would be somewhat greater than the $2.4 billion of 1985, but would decline substantially thereafter. Of course, if interest rates were lower or disbursement occurred faster, net transfer projections would be higher.

10 The financial data reported in this section through fiscal year 1985 are from *The World Bank Annual Report 1985* (Washington, D.C.: 1985). Future projections are the author's unless otherwise reported.

11 The rate charged on variable-rate loans in the second half of 1985 was 8.82 per cent.

12 By 1990, outstanding loans would total about $79 billion. Without more capital subscriptions, lending capacity would increase from $64 billion to $67 billion, leaving a gap of $12 billion to be filled.

13 In judging the riskiness of its bonds, the bond market undoubtedly also pays attention to the Bank's liquidity, quality of operations, and refusal to engage in reschedulings.

14 If the quality of the Bank's loan portfolio were a very important factor in determining the risk of holding World Bank bonds, the spread or risk-premium would have increased when major borrowers such as Mexico and Brazil went into debt crises. This did not happen.

15 In 1985, interest charges were $175 million, repayments were $99 million, and World Bank transfers $100 million. Administrative expenses were $273 million. The financial data reported in this section through fiscal year 1985 are from *The World Bank Annual Report 1985*, op. cit.

16 This is a realistic measure of the grant element during the 1970s when inflation (and hence, the discount rate) was high. If world interest rates in the future were to average 5 per cent, the grant element would fall to 64 per cent.

17 This would have the effect of reducing the grant element, which we assume is politically important to the donors. If the member countries agreed, the interest subsidy component could vary among borrowing countries depending on income level or debt-servicing ability.

18 Some previous proposals for interest subsidization have suggested that the subsidy be paid out of World Bank profits. We reject this on two counts. First, unless the lending program is very small, the draw on World Bank profits could not be sustained for long. Having a small facility undermines the whole objective. Second, World Bank profits can be used to leverage World Bank borrowing; diverting them to this purpose would implicitly make the non-IDA developing countries partial funders of the subsidy, which is objectionable on equity and other grounds.

[19] Under the present IDA arrangements, net lending and net transfers are almost identical because the interest rate is only 0.75 per cent. Since interest payment under this version of an interest-subsidy facility would be substantial, net lending would be larger than net transfers.

[20] The 9-per cent cost of borrowing is based on an assumption that interest rates on government long-term securities will average 7.5 per cent and that these bonds would have a spread of 1.5 per cent. This is a much larger spread than the World Bank pays and reflects additional risk. This may be too conservative an assumption given the backing of one-to-one guarantees.

[21] Since resources are fungible, proper appraisal of a loan may involve more than a simple cost-benefit analysis of a particular project. This issue is closely related to the question of the balance between project and non-project lending.

Chapter 6

The Technological Impact of World Bank Operations

Howard Pack

The technological performance of the World Bank is a major determinant of its overall impact as a development institution.[1] In addition to its role of supplementing the overall resources of developing countries, the Bank provides relevant guidance with respect to the technical problems encountered in individual projects and changes in economic policy. The benefit of any additional project investment undertaken or policy changes made possible depends critically on a number of economic-technical dimensions, such as the productivity achieved by a given investment or change in policy regime, its employment effect, or its impact on specific policy objectives (for example, the provision of clean water). Many of the Bank's actions reflect sensitivity to these dimensions. Nevertheless, in some activities (for example, industrial lending), the Bank has been less attentive to areas of potential improvement that have been explored by analysts within and outside the Bank. Although significant changes in policy appear to be under way, the extent of alteration is unclear. This chapter provides a brief overview of some major technological activities of the World Bank—using this designation for the entire World Bank group[2]—and suggests improvements in several areas.

In assessing the performance of the World Bank with respect to its technological impact, it is necessary to distinguish between two types of policies—implicit and explicit—that affect the adoption of specific technologies within developing countries. Wage levels, interest and foreign-exchange rates, the varying levels of tariff and

161

other protective measures across sectors, and various incentive devices (such as tax holidays and depreciation rates) affect the technological choices made by a variety of economic agents in all sectors. Insofar as World Bank actions affect any of these economic variables, there is an *implicit* policy with respect to technology. Thus structural adjustment loans may require recipients to end artificial limitations on the height of interest rates; the resulting increase in interest rates may discourage individual firms or government agencies from adopting technologies that require large amounts of capital.

In contrast, *explicit* policies reflect a direct effort to influence the technology chosen in a specific project. Explicit policies undertaken by the Bank include the financing of efforts to develop new seed varieties, the experimental investigation of alternative methods of road construction, and financing of the design of new water supply and sanitary engineering systems appropriate to conditions in less-developed countries.

The World Bank has engaged in many important activities in both spheres. Explicit technological efforts have been briefly noted in the preceding paragraph. The Bank's research staff have been among the leaders in the international research community in the analysis of the impact of prices on economic activity. Much of the research effort has been diffused within the project and regional staffs, which now routinely employ such concepts as the domestic resource cost of a project. The conditions imposed in structural adjustment loans typically reflect knowledge obtained from the investigation of implicit policies.

A Sectoral Review of World Bank Activities[3]

The Agricultural Sector

Until the late 1960s, agriculture was not a major recipient of Bank lending despite the fact that much of the poverty in developing countries occurred in this sector. More recently, agriculture's share in total lending has increased considerably, reaching 27 per cent of World Bank lending in 1979–83.[4] Three types of loans are provided: 1) to finance the *purchase of farm inputs*; 2) to build *physical infrastructure* such as dams, irrigation facilities, and roads; and 3) to *develop institutions* (for example, collectives and rural extension services). While all of these activities are useful, there is a limited technological component except in the last group.

The Bank is also an important contributor and perhaps the catalytic institution in organizing the Consultative Group on International Agricultural Research (CGIAR). This consortium sponsors thirteen international centers that undertake agricultural research relevant for developing countries, including research on topics such as plant genetics and appropriate agricultural policies. The structure of CGIAR might serve as a model for technical efforts in other areas.[5]

Civil Works

About 40 per cent of World Bank loans have gone to civil works, including those activities (for example, rural roads) whose functional lending category is agriculture.[6] The Bank and the International Labour Office have carried out pioneering research to ascertain the scope of alternative technologies that can be employed in civil construction. Given the magnitude of outlays on civil works in most developing countries, more labor-intensive methods of construction offer an important opportunity for the provision of productive employment for the underemployed, particularly those in rural areas who are underemployed.[7] A key issue is whether labor-intensive production techniques are economically efficient—that is, whether they permit production costs as low as those obtained with more mechanized methods. While the various Bank and ILO studies concluded that a significant amount of economically efficient substitution is possible, provided that some feasible productivity growth is achieved in labor-intensive methods, it is difficult to determine the extent to which these results have been considered or incorporated in new Bank projects. Where unconventional production technologies are considered, investigation of their suitability and changes in project bidding and review are necessary and require more intensive staff involvement at the World Bank. Pursuit of a project configuration that leads to greater national income and better distributional outcomes in the borrowing country may conflict with the objective of increasing total disbursements. In this and other cases considered below, the greater time requirements of lower-cost labor-intensive projects might prevent the Bank staff— given present staff size—from disbursing as much money as current policy dictates.

The adoption of labor-intensive production methods, where economically efficient in World Bank projects, would have a particularly great benefit in that the Bank's seal of approval would carry significant weight in many developing countries and would thus influence their own decisions. In this and other cases noted below, the total impact of a specific Bank policy could be multiplied considerably by the imitation engendered.

Water Supply and Waste Disposal

It is estimated that two billion people in developing countries do not have access to safe water and sanitary waste disposal.[8] This lack of access is concentrated in rural areas but inevitably occurs in poorer urban ones as well. In recent years, the Bank has increased lending for these activities as well as for efforts to devise new low-cost means of delivery of both services. The strictly technical activities involved include analysis of the need for improved services, the development of new technologies, the diffusion of knowledge about them, and the attempt to embed the capital facilities within an expanded social matrix including housing, health, education, and nutrition programs. In all of these areas, the Bank has made innovative contributions; one example is the financing of site and service projects for urban housing. Nevertheless, the impact on the poor of the improved understanding of issues in these areas and of the greater availability of appropriate technologies is unclear.[9] The diffusion of improved social services for poor populations is not a high-priority issue for most developing-country governments, and it is unclear that the Bank has been able to overcome this diffidence.

Industry

The World Bank contains two major sources of lending for industry: the IBRD and the International Finance Corporation (IFC). In both cases, a high percentage of lending is directed toward large-scale industry. Financing of industry constitutes about 15 per cent of Bank lending and is about equally divided between large-scale industry and small- and medium-scale enterprises.[10] Bank attitudes with respect to this rapidly growing sector can help to establish an acceptable scenario of desirable growth patterns in both the sectors of expansion and the nature of technology choices. In particular, policy-based lending that encourages the movement of critical prices toward levels that conform to the scarcity value of resources encourages the expansion of sectors in conformity with comparative advantage and a choice of technology consistent with the country's factor endowment. Industrial performance can also be improved by non-price-denominated policies.

In general, the World Bank has not been technically innovative with respect to industry. Unlike its efforts in agriculture, there has been little concern with the generation of innovative technology, particularly that which would be appropriate for small-scale enterprise, although such efforts have recently begun, particularly with respect to Africa. Nor has there been a systematic effort to encourage the search for and adoption of least cost technology for larger firms that is more labor-intensive than that currently being installed.

An Evaluation of Explicit Technology Policies

The preceding brief survey suggests a range of existing World Bank activity that is impressive. Can the Bank exert an even greater and qualitatively superior effect on the technology available to and employed in developing countries? This depends partly on developing-country adoption of policies that will encourage acceptance and diffusion of both existing and still-to-be-developed technologies. The economic policies conducive to such adoption are discussed later in this chapter. This section is devoted to setting out a framework that defines the appropriate scope for World Bank technological activity, suggesting that some activities are more appropriate than others, and indicating areas in which new initiatives are justified on the basis of two criteria: appropriability and the existence of economies of scale.

Appropriability

Many of the activities described earlier might best be characterized as efforts to redress some failures in the existing mechanisms for generating technological change. The public financing of CGIAR's agricultural research parallels publicly supported agricultural research in many individual countries. The location of agricultural research in the public sector reflects a specific characteristic of the results of such effort—namely, the difficulty of the innovator in appropriating the benefits. Subsidized research is warranted where the knowledge of the activity is *not* easily "appropriable." Appropriability of the benefits of an activity is one useful guideline to desirable areas for World Bank initiatives.

Economies of Scale

A second—not necessarily mutually exclusive—criterion is the existence of large initial costs in undertaking an activity but low marginal costs in diffusing the benefits. The knowledge obtained by the World Bank in its investigation of alternative technologies for civil construction resulted from a costly series of field investigations. Yet once the knowledge was obtained and codified, it could be diffused to potential users at relatively low costs. Replication of the field work by many countries would not be justified, given its expense and the low cost of diffusing the results. Similarly, searching the extensive literature on alternative methods of providing clean water is very expensive, yet the dissemination of the knowledge obtained is relatively cheap. More generally, high fixed costs and low marginal costs in generating and diffusing either hardware or knowledge provides a prima facie case for the Bank's considering the activity to be one that might well fall within its domain.

Despite the Bank's investment in determining alternative technologies for construction, there is still relatively little activity that employs the more labor-intensive alternatives. This in part reflects the fact that such alternatives are not appropriate for some types of construction, and in part that local governments are not receptive to employing them. Moreover, international contractors are often not interested in these technologies, presumably wishing to avoid having to manage the work of large groups of local laborers. World Bank-financed construction projects offer opportunities to augment the employment impact of such projects while reducing their cost.

Suggested Changes Employing the Appropriability Criterion

Under the appropriability criterion, some current World Bank activities are probably not justifiable, whereas other potential activities not currently undertaken might prove highly beneficial to developing countries. Recent loans to foster industrial-sector technological development—for example, a project to encourage the growth of the semiconductor industry in the Republic of Korea—have been partly financed by Bank efforts. Given the small number of very large firms involved in that sector, the benefits will accrue to a well-defined and known set of firms. Under such conditions, there can be little justification for Bank financing.[11] While it is possible that some benefits will occur that are not captured by the innovating firms, the Bank's stance should be one of skepticism. Instead, other proposals for financing technological development where such development has high appropriability should be subjected to careful evaluation.

At the other end of the spectrum of industrial innovation, the World Bank has done little to encourage innovation appropriate for the tiny firms that inevitably will provide most of the employment for new members of the labor force in most developing countries over coming decades. Projections of labor-force growth and investment levels indicate that most new entrants to the labor force will have to be absorbed in occupations in which they will have a very small amount of capital. Little innovation has been undertaken in either developed or developing countries to improve the productivity of the typically simple tools used in both the rural and urban small-scale sector.

In contrast to agriculture, small-scale industrial innovation has received limited funding both within developing countries and at the international level. Yet the potential gains are not necessarily inferior to those that have been obtained from agricultural research (in which rates of return between 40 and 80 per cent a year have been calculated). Innovations that could benefit the small-scale sector are likely to be relatively simple to copy, and thus the benefit to individual firms undertaking such research are likely to be low. Moreover, once the initial costs of innovation have been incurred, the cost of diffusion of new designs is likely to be low, further strengthening the argument for Bank financing. These characteristics suggest the desirability of an effort along the lines of CGIAR for the small-scale industrial sector. Such a program would require funding research into the design of improved equipment and field testing to examine the possibility of unanticipated social effects or hindrances to acceptance, as well as the coordination of the work of existing research institutes.

The Bank has exhibited considerable skill in eliciting appropriate innovative activity in areas such as water supply and sanitary waste disposal, and the organizational skills learned in these activities should be deployed in the generation of appropriate small-scale industrial innovation.

Implicit Policies

It is now well established that economic policies exert a considerable technological effect. Thus, for example, the maintenance of overvalued exchange rates artificially reduces the cost in domestic currency of expensive imported equipment in activities ranging from water supply to the establishment of new industrial plants. Physically efficient and economically preferable lower-cost equipment is also discriminated against by ceilings on interest rates, accelerated depreciation allowances, tax holidays, and other investment incentives often introduced by governments in the mistaken belief that industrial investment is characterized by low profitability. There is also evidence that high rates of protection, whether by tariffs or import quotas, may result in excessively capital-intensive methods of production as well as low productivity. Finally, high minimum wages in large-scale private and public enterprises also encourage the purchase of unduly expensive equipment that has the effect of displacing labor.

The impact of such inappropriate economic policies differs among and within sectors. There is extensive evidence that inappropriate prices have encouraged outcomes such as the following:

the premature introduction of tractors in many developing countries; the expansion of industrial sectors such as steel, which inherently offer few employment opportunities; the choice within industrial sectors of very mechanized methods of production where more labor-intensive ones exist; and the deployment of techniques of construction in roads and other public works that use less labor than should be used.

The World Bank has been in the forefront in emphasizing the importance of these factors in its dialogue with developing-country governments, particularly in connection with sector adjustment and structural adjustment loans (SALs). Nevertheless, it is not clear that the impact of such dialogue has done much to alter the pattern of price distortions. Bank officials suggest that recipients of SALs often appear capable of avoiding or delaying many of the changes in critical prices expected as a condition of such loans.[12] But the pricing policies of recipient countries are not the only policies that affect technological decisions. Loans favoring one sector rather than others, or large projects rather than small ones, also influence the mix of technology. Project evaluation that concentrates on the rate of return on additions to capacity but neglects other potential sources of increased output may have a negative impact on the productivity with which existing technology is employed. And the absence of institutions to disseminate information about appropriate technology, including used equipment, also affects technology choices.

The following discussion of these and other questions about the impact of implicit technology policies concentrates on the industrial sector for a number of reasons. First, the *technological* impact of pricing policies mainly affects the industrial sector—although it certainly also has repercussions on non-industrial activities. Second, the Bank's efforts in other sectors mainly have been explicit efforts at developing and disseminating technology—for example, in agriculture through the CGIAR, and in civil construction through the development of alternative methods of production. Third, given projected rates of labor-force growth and the limited absorptive capacity of agriculture in most countries, industrial employment in both rural and urban areas will have to absorb a greater percentage of new labor-force entrants than has been true in the past. Substantial employment growth and simultaneous growth in industrial productivity constitute an important agenda for the Bank's efforts in this sector.

Sectoral Choices Within Industry

The initiation of industrial projects by sector presumably lies, as it should, with the developing country. Yet many industrial loans financed by the IBRD and the IFC have been to sectors whose economic viability is dubious. For example, a considerable part of IFC lending has been directed to such sectors as iron and steel, chemical and petrochemical products, pulp and paper, and motor vehicle manufacturing.[13] IBRD loans have also been made to such sectors. The development of such intrinsically capital-intensive sectors is not in the interest of most developing countries. Because of their relative scarcity of capital and an abundant supply of unskilled labor, these countries can gain greater private and social returns through industrial sectors that conserve physical capital while employing considerable amounts of unskilled labor. In the early stages of their development, rapidly industrializing countries such as Korea and Taiwan correctly concentrated on such labor-intensive commodities as sports-equipment, clothing, and plywood production. The private profitability, where it exists, of the typical capital-intensive industrial project in poor developing countries is made possible by a set of favorable alterations introduced by government policy in the price of outputs and inputs. At undistorted prices, these ventures would exhibit operating losses.[14] The loans have financed projects far inferior in their returns to the economy than others available but neglected.

Although loan requests originate in the developing countries, the acquiescence of the IBRD and the IFC to many of these requests reinforces the predilections of domestic policy makers that considerably distort the development process even given their *own* professed goals. In one Sub-Saharan country, for example, a pulp and paper plant that cost $250 million was partly financed by the IBRD in the late 1970s. This one plant accounted for 15 per cent of the government's planned industrial development over a five-year period, yet it provided only one thousand jobs—a cost per job of $500,000. Not surprisingly, the plant is not doing well—and there are many other similar examples.

Even if a project passes through the World Bank's own internal review process, which includes the calculation of social rates of return, it may be that this process contains an inherent optimistic bias. Where Bank staff perceive themselves to be under pressure to achieve high target rates of lending, it may be easier to make a small number of large loans whose realized rate of return will be lower than the forecast presented to Bank management. This pressure could be partly alleviated by a larger staff. Nevertheless, with a given staff size, there may be a quality-quantity tradeoff. The responsibility for poorly conceived loans ultimately rests with the borrowers, but the Bank, as the repository of considerable acumen in this area, should not validate misguided developing-country policy making. Yet the pressure on Bank staff to do precisely this is often present.

Large-Scale versus Small-Scale Lending

About half of the World Bank's direct financing of industrial projects is for large-scale manufacturing plants, with the remainder, often channeled through industrial development banks, going to small- and medium-scale enterprises (SMEs). Given the well-documented finding that small- and medium-scale enterprises are typically more economically efficient and provide more employment per unit of investment, these proportions should be altered, so as to increase funding for these producers.

Again, the quantity-quality tradeoff arises. The Bank staff does not have the ability to directly supervise loans to individual firms, and developing-country intermediaries such as industrial development banks possess a limited skill base—both quantitatively and qualitatively. Thus a strong argument exists for increasing the number of high-quality loan officers in developing-country public financial institutions. Currently, some efforts in this direction are being undertaken by the Economic Development Institute; these should be expanded significantly. Although such an effort will not be a major absorber of Bank loans, it is likely to have significant long-term beneficial effects. In the interim, a reduction in large-scale lending may be an appropriate measure—even if such a policy reduces net Bank lending. There are no benefits from lending to projects whose most probable realized economic rates of return are low, even though *ex ante* calculations, often containing an optimistic bias, indicate adequate rates of return.

New Industrial Projects versus Rehabilitation

The typical Bank industrial-sector project finances the construction of a new factory. A growing segment of lending is devoted to rehabilitation loans for new equipment to alleviate bottlenecks and to measures to improve the productivity of existing plants in the sector. Nevertheless, rehabilitation loans remain quantitatively small, and a considerable percentage of the funds allocated under them is devoted to the purchase of additional equipment even in sectors in which existing machinery is as modern as in much more efficient sectors in other countries. Evidence suggests that the following are desirable components in analyzing new industrial projects: 1) an evaluation of the recent evolution of productivity in sectors in which new plants are proposed;[16] 2) a comparison of the level of output of the plants in the sector to the level that could be realized with existing plant and equipment and improved productivity; 3) an estimate of whether the increased output forthcoming from improved productivity could eliminate the need for a new plant. If these steps suggest that rehabilitation of the sector is more desirable than the construction of a new plant, policies to encourage improved productivity can be made part of structural adjustment loans. Existing SALs often have provided a large component for additional purchases of equipment even where existing machinery is employed insufficiently. Old wine appeared in new bottles. Appropriate policy measures include specific technical aid to help firms improve their productivity, as well as a set of more conventional policies such as reduced protection against imports to provide an incentive for the effective use of aid and to help ensure that the benefits of improved productivity are passed on also to consumers instead of accruing solely to the owners and workers in an industry as increased income.

Again, implementation of such a change in evaluation procedures and lending policies at the Bank would almost surely result in a considerable diminution in the magnitude of current industrial-sector lending, although the rate of return on the entire industrial portfolio probably would increase. As currently constituted, the Bank staff is too small to carry out the proposed evaluation procedures. Moreover, strong objections from borrowers would almost certainly ensue. Recipient governments may object to sole reliance on productivity enhancement in existing factories insofar as new plants provide a method of securing political support in specific regions and a general source of patronage to sustain popularity. Despite these problems, continued growth in lending designed to secure greater productivity is desirable. The benefit-cost ratio of achieving additional expansion of output is certainly greater from projects designed to improve productivity than from adding to physical capacity. An important consideration is the much smaller debt service required by the former option.

The Choice of Technology and Employment Creation

Among the major problems facing the industrial sector in most developing countries is the creation of productive jobs for the burgeoning population. Given the rapid growth of the labor force and the limited availability of arable land, non-agricultural pursuits must provide a significant number of new jobs. The absolutely small size of the large-scale manufacturing sector in many countries militates against its being a major employer of new labor-force entrants. Nevertheless, even where manufacturing provides only 10 per cent of total national employment, it accounts for a considerably greater percentage of modern sector employment; a substantial increase in its labor intensity could eliminate a large fraction of open unemployment and contribute to the absorption of poorer workers currently underemployed in the urban informal sector.

The generation of a greater number of jobs per dollar of investment in Third World developing-country manufacturing requires that attention be paid to the possibilities of cost-effective substitution of labor for machinery. Engineering and economic analyses have demonstrated that substantial gains in output, employment, and profits can be realized by a suitable choice of technology. The Bank already encourages the realization of such gains via policy changes required as part of policy-based lending. Beyond enforcing changes in the prices of inputs and outputs, the Bank can pursue additional policies that lie on the border between explicit and implicit policies, including expanded feasibility studies, encouragement of international trade in *used* equipment, and promotion of the manufacture of appropriate machinery.

Guidelines for Feasibility Studies

The Bank finances industrial projects both directly through its own lending and indirectly through development finance corporations. Although the choice of technology receives some attention, it is not accorded a high priority. One way to increase the range of choices considered for projects would be to alter the nature of the feasibility studies currently submitted by consulting engineers. Specifically, these could be required to: present a detailed costing for several alternative technologies, provide a profile of production techniques in several countries at different stages of development, and indicate why techniques differing from those ultimately recommended were judged unsuitable. Another method to increase the range of technological choice would require parallel efforts by two consulting engineering firms—one from a developed country and one from a developing country. Because the range of knowledge possessed by these firms generally appears to be limited to a few equipment producers in one or two countries, Third World-based consulting engineers are more familiar with machinery produced in developing countries, or less-expensive equipment available from developed countries.

Both changes in practice would generate useful side benefits. Consulting engineers, by having to provide alternatives, would enable lending institutions to accumulate a 'shelf' of technologies against which future feasibility studies could be checked. Encouraging the employment of Third World-based consulting engineers should increase their competence and provide important incentive to local machinery manufacturers, who might thus begin to perceive heretofore neglected opportunities for exporting to other developing countries.

Encouraging Trade in Used Equipment

In the industrial sectors of many developing countries, the purchase of used equipment provides a significant opportunity to reduce capital-intensity and increase employment. In developed countries, many firms routinely buy used equipment whereas firms in developing countries face difficulties if they attempt to do so. Problems are encountered in identifying high-quality used equipment, in obtaining financing, and in ensuring that initial performance can be reestablished after machinery is disassembled, transported, and reinstalled. While individual firms face risks, the social return in terms of greater output and employment from a given level of investment may be substantial.[17]

The Bank can help to overcome some of the obstacles by, for example: encouraging consulting engineers to investigate the availability of appropriate used equipment, helping to establish a clearinghouse to identify high-quality machinery, convincing recipient governments to remove prohibitions on the import of used machinery, encouraging governments to establish central insurance funds to cover some of the risks faced by individual firms, and financing the foreign-exchange component of such programs.

Encouraging the Production of Appropriate Machinery

Currently, insufficient effort is being made to increase the productivity of labor-intensive medium- and large-scale equipment except by a few private voluntary organizations. Since any success in these endeavors is likely to be relatively easy to emulate, it is argued that such research should be publicly subsidized at the international level. The Bank's efforts in catalyzing CGIAR provide a precedent for encouraging research, much of whose benefit is not appropriable. In principle, the required research could take place in either developed or developing countries—as could the ultimate production of such equipment. Whatever the locus of machine production, the major beneficiaries will be the users of equipment in the developing countries.

Training

In many areas of the world, most notably in the Sub-Saharan African countries, a shortage of skilled analysts and administrators hampers development efforts. The missing skills are those which are typically taught in the developed countries' Master's degree programs in business administration, engineering, and public policy. Relatively small numbers of trainees—even twenty or so a year—can have an enormous impact on the quality of developing-country performance within a decade. Although the Bank has provided high-quality education through its Economic Development Institute, there are strong arguments for augmenting this effort with formal degree training at established universities.

Regional centers of excellence should also be supported. A small number that were financed by the Ford and Rockefeller Foundations, particularly in East Africa, had a substantial beneficial impact on the quality of policy making. As private foundations withdrew from such activities, however, the quantity and quality of new decision makers declined. The rate of return on efforts to reinvigorate such regional Third World centers is likely to be enormous.

Conclusions

In many of its activities that contain a technological element, the Bank has exhibited a concern with innovative efforts. Thus, it has helped to finance international agricultural research centers, encouraged the provision of agricultural extension services, financed efforts to encourage low-cost housing, and funded experiments designed to determine the feasibility of labor-intensive construction methods. Its industrial lending programs have not been characterized by the same degree of innovation, although recently there has been some movement in this direction. Industrial lending is not currently a major area of funding by the World Bank, but the sector is of great importance for future progress in the developing countries insofar as it is well documented that as per capita income grows, the relative importance of manufacturing rises.

The major issues facing developing-country governments with respect to industry are the improvement of productivity and the generation of new jobs. Yet the Bank's efforts have largely been limited to the financing of new large-scale factories, with only cursory attention being given to employment generation and to improving productivity in existing plants. Greater attention to these considerations would require a larger staff and might lead to a smaller total lending program for a transition period. Maintaining the current level of industrial-sector lending may imply failure to undertake alternative, smaller projects with higher social rates of return.

Notes

[1] "Technology," as used in this chapter, refers to the methods of production and organization of economic activity.

[2] The "World Bank group" consists of the International Bank for Reconstruction and Development (IBRD)—which is the World Bank itself—the International Development Association (IDA), and the International Finance Corporation (IFC).

[3] This section relies heavily on a number of World Bank documents, including: *Technology and Science in World Bank Operations*, 1982; Charles Weiss, Jr., *Science, Technology and The World Bank*, 1983; Charles Weiss, Jr. and Nicolas Jequier, eds., *Technology, Finance, and Development* (Lexington, Mass.: Lexington Books, 1984).

[4] See Graham Donaldson, "Technology in Agricultural Development," in Weiss and Jequier, op. cit. Most of the statements in this section about the scope of World Bank operations in agriculture are based on Donaldson's very useful survey.

[5] For a detailed description of the financing and structure of CGIAR, see John K. Coulter, "The Consultative Group on International Agricultural Research," in Weiss and Jequier, op. cit.

[6] Coukis and N. Jequier, "Civil Works Construction," in Weiss and Jequier, op. cit.

[7] A summary of most of the results of the studies, including the outcome of seminars discussing the project, is contained in "The Study of Labor and Capital Substitution in Civil Engineering Construction," Transportation Department, The World Bank (Washington, D.C.: World Bank, 1978).

[8] Julian Bharier, "Water Supply and Waste Disposal," in Weiss and Jequier, op. cit. This section is based on Bharier's paper.

[9] On the role of the Bank in urban housing, education, and health, see the papers by Werlin, Lethem, and Lucas in Weiss and Jequier, op. cit.

[10] For IFC figures, see *International Finance Corporation, 1985 Annual Report*, p. 124. Industrial lending includes that noted under industry as well as that to development finance companies and small-scale enterprises.

[11] While it might be argued that the Bank can learn about specific, leading industrial-development problems from such financing, there are alternative and better means for doing so.

[12] This of course has also been true of the conditions imposed by the IMF. See, for example, John Williamson, ed., *IMF Conditionality* (Washington, D.C.: Institute for International Economics, 1983).

[13] H. Geoffrey Hilton, "The International Finance Corporation," in Weiss and Jequier, op. cit.

[14] Nor is it an argument in favor of such projects that their loans are eventually repaid.

[15] Much of the recent documentation of these statements comes from the research of the Bank's staff that corroborates evidence obtained in many countries over the last quarter-century. See, for example, Dennis Anderson, "Small Industry in Developing Countries," *World Development*, Vol. 10, No. 11 (November 1982), Mariluz Cortes, R. Albert Berry, and A. Ishaq, *What Makes for Success in Small and Medium Scale Enterprises: The Evidence from Colombia*, Development Research Department, The World Bank, 1985; I.M.D. Little, Dipak Mazumdar, and John Page, *The Small Scale Sector in India*, Development Research Department, The World Bank, 1985.

[16] Bank staff members have occasionally carried out such evaluations. See, for example, "Tanzania, Basic Economic Report, Annex V, East Africa Country Programs I," December 1977.

[17] See, for example, Cortes, Berry, and Ishaq, op. cit., Chapter 3.

About the Overseas Development Council and the Contributors

The Overseas Development Council is a private, non-profit organization established in 1969 for the purpose of increasing American understanding of the economic and social problems confronting the developing countries and of how their development progress is related to U.S. interests. Toward this end, the Council functions as a center for policy research and analysis, a forum for the exchange of ideas, and a resource for public education. The Council's current program of work encompasses four major issue areas: trade and industrial policy, international finance and investment, development strategies and development cooperation, and U.S. foreign policy and the developing countries. ODC's work is used by policy makers in the Executive Branch and the Congress, journalists, and those concerned about U.S.-Third World relations in corporate and bank management, international and non-governmental organizations, universities, and educational and action groups focusing on specific development issues. ODC's program is funded by foundations, corporations, and private individuals; its policies are determined by a governing Board and Council. In selecting issues and shaping its work program, ODC is also assisted by a standing Program Advisory Committee.

Victor H. Palmieri is Chairman of the ODC, and J. Wayne Fredericks is Vice Chairman. The Council's President is John W. Sewell.

The Editors

Between Two Worlds: The World Bank's Next Decade is the seventh volume in the Overseas Development Council's series of policy books, U.S.-Third World Policy Perspectives. The co-editors of the series—sometimes collaborating with guest editors contributing to the series—are Richard E. Feinberg and Valeriana Kallab.

Richard E. Feinberg, vice president of the Overseas Development Council and co-editor of and a frequent contributing author to the Policy Perspectives series, directed the ODC policy research project resulting in this volume. Before joining ODC in 1981, Dr. Feinberg served as the Latin American specialist on the Policy Planning Staff of the U.S. Department of State, and as an international economist in the Treasury Department and with the House Banking Committee. Dr. Feinberg is the author of numerous books as well as journal and newspaper articles on U.S. foreign policy, Latin American politics, and international and economic and financial issues. His most recent book is the *The Intemperate Zone: The Third World Challenge to U.S. Foreign Policy* (1983).

Valeriana Kallab is vice president and director of publications of the Overseas Development Council and series co-editor of the ODC's U.S.-Third World Policy Perspectives series. She has been responsible for ODC's published output since 1972. Before joining ODC, she was a research editor and writer on international economic issues at the Carnegie Endowment for International Peace in New York. She was co-editor (with John P. Lewis) of *U.S. Foreign Policy and the Third World: Agenda 1983* and (with Guy F. Erb) of *Beyond Dependency: The Third World Speaks Out.*

Contributing Authors

Gerald K. Helleiner is professor of economics at the University of Toronto, where he teaches international and development economics. He has previously taught and conducted research at Yale University's Economic Growth Center, the Institute of Development Studies (Sussex, U.K.), Oxford University, the University of Ibadan, and the University of Dar es Salaam. Dr. Helleiner is the author of numerous books and articles on international development issues and editor of *The IMF and Africa* (1986) and *For Good or Evil: Economic Theory and North-South Negotiations.* He was chairman of the Commonwealth Finance Ministers' study group that in 1983 produced *Towards a New Bretton Woods, Challenges for the World Financial and Trading System.* Dr. Helleiner is currently deputy chairman of the board of the North-South Institute (Ottawa), a member of the executive committee of the International Development Center (Ottawa), and a member of the Overseas Development Council's program advisory committee. He has served as a consultant to many development organizations, including the World Bank, the United Nations Conference on Trade and Development (UNCTAD), the International Labour Office (ILO), the Group of Twenty-four, the Commonwealth Secretariat, and the Brandt Commission.

Joan M. Nelson is a visiting fellow at the Overseas Development Council. She has long been concerned with various aspects of the politics of development. After serving during the 1960s on the Policy Planning Staff of the U.S. Agency for International Development (AID), she taught at the Massachusetts Institute of Technology and at the Johns Hopkins School of Advanced International Studies. She has also been a consultant to the World Bank and to AID. Joan Nelson's publications include: "The Politics of Stabilization," in Richard E. Feinberg and Valeriana Kallab, eds., *Adjustment Crisis in the Third World*, ODC U.S.-Third World Policy Perspectives No. 1 (1984); *Access to Power: Politics and the Urban Poor in Developing Nations* (1979); (with Samuel P. Huntington) *No Easy Choice: Political Participation in Developing Nations* (1976); and *AID, Influence, and Foreign Policy* (1968).

Sheldon Annis is a visiting fellow at the Overseas Development Council and is writing a book on the relationship between grassroots organizations and the public sector in middle-income Latin American countries. Formerly he was senior research officer at the Inter-American Foundation, where, among other responsibilities, he edited the journal, *Grassroots Development*. Dr. Annis has served as a consultant on poverty issues for the U.S. Agency for International Development (AID), the World Bank, and private voluntary organizations. He recently completed writing *God and Production in a Guatemalan Town* (to be published by the University of Texas Press), and editing *Direct to the Poor: A Reader in Grassroots Development* to be published by Pergamon Press).

John F. H. Purcell is a vice president in the Corporate Bond Research group at Salomon Brothers. He heads the unit responsible for political and economic credit assessment of the major sovereign and supranational borrowers in the international financial markets. Before joining Salomon Brothers in 1983, Dr. Purcell was vice president in the International Economics group at Bankers Trust Company in charge of Latin American political assessment. Until 1979, he was professor of political science at California State University, Fullerton. Dr. Purcell has been a consultant to the Rockefeller Foundation on U.S.-Mexican relations and has had extensive research experience in Mexico and other Latin American countries. He is the author of numerous articles on politics and policy in Latin America.

Michelle B. Miller is an analyst in the Corporate Bond Research group at Salomon Brothers. She is responsible for political and economic assessment of the multilateral development banks and other sovereign and supranational credits. Prior to joining Salomon Brothers, Ms. Miller was European desk officer at Multinational Strategies, Inc., a political and economic consulting firm, where she covered Europe and Canada and completed projects on international financial institutions. Ms. Miller is rapporteur for the U.S.- Canada Business Seminars series, sponsored by the Americas Society/Canadian Affairs and the Pace Institute for U.S.-Canada Business Studies. She has also worked in the State Department's Bureau of Northern European Affairs.

Charles R. Blitzer is principal research associate and coordinator of developing-country studies at the Energy Laboratory of the Massachusetts Institute of Technology. He is also visiting professor of economics at the Fletcher School of Law and Diplomacy. Dr. Blitzer was senior adviser to the director of the U.S. International Development Cooperation Agency (IDCA) from 1979 to 1981, and a staff member at the World Bank from 1971 to 1979. Dr. Blitzer has also taught at the Johns Hopkins University and the University of California at Berkeley. His research interests include development planning and policy, international trade and finance, the relationship of energy to macro-economics and development strategies, contracting and financial issues involving oil and gas exploration, and foreign aid policy. He has published widely on these and other topics in development economics.

Howard Pack is professor of city and regional planning and economics at the University of Pennsylvania and director of the Program in Appropriate Technology. He has written about many issues arising during the process of industrialization, including the choice of appropriate technology, the role of the capital-goods sector, and the determinants of industrial productivity. He has been a consultant to the U.S. Agency for International Development (AID), the International Labour Office (ILO), the United Nations Conference on Trade and Development (UNCTAD). Appropriate Technology International, and other development agencies. From 1977 to 1979, he was a member of the Development Research Department of the World Bank and has frequently served as a World Bank consultant.

Overseas Development Council

Board of Directors*

Chairman: Victor H. Palmieri
Chairman, The Palmieri Company
Vice Chairman: J. Wayne Fredericks
Ford Motor Company

Marjorie C. Benton
Chairman of the Board
Save the Children Federation

William H. Bolin
San Francisco, California

Thornton F. Bradshaw
Chairman of the Board
RCA Corporation

William D. Eberle
President
Manchester Associates, Ltd.

Thomas L. Farmer**
Prather, Seeger, Doolittle and Farmer

Roger Fisher
Harvard Law School

Stephen J. Friedman
Executive Vice President
E. F. Hutton & Co., Inc.

John J. Gilligan
Chairman, Institute for Public Policy
University of Notre Dame

Edward K. Hamilton
President
Hamilton, Rabinovitz,
and Alschuler, Inc.

Frederick Heldring
Deputy Chairman
Philadelphia National Bank

Susan Herter
Santa Fe, New Mexico

Ruth J. Hinerfeld
Former President, The League
of Women Voters of the USA

Joan Holmes
Executive Director
The Hunger Project

Robert D. Hormats
Vice President
International Corporate Finance
Goldman, Sachs & Co.

Jerome Jacobson
President
Economic Studies, Inc.

William J. Lawless
President
Cognitronics Corporation

C. Payne Lucas
Executive Director
Africare

Paul F. McCleary
Associate General Secretary
General Council on Ministries of the
United Methodist Church

Robert S. McNamara

Lawrence C. McQuade
Executive Vice President
W. R. Grace & Co.

William G. Milliken
Former Governor
State of Michigan

Alfred F. Miossi
Executive Vice President
Continental Illinois National Bank
and Trust Company of Chicago

Merlin E. Nelson
Kleinwort, Benson (International)

Jane Cahill Pfeiffer
Former Chairman, NBC, Inc.

John W. Sewell**
President
Overseas Development Council

Daniel A. Sharp
Director, International Relations
and Public Affairs
Xerox Corporation

*Board members are also members of the Council.
**Ex Officio.

Council

Robert O. Anderson
Atlantic Richfield Company

Robert E. Asher
Washington, DC

William Attwood
New Canaan, Connecticut

Marguerite Ross Barnett
The City University of New York

Douglas J. Bennet
National Public Radio

Edward G. Biester, Jr.
Judge, Court of Common Pleas
Doylestown, Pennsylvania

Jonathan B. Bingham
Former Member, U.S. House of
Representatives

Eugene R. Black
Scandinavian Securities
Corporation

Robert R. Bowie
Washington, DC

Harrison Brown
Albuquerque, New Mexico

Lester R. Brown
Worldwatch Institute

John C. Bullitt
Shearman & Sterling

Goler T. Butcher
Howard University Law School

Frank C. Carlucci
Sears World Trade, Inc.

Lisle C. Carter, Jr.
Verner, Liipfert, Bernhard,
McPherson and Hand

Kathryn D. Christopherson
Louisville, Kentucky

George J. Clark
Citibank, N.A.

Harlan Cleveland
Hubert H. Humphrey Institute of
Public Affairs
University of Minnesota

Frank M. Coffin
Chief Judge, United States Court of
Appeals for the First Circuit

John C. Culver
Arent, Fox, Kinter, Plotkin & Kahn

Ralph P. Davidson
Time Incorporated

Richard H. Demuth
Surrey & Morse

William T. Dentzer, Jr.
Depository Trust Company

John Diebold
The Diebold Group

Albert Fishlow
University of California at Berkeley

Luther H. Foster
Alexandria, Virginia

Arvonne Fraser
Hubert H. Humphrey Institute of
Public Affairs
University of Minnesota

Orville L. Freeman
Popham, Haik, Schnobrich,
Kaufman & Doty, Ltd.

Richard N. Gardner
Columbia University School of Law
and International Organization

Peter C. Goldmark
Times Mirror Co.

Katharine Graham
The Washington Post Company

James P. Grant
UNICEF

Arnold C. Harberger
University of Chicago

Theodore M. Hesburgh, C.S.C.
University of Notre Dame

Philip Johnston
CARE

Peter T. Jones
University of California at Berkeley

Vernon E. Jordan
Akin, Gump, Strauss, Hauer & Feld

Nicholas deB. Katzenbach
IBM Corporation

Philip H. Klutznick
Klutznick Investments

J. Burke Knapp
Portola Valley, California

Peter F. Krogh
Georgetown University

Geraldine Kunstadter
New York City Commission for the
United Nations

Walter J. Levy
Research & Social Service
Foundation

George N. Lindsay
Debevoise & Plimpton

Harald B. Malmgren
Malmgren, Inc.

Edwin M. Martin
Population Crisis Committee

William McSweeny
Occidental International

John W. Mellor
International Food Policy Research Institute

Robert R. Nathan
Robert Nathan Associates

Rev. Randolph Nugent
General Board of Global Ministries United Methodist Church

Joseph S. Nye
John F. Kennedy School of Government Harvard University

Richard Ottinger
Pace University Law School

Daniel S. Parker
Charleston, South Carolina

James A. Perkins
International Council for Educational Development

John Petty
Chairman and Chief Executive Officer Marine-Midland Bank, N.A.

James J. Phelan
The Chase Manhattan Bank, N.A.

Samuel D. Proctor
Rutgers University

Charles W. Robinson
Energy Transition Corporation

William D. Rogers
Arnold & Porter

J. Robert Schaetzel
Washington, DC

David H. Shepard
Cognitronics Corporation

Eugene Skolnikoff
Massachusetts Institute of Technology

Davidson Sommers
Webster & Sheffield

Joan E. Spero
American Express Company

Stephen Stamas
Exxon Corporation

C. M. van Vlierden
San Francisco, California

Alan N. Weeden
Investment Banker

Clifton R. Wharton, Jr.
State University of New York

Thomas H. Wyman
CBS, Inc.

Andrew Young
Mayor, Atlanta, Georgia

George Zeidenstein
The Population Council

Barry Zorthian
Alcade, Henderson, O'Bannon & Rousselot

ODC Program Advisory Committee

John P. Lewis, Chairman
*Woodrow Wilson School of Public
and International Affairs,
Princeton University*

Lawrence J. Brainard
Bankers Trust Company

Shahid Javed Burki
The World Bank

Albert Fishlow
University of California

James Galbraith
*Lyndon B. Johnson
School of Public Affairs,
University of Texas at Austin*

Jeffrey Garten
Shearson Lehman American Express

Denis Goulet
University of Notre Dame

Davidson R. Gwatkin
The World Bank

Catherine Gwin

Edward K. Hamilton
*Hamilton Rabinovitz,
and Alschuler, Inc.*

G. K. Helleiner
University of Toronto

Albert O. Hirschman
*Institute for Advanced Study,
Princeton, New Jersey*

Robert D. Hormats
Goldman, Sachs & Company

Michael M. Horowitz
*Institute for Development
Anthropology, Inc.
State University of New York*

Gary Hufbauer
*School of Foreign Service,
Georgetown University*

Peter B. Kenen
Princeton University

John W. Mellor
*International Food Policy Research
Institute*

Theodore H. Moran
*Landegger Program,
School of Foreign Service
Georgetown University*

Henry Nau
George Washington University

Kenneth A. Oye
Princeton University

Dwight H. Perkins
*Institute for International Development,
Harvard University*

Gustav Ranis
*Economic Growth Center,
Yale University*

Ronald K. Shelp
Celanese Corporation

Robert Solomon
The Brookings Institution

Joan E. Spero
American Express Company

Lance Taylor
Massachusetts Institute of Technology

Norman Uphoff
Cornell University

Nadia Youssef
UNICEF

Overseas Development Council
1717 Massachusetts Ave., N.W.
Washington, D.C. 20036
Tel. (202) 234-8701

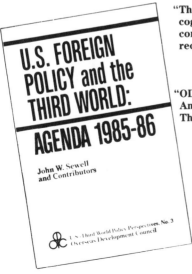

U.S. FOREIGN POLICY AND THE THIRD WORLD: AGENDA 1985-86

John W. Sewell, Richard E. Feinberg, and Valeriana Kallab, editors

> "high-quality analysis ... has made the ODC's *Agenda* series necessary reading for anyone interested in American foreign policy or development issues"
> —Joseph S. Nye
> Professor of Government and Public Policy
> John F. Kennedy School of Government
> Harvard University

> "This year's volume begins with an interesting balance sheet of the Reagan administration's 'reassertionist' approach ... All [chapters] are full of ideas ... for policy-making."
> —*Foreign Affairs*

The Overseas Development Council's 1985-86 *Agenda*—the tenth of its well-known annual assessments of U.S. policy toward the developing countries—analyzes the record of the Reagan administration's first term and identifies the main issues currently looming in this area of U.S. foreign policy. The losses and gains of the administration's "reassertionist" approach are tallied both in terms of its own expressed objectives and in terms of broader, longer-term criteria for advancing U.S. economic, security, and humanitarian interests in the Third World.

Contents:

Overview: Testing U.S. Reassertionism: The Reagan Approach to the Third World
Paul R. Krugman—U.S. Macro-Economic Policy and the Developing Countries
Richard E. Feinberg—International Finance and Investment: A Surging Public Sector
Steve Lande and Craig VanGrasstek—Trade with the Developing Countries: The Reagan Record and Prospects
John W. Sewell and Christine E. Contee—U.S. Foreign Aid in the 1980s: Reordering Priorities
Anthony Lake—Wrestling with Third World Radical Regimes: Theory and Practice
Stuart Tucker—Statistical Annexes

John W. Sewell has been president of the Overseas Development Council since January 1980. From 1977 to 1979, he was the Council's executive vice president, directing ODC's program of research and public education. Prior to joining ODC in 1971, he was with the Brookings Institution, and served in the U.S. Foreign Service. A contributor to several of ODC's past *Agenda* assessments of U.S. policies and performance in U.S.-Third World relations, he was also recently a co-author of *Rich Country Interests and Third World Development* and of *The Ties That Bind: U.S. Interests in Third World Development*

ISBN: 0-88738-042-5 (cloth)   **$19.95**
ISBN: 0-87855-990-6 (paper)   **$12.95**
1985   **242 pp.**

Available Fall 1986
THE UNITED STATES AND MEXICO: FACE TO FACE WITH NEW TECHNOLOGY
Cathryn L. Thorup and contributors

Rapid technological advance is fast changing the nature of the relationship between the industrial countries and the advanced developing countries. This volume explores the meanings of this change close to home—as it affects the U.S.-Mexican relationship.

What is the impact of the new technology on trade, investment, and labor flows between the United States and Mexico? Will development of a stronger Mexican industrial sector constitute an aid or a threat to specific U.S. industries? While demand for the middle-technology goods that countries such as Mexico can produce is growing in the United States, the debt crisis and the high dollar make procuring the high-technology capital goods necessary for this effort difficult and expensive.

An overview essay explores the impact of technological change upon conflicts between the economic and political objectives of the two countries and ways in which the coordination of national policies might be maximized. The authors—representing a mix of government and business experience in both countries—offer specific recommendations on improving the efficiency of bilateral economic interaction, reducing the adjustment costs of technological change, and avoiding diplomatic tensions between the two nations.

Contents:

Cathryn L. Thorup—Overview
Alan Madian—The New Competition: Technology and the Changing Industrial Balance
Mauricio de Maria y Campos—Bilateral Implications of Mexico's Development Strategy
James K. Galbraith—Implications of U.S. Macro-Economic Strategy and Trends in Industrial Structure for Economic Relations with Advanced Developing Countries
María Patricia Fernández Kelly—Technology and Employment Along the U.S.-Mexico Border: Implications for National Development
James P. Womack—Prospects for the U.S.-Mexican Relationship in the Auto Sector
Susan Sanderson—Impacts of Automated Manufacturing Technologies on Mexico's Offshore Assembly
Cassio Luiselli—Bio-Technological Change in Agriculture and Nutrition
Joan Brodovsky—The Mexican Pharmaceutical and Pharmochemical Industries

Cathryn L. Thorup is director of the Overseas Development Council's U.S.-Mexico Project, a policy-oriented, Washington-based forum for the exchange of ideas among key actors in the bilateral relationship. She is the author of many articles on conflict management in the U.S.-Mexican relationship, on Mexico's attempts to diversify its foreign investments, on the Reagan administration and Mexico, and on U.S.-Mexican policies toward Central America.

ISBN: 0-88738-120-0 (cloth)   **$19.95**
ISBN: 0-87855-663-6 (paper)   **$12.95**

INVESTING IN DEVELOPMENT: NEW ROLES FOR PRIVATE CAPITAL?

Theodore H. Moran and contributors

The tone of the debate about foreign direct investment in Third World development has changed dramatically since the 1970s. There are expectations in both North and South that multinational corporations can play a key role in restoring growth, replacing aid, providing capital to relieve the burden on commercial bank lending, and (together with the private sectors in the local economies) lead to an era of healthier and more balanced growth.

To what extent are these expectations justified? This volume provides a reassessment of the impact of multinational corporate operations on Third World development. It covers not only direct equity investment in natural resources and manufacturing, but non-equity arrangements extending to agriculture and other sectors as well. It examines whether the efforts of less developed countries to attract and control multinational corporations have constituted a serious "distortion" of trade that threatens jobs in the home nations. It analyzes the link between international companies and the "umbrella" of World Bank co-financing as a mechanism to reduce risk. Finally, it attempts to estimate how much of the "gap" in commercial bank lending might plausibly be filled by direct corporate investment over the next decade.

In each case, it draws policy conclusions for host governments, for home governments (focused particularly on the United States), for multilateral institutions such as the World Bank and the agencies of the United Nations, and for the multinational firms themselves.

Contents

Theodore H. Moran—Overview: The Future of Foreign Direct Investment in the Third World

Dennis J. Encarnation and Louis T. Wells, Jr.—Evaluating Foreign Investment

Vincent Cable and Bishakha Mukheriee—Foreign Investment in Low-Income Developing Countries

David J. Glover—Multinational Corporations and Third World Agriculture

Charles P. Oman—New Forms of Investment in Developing Countries

Stephen Guisinger—Host-Country Policies to Attract and Control Foreign Investment

David J. Goldsbrough—Investment Trends and Prospects: The Link with Bank Lending

Theodore H. Moran is director of Georgetown University's Landegger Program in International Business Diplomacy as well as professor and member of the Executive Council of the Georgetown University School of Business Administration. A former member of the Policy Planning Staff of the Department of State with responsibilities including investment issues, Dr. Moran has since 1971 been a consultant to corporations, governments, and multilateral agencies on investment strategy, international negotiations, and political risk assessment. His publications include many articles and five major books on the issues explored in this new volume. He is a member of the ODC Program Advisory Committee.

ISBN: 0-88738-044-3 (cloth)   **$19.95**
ISBN: 0-88738-644-X (paper)   **$12.95**

DEVELOPMENT STRATEGIES RECONSIDERED

John P. Lewis and Valeriana Kallab, editors

"First-rate, comprehensive analysis—presented
in a manner that makes it extremely valuable
to policy makers."
—Robert R. Nathan
Robert Nathan Associates

Important differences of opinion are emerging about the national strategies best suited for advancing economic growth and equity in the difficult global adjustment climate of the late 1980s.

Proponents of the "new orthodoxy"—the perspective headquartered at the World Bank and favored by the Reagan administration as well as by a number of other bilateral donor governments—are "carrying forward with redoubled vigor the liberalizing, pro-market strains of the thinking of the 1960s and 1970s. They are very mindful of the limits of government." And they are "emphatic in advocating export-oriented growth to virtually all comers."

Other prominent experts question whether a standardized prescription of export-led growth can meet the needs of big low-income countries in the latter 1980s as well as it did those of small and medium-size middle-income countries in the 1960s and 1970s. They are concerned about the special needs of low-income Africa. And they see a great deal of unfinished business under the heading of poverty and equity.

In this volume, policy syntheses are proposed to reconcile the goals of growth, equity, and adjustment; to strike fresh balances between agricultural and industrial promotion and between capital and other inputs; and to reflect the interplay of democracy and development.

Contents:
John P. Lewis—Development Promotion: A Time for Regrouping
Irma Adelman—A Poverty-Focused Approach to Development Policy
John W. Mellor—Agriculture on the Road to Industrialization
Jagdish N. Bhagwati—Rethinking Trade Strategy
Leopoldo Solis and Aurelio Montemayor—A Mexican View of the Choice Between Inward and Outward Orientation
Colin I. Bradford, Jr.—East Asian "Models": Myths and Lessons
Alex Duncan—Aid Effectiveness in Raising Adaptive Capacity in the Low-Income countries
Atul Kohli—Democracy and Development

John P. Lewis, guest editor of this volume, is professor of economics and international affairs at Princeton University's Woodrow Wilson School of Public and International Affairs. He is simultaneously senior advisor to the Overseas Development Council and chairman of its Program Advisory Committee. From 1979 to 1981, Mr. Lewis was chairman of the OECD's Development Assistance Committee. He has served as a member of the U.N. Committee for Development Planning. For many years, he has alternated between academia and government posts, with collateral periods of association with The Brookings Institution and The Ford Foundation.

ISBN: 0-88738-044-1 (cloth)   **$19.95**
ISBN: 0-87855-991-4 (paper)   **$12.95**
1986   **208 pp.**

HARD BARGAINING AHEAD: U.S. TRADE POLICY AND DEVELOPING COUNTRIES

Ernest H. Preeg and contributors.

U.S.-Third World trade relations are at a critical juncture. Trade conflicts are exploding as subsidies, import quotas, and "voluntary" export restraints have become commonplace. The United States is struggling with record trade and budget deficits. Developing countries, faced with unprecedented debt problems, continue to restrain imports and stimulate exports.

For both national policies and future multilateral negotiations, the current state of the North-South trade relationship presents a profound dilemma. Existing problems of debt and unemployment cannot be solved without growth in world trade. While many developing countries would prefer an export-oriented development strategy, access to industrialized-country markets will be in serious doubt if adjustment policies are not implemented. Consequently, there is an urgent need for more clearly defined mutual objectives and a strengthened policy framework for trade between the industrialized and the developing countries.

In this volume, distinguished practitioners and academics identify specific policy objectives for the United States on issues that will be prominent in the new round of GATT negotiations.

Contents:

Ernest H. Preeg—Overview: An Agenda for U.S. Trade Policy Toward Developing Countries
William E. Brock—Statement: U.S. Trade Policy Toward Developing Countries
Anne O. Krueger and Constantine Michalopoulos—Developing-Country Trade Policies and the International Economic System
Henry R. Nau—The NICs in a New Trade Round
C. Michael Aho—U.S. Labor-Market Adjustment and Import Restrictions
John D. A. Cuddy—Commodity Trade
Adebayo Adedeji—Special Measures for the Least Developed and Other Low-Income Countries
Sidney Weintraub—Selective Trade Liberalization and Restriction
Stuart K. Tucker—Statistical Annexes

Ernest H. Preeg, a career foreign service officer and recent visiting fellow at the Overseas Development Council, has had long experience in trade policy and North-South economic relations. He was a member of the U.S. delegation to the GATT Kennedy Round of negotiations and later wrote a history and analysis of those negotiations, *Traders and Diplomats* (The Brookings Institution, 1969). Prior to serving as American ambassador to Haiti (1981-82), he was deputy chief of mission in Lima, Peru (1977-80), and deputy secretary of state for international finance and development (1976-77).

ISBN: 0-88738-043-3 (cloth)   **$19.95**
ISBN: 0-87855-987-6 (paper)   **$12.95**
1985   **220 pp.**

UNCERTAIN FUTURE: COMMERCIAL BANKS AND THE THIRD WORLD

Richard E. Feinberg and Valeriana Kallab, editors

> "useful short papers by people of differing backgrounds who make quite different kinds of suggestions about how banks, governments and international bodies ought to behave in the face of the continuing debt difficulties"
> —*Foreign Affairs*

> "the very best available to academia and the general public . . . on the criteria of reader interest, clarity of writing, quality of the research, and on that extra something special that sets a work apart from others of similar content"
> —James A. Cox, Editor
> *The Midwest Book Review*

The future of international commercial lending to the Third World has become highly uncertain just when the stakes seem greatest for the banks themselves, the developing countries, and the international financial system. Having become the main channel for the transfer of capital from the North to the South in the 1970s, how will the banks respond in the period ahead, when financing will be urgently needed?

The debt crisis that burst onto the world stage in 1982 is a long-term problem. New bank lending to many developing countries has slowed to a trickle. The combination of high interest rates and the retrenchment in bank lending is draining many developing countries of badly needed development finance. While major outright defaults now seem improbable, heightened conflict between creditors and debtors is possible unless bold actions are taken soon.

New approaches must take into account the interests of both the banks and developing-country borrowers. No single solution can by itself resolve the crisis. A battery of measures is needed—reforms in macroeconomic management, in the policies of the multilateral financial institutions, in bank lending practices as well as information gathering and analysis, and in regulation.

Contents:

Richard E. Feinberg—Overview: Restoring Confidence in International Credit Markets
Lawrence J. Brainard—More Lending to the Third World? A Banker's View
Karin Lissakers—Bank Regulation and International Debt
Christine A. Bogdanowicz-Bindert and Paul M. Sacks—The Role of Information: Closing the Barn Door?
George J. Clark—Foreign Banks in the Domestic Markets of Developing Countries
Catherine Gwin—The IMF and the World Bank: Measures to Improve the System
Benjamin J. Cohen—High Finance, High Politics

ISBN: 0-88738-041-7 (cloth)   **$19.95**
ISBN: 0-87855-989-2 (paper)   **$12.95**
1984   **144 pp.**

ADJUSTMENT CRISIS IN THE THIRD WORLD

Richard E. Feinberg and Valeriana Kallab, editors

**"major contribution to the literature on the
adjustment crisis"**
—B. T. G. Chidzero
Minister of Finance, Economic Planning
and Development Government of Zimbabwe

**"The adjustment crisis book has really stirred
up some excitement here"**
—Peter P. Waller
German Development Institute (Berlin)

"good collection of papers"
—*Foreign Affairs*

Just how the debt and adjustment crisis of Third World countries is handled, by them and by international agencies and banks, can make a big difference in the pace and quality of *global* recovery.

Stagnating international trade, sharp swings in the prices of key commodities, worsened terms of trade, high interest rates, and reduced access to commercial bank credits have slowed and even reversed growth in many Third World countries. Together, these trends make "adjustment" of both demand and supply a central problem confronting policy makers in most countries in the mid-1980s. Countries must bring expenditures into line with shrinking resources in the short run, but they also need to alter prices and take other longer-range steps to expand the resource base in the future—to stimulate investment, production, and employment. Already low living standards make this an especially formidable agenda in most Third World nations.

What can be done to forestall the more conflictive phase of the debt crisis that now looms ahead? How can developing countries achieve adjustment *with growth?* The contributors to this volume share the belief that more constructive change is possible and necessary.

Contents:

Richard E. Feinberg—The Adjustment Imperative and U.S. Policy
Albert Fishlow—The Debt Crisis: Round Two Ahead?
Tony Killick, Graham Bird, Jennifer Sharpley, and Mary Sutton—
The IMF: Case for a Change in Emphasis
Stanley Please—The World Bank: Lending for Structural Adjustment
Joan M. Nelson—The Politics of Stabilization
Colin I. Bradford, Jr.—The NICs: Confronting U.S. "Autonomy"
Riordan Roett—Brazil's Debt Crisis
Lance Taylor—Mexico's Adjustment in the 1980's: Look Back Before Leaping Ahead
DeLisle Worrell—Central America and the Caribbean: Adjustment in Small, Open
Economies

ISBN: 0-88738-040-9 (cloth)   **$19.95**
ISBN: 0-87855-988-4 (paper)   **$12.95**
1984   **220 pp.**